Shakespeare and the Problem of Adaptation

D1547465

Shakespeare's plays continue to be circulated on a massive scale in a variety of guises – as editions, performances and adaptations – and it is by means of such productions that we come to know his drama. *Shakespeare and the Problem of Adaptation* addresses fundamental questions about this process of identification, making use of the fraught category of adaptation to explore how we currently understand the Shakespearean work. To adapt implies there exists something to alter, but what constitutes the category of the 'play', and how does it relate to adaptation? How do 'play' and 'adaptation' relate to drama's twin media, text and performance? What impact might answers to these questions have on current editorial, performance and adaptation studies?

Margaret Jane Kidnie argues that 'play' and 'adaptation' are provisional categories – mutually dependent processes that evolve over time in accordance with the needs of users. This theoretical argument about the identity of works and the nature of text and performance is pursued in relation to diverse examples, including theatrical productions by the Royal Shakespeare Company, the BBC's *ShakespeaRe-Told*, the Reduced Shakespeare Company, and recent print editions of the complete works. These new readings build up a persuasive picture of the cultural and intellectual processes that determine how what is deemed 'authentically' Shakespearean is distinguished from the fraudulent and adaptive. Adaptation thus emerges as the conceptually necessary but culturally problematic category that results from partial or occasional failures to recognize a shifting work in its textual-theatrical instance.

Margaret Jane Kidnie is Associate Professor of English at the University of Western Ontario, Canada. She has edited early modern drama and prose, and has published widely on performance, adaptation, textual studies and editorial practice. She is currently editing *A Woman Killed with Kindness* for the Arden Early Modern Drama series.

Shakespeare and the Problem of Adaptation

Margaret Jane Kidnie

 Routledge
Taylor & Francis Group

LONDON AND NEW YORK

First edition published 2009
by Routledge
2 Park Square, Milton Park, Abingdon, Oxon OX14 4RN

Simultaneously published in the USA and Canada
by Routledge
270 Madison Ave, New York, NY 10016

Routledge is an imprint of the Taylor & Francis Group, an informa business

© 2009 Margaret Jane Kidnie

Typeset in Baskerville by
Taylor & Francis Books
Printed and bound in Great Britain by
TJ International Ltd, Padstow, Cornwall

All rights reserved. No part of this book may be reprinted or
reproduced or utilised in any form or by any electronic, mechanical, or
other means, now known or hereafter invented, including
photocopying and recording, or in any information storage or retrieval
system, without permission in writing from the publishers.

British Library Cataloguing in Publication Data
A catalogue record for this book is available from the British Library

Library of Congress Cataloging-in-Publication Data
Kidnie, Margaret Jane.
    Shakespeare and the problem of adaptation / Margaret Jane
Kidnie. – 1st ed.
        p. cm.
    Includes bibliographical references (p.) and index.
    1. Shakespeare, William, 1564–1616–Adaptations – History and
criticism. 2. Shakespeare, William, 1564–1616–Stage history. 3.
English drama – Adaptations. I. Title.
    PR2880.A1.K45 2008
    822.3'3 – dc22
                                                    2008023496

ISBN 13: 978-0-415-30867-0 (hbk)
ISBN 13: 978-0-415-30868-7 (pbk)
ISBN 13: 978-0-203-16771-7 (ebk)

Dedicated to the memory of
Beth Kidnie (1957–2000)

Contents

Illustrations

Acknowledgements

Shakespeare and the Problem of Adaptation has been a project I've lived with for a few years now, and I've been grateful throughout that time for the support and assistance of many friends and colleagues. James Purkis, at one time or another, heard and discussed with me probably every idea I had along the way about adaptation, and he offered encouragement, suggested secondary reading and possible new directions, and, most valuably, told me when he thought I'd got it wrong. Lukas Erne and Sonia Massai generously read through the completed manuscript in draft version, offering me detailed and immensely useful suggestions for final revisions, while Barbara Hodgdon and Jill Levenson offered frequent sounding-boards for ideas about text, performance, and adaptation, especially as they were beginning to take shape. And I can't thank Bruce Smith enough for once asking me what a performance is a performance of – it was probably at that moment that the project finally snapped into focus. I've further benefited from the contributions made by three exemplary research assistants: Andrew Moore helped to check citations and research the production history of *Harlem Duet*, Eleanor Collins provided preliminary information from England about the interactive segment of the *ShakespeaRe-Told* website that could not be streamed by the BBC to a computer in Canada, and Elan Paulson prepared a superb draft version of the index.

Shelly Scott kindly allowed me to read her 1997 University of Toronto doctoral dissertation, 'Feminist Theory and Nightwood Theatre', in preparation for my work on *Harlem Duet*, and I'm further indebted to Nightwood Theatre for sharing with me their copy of Scott's dissertation. I'm also grateful to Nightwood Theatre for helping me to track down archival information relating to the Tarragon production of *Harlem Duet*. Karen Robinson and Nigel Shawn Williams (Billie and Othello in the 2006 Stratford Festival production of *Harlem Duet*) found time in an already hectic production schedule to be interviewed about the Stratford production, and Bonnie Brown, producer of *The National* for CBC TV News, generously provided me with a transcript of the feature they ran on Djanet Sears and the Stratford Festival in the spring of 2006. Ex Machina welcomed me to La Caserne Dalhousie, providing me with access to archival materials relating to *Elsinore* and Lepage's other one-man productions, while Richard-Max Tremblay very kindly gave me permission to reproduce one of his superb photographs of *Elsinore*. Sylvia Morris, Head of Library and Information Resources at the Shakespeare Birthplace Trust, Stratford-upon-Avon, offered crucial research support on the Warchus and Dench productions. I would also like to extend heartfelt thanks to Polly Dodson and Liz Thompson for being such supportive and patient editors, and to Emma Nugent, Anna Callander, Fintan Power, and the rest of the Routledge production team for their hard work. The publisher's external readers provided invaluable suggestions and feedback on the finished manuscript.

Parts of Chapter 3 were first published as '"There's magic in the web of it": Seeing Beyond Tragedy in *Harlem Duet*', in the *Journal of Commonwealth Literature* 36:2 (2001): 29–44, reprinted in *African-Canadian Theatre*, ed. Maureen Moynagh, Critical Perspectives on Canadian Theatre in English, Vol. II (Toronto: Playwrights Canada Press, 2005), pp. 40–55. This article has been very heavily revised for publication here. Segments from the study of Lepage's *Elsinore* in Chapter 3 were previously published as 'Dancing with Art: Robert Lepage's *Elsinore*', in *World-wide Shakespeares: Local Appropriations in Film and Performance*, ed. Sonia Massai (London: Routledge, 2005), pp. 132–40, while a few paragraphs on the Reduced Shakespeare Company in the final chapter appeared as part of 'Citing Shakespeare', in *Shakespeare: Remembering Performance*, ed. Peter Holland (Cambridge: Cambridge University Press, 2006), pp. 117–32. *Shakespeare and the Problem of Adaptation* was made possible through the award of a three-year Standard Research Grant from the Social Sciences and Humanities Research Council of Canada, and through a half-year sabbatical in 2005 from the University of Western Ontario. I'm indebted to both institutions for their research support.

Introduction

The problem of adaptation

Matthew Warchus's production of *Hamlet* for the Royal Shakespeare Company in 1997, starring Alex Jennings, was one of those shows able to animate a familiar debate about how Shakespeare's plays might or should work on stage. It was a controversial modern-dress production that made noticeable cuts to famous lines, speeches, and characters, with much of the material that remained boldly rearranged and intercut. Simon Russell-Beale, himself starring in the role three years later at the Royal National Theatre in London, describes this 'extremely chic, exhilarating production' as the best he has seen: 'I remember at the end of the show muttering to a friend, with all the generosity I could muster, "Well, he's cracked it"'.[1] Reviewers at the time, however, saw it as rather more problematic. Part of what interests me about this staging is precisely the way it exposed conflicting opinions among spectators about what they think *Hamlet* in performance should be. I return to a fuller discussion of this show in the second chapter, but for the moment wish simply to highlight the discourse of 'survival' which became something of a refrain in the commentary offered by the production's supporters and critics alike. As David Nathan put it, 'I liked a lot of it and Hamlet the play survives'.[2] Nicholas de Jongh, less enthusiastically and drawing on a metaphor that suggests that Warchus's ill-advised choices amount in effect to an action of battery, granted that 'the play will make a complete recovery', while Charles Spencer, noting that this (in his opinion) flawed production nonetheless has its merits, took comfort from the realization that after all '[i]t's not like defacing a painting, a permanent act of vandalism. The plays will always be there.'[3] Even Jennings, speaking in an interview before the show opened, sought to counter public anxiety about a cut text – the cast had already received a letter of complaint from an irate local headmaster – by noting that 'the play will still be there in four years' time for somebody to do the full-length version again'.[4]

The idea that *Hamlet* 'survives' performance, recurrent in these comments, seems enabled by the unspoken belief that the play exists somewhere – or rather, somewhere *else* – apart from its (or perhaps just this) production. It may not be housed in one place like a painting or carved sculpture, yet it is nonetheless an object against which one can take the measure of its theatrical treatments, outlandish or otherwise. It is sometimes assumed, perhaps for lack of a better alternative, that the printed text of Shakespeare's plays provides the fixed point against which theatrical production can be monitored.[5] In practice, however, appeals to the text are hampered by an inability to determine what constitutes the text of *Hamlet*, or any other play. As I will argue in the opening chapter, perceptions of a textual original necessarily extend well beyond any single text or document, providing the standard against which not only performance but a range of printed texts, from the First Folio or earliest quarto to the most recent New Cambridge or Arden 3 editions, can themselves be assessed in terms of their supposed accuracy. *Shakespeare and the Problem of Adaptation* proposes that a play, for all that it carries the rhetorical and ideological force of an enduring stability, is not an object at all, but rather a dynamic *process* that evolves over time in response to the needs and sensibilities of its users. The chapters that follow explore some implications of this argument, especially as they help to shape, in turn, conceptions of adaptation.

This book began life with the Warchus production of *Hamlet*, and it was at first conceived as a study of Anglo-North American Shakespearean theatrical adaptations. My goal was to consider the adaptive strategies of various playwrights and theatre practitioners in an effort to interpret the politics of production around the turn of the twenty-first century. Stimulated by the exponential growth of critical studies in this field in the thirty years since the publication of Ruby Cohn's *Modern Shakespeare Offshoots*, I set about identifying recent instances of adaptation that seemed typical of a modern or even 'postmodern' dynamic of open-ended, dialectical engagement with the canon. However, and as the project continued to evolve, my interests shifted to the rather more basic question of how one determines *which* shows and texts form the proper subject of a study of adaptation. To consider again the variety of responses met by the Warchus production of *Hamlet*, how might one differentiate adaptation from straightforward – or relatively straightforward, or even just acceptably straightforward – production in a reception climate where one not infrequently hears at least some spectators challenge a particular staging as 'not' Shakespeare?

Perhaps surprisingly in light of the many excellent monographs and articles that have been published on Shakespearean adaptation, the issue of what should 'count' as adaptation is often taken for granted. Depending on the study, the term seems, relatively unproblematically, to describe Shakespeare on film, in performance, or in translation, to group together new drama that has overt or at least perceptible links to the canon, or to function to safeguard the very category of 'Shakespearean' by explicitly marking just some theatrical representations as standing at a distance from what the critic considers genuine production. The difficulties, however, in distinguishing between Shakespeare and new drama 'based on' Shakespeare are immediately evident in stagings such as Charles Marowitz's *Hamlet* or Robert Lepage's *Elsinore* which cut and rearrange lines and scenes already familiar to spectators from the three printed versions published in the twenty years between 1603 and 1623.[6] Is the difference between Marowitz's and Lepage's directorial strategies and those used by most modern directors a matter of degree, or is every staging, perhaps, an adaptation? If the former, then at what point does theatrical production become adaptive?

Cohn is particularly alert to the variety of ways Shakespeare's drama can be produced/adapted, figuring the vast range of examples she considers in her book as a sort of metaphorical family tree, branching ever further away from the body, or corpus, of a common ancestor. All of these plays are, to use Cohn's term, 'offshoots', but she goes on to register their relative proximity to a Shakespearean progenitor through categorization under one of three headings. A 'reduction/emendation' sees lines and words cut or altered, an 'adaptation' involves the addition of new material alongside substantial cutting and rearrangement, while a 'transformation', the most extreme mode of innovation, offers characters 'simplified or trundled through new events, with the ending scrapped'.[7] Of particular relevance to my study is Cohn's implicit *a priori* assumption that one can identify a modern staging or published text that has 'shot off' to become an at least partly independent creation; her position, in other words, seems to be that we all know an adaptation of Shakespeare when we encounter it.

This view that adaptations somehow declare their status as adaptations is integral to Linda Hutcheon's more recent analysis of the phenomenon as both product and readerly/writerly process in *A Theory of Adaptation*. For Hutcheon, adaptation is simultaneously:

- An acknowledged transposition of a recognizable other work or works
- A creative *and* an interpretive act of appropriation/salvaging
- An extended intertextual engagement with the adapted work.[8]

Led by a levelling impulse that refuses to equate 'derivation' and 'derivative' and so offering a timely corrective to a long tradition of fidelity study, Hutcheon advances a theoretical model of intertextuality that seeks to interpret an adaptation as 'its own palimpsestic thing'.[9] This approach richly complicates the interpretative relationship between an adaptation and the work it adapts. No longer motivated by a need to defend or attack – or even necessarily to account for – perceived departures from a supposed origin or 'source', the critic's goal is instead to trace a potential *web* of relations in which connected instances participate. Hutcheon's theoretical perspective resonates with priorities expressed in some other recent studies of adaptation. Commenting on the complex cultural dialogues pursued in part by means of adaptation, Julie Sanders, for example, notes that postcolonial appropriations of *The Tempest* and *Othello* 'are often as much in dialogue with other adaptations as with the Shakespearean sourcetext'.[10] From this perspective, and as Sarah Cardwell argues in *Adaptation Revisited*, to push too insistently at the details of how the textual fabric of a particular novel such as *The Fortunes and Misfortunes of Moll Flanders* has been altered for television can be misleading. A literary bias prevents one from realizing the extent to which this sort of cross-media adaptation is shaped less by the demands of the novel's supposed essence than by the history and evolving generic conventions of classic-novel television adaptation.[11]

The difficulty, however, is that while addressing adaptation as something like an independent art form opens up areas of investigation not available to more traditional compare-and-contrast methods, these studies tend to assume that there exists a relatively stable distinction between work and adaptation. Thus, and in a manner already familiar from Cohn's much earlier study, Hutcheon's three-pronged definition requires that one already know what constitutes the body of study. Adaptation is 'an *acknowledged* transposition' (my emphasis) that offers an extended engagement with a work that is described as already 'adapted' and so identified as something creatively distinct from the subject of Hutcheon's analysis. However, quite how one arrives at a perception of the adapted work and its adaptations is a point Hutcheon never addresses. *A Theory of Adaptation* addresses a wide variety of creative adaptations, and perhaps for that reason focuses primarily on transfers between media – novels that are turned into films, or graphic novels into video games. These sorts of 'acknowledged transposition[s]', frequently signalled by the phrase 'based on a book', help to make adaptation seem readily visible as its own category. Hutcheon's important contribution is thus to prompt us to reconsider *how* one might analyse adaptation, but it equally begs important questions about how one recognizes old works as new.

Daniel Fischlin and Mark Fortier take a very different approach to issues of adaptation and intertextuality in their ambitious and wide-ranging 'General Introduction' to *Adaptations of Shakespeare*. Tackling head-on problems of categorization raised, for instance, by transfers across media, Shakespearean source materials, and postcolonial appropriations, Fischlin and Fortier comment that they decided to use adaptation '[f]or lack of a better term' to describe the phenomenon of 'recontextualization' that characterizes the way writers, directors, and editors accommodate Shakespeare's plays to new audiences.[12] The definition of adaptation at which they finally arrive is striking, precisely because it is so inclusive:

> Adaptation as a material, performance practice can involve both radical rewritings, and a range of directorial and theatrical practices … One of the other ways in which Shakespeare is made fit is through criticism, itself a form of adaptive undertaking by virtue of its intertextual dependence on a source text. A related area that concerns adaptive practice has to do with how editorial practices that seek to stabilize or destabilize texts literally adapt Shakespeare, making him conform to a particular editorial vision.[13]

Fischlin and Fortier address the problem of how one knows one is faced with adaptation by arguing, in effect, that *any* modern or historical production of Shakespeare, whether theatrical, critical, or editorial, is an adaptation, part of an ongoing process of making Shakespeare 'fit'. This position resists the temptation to impose on particular case studies critically arbitrary boundaries. However, by finding adaptation potentially everywhere, Fischlin and Fortier are in danger of emptying the term of meaning, making it simply synonymous with production. Even more to the point, such an account fails to acknowledge that in everyday and specialist usage people feel able, and some are even determined, to flag not all but specifically *some* Shakespearean production(s) as 'not quite' Shakespeare. Collapsing adaptation into production neglects a crucial feature of the phenomenon – precisely the widespread critical ability to discriminate between Shakespeare and Shakespearean adaptation, whether these judgements are made by academics, students, theatregoers, theatre practitioners, or interested general readers.

By first addressing as a theoretical problem the question of what constitutes adaptation, and subsequently treating adaptation as a necessarily provisional category of study, this book seeks to achieve a few related goals. First, it challenges sometimes unspoken assumptions that adaptation is synonymous with performance, or that performance is somehow more vulnerable than text to adaptive practices. Second, it seeks to define adaptation not in terms of a tension between text and performance, but in a reciprocal relation to the Shakespearean 'work' (the term I use throughout this study to describe the play as process). My argument is that adaptation as an evolving category is closely tied to how the work modifies over time and from one reception space to another. Finally, this book shows how an understanding of the work as an ongoing process rather than a fixed object makes alternative critical practices potentially available to adaptation studies since the 'work as process' reshapes in significant ways the politics of reception.

In contrast to some other studies of adaptation, *Shakespeare and the Problem of Adaptation* limits its examples and case studies to drama (as opposed to including, for instance, novels, graphic novels, operettas, or video games) since drama presents certain consistent and fundamental generic difficulties to adaptation studies. The peculiar problems associated with an art form that exists simultaneously in two media – text and performance – are not infrequently glossed over, usually in favour of reading performance as an inherently adaptive strategy. This is perhaps because the way to accommodate drama most readily within the broader field of adaptation studies is simply to treat the relation between script and performance as analogous to the relation between novel and film. Cardwell, for example, usefully troubles a notion of origins by challenging the exclusive priority given to Shakespeare's version of the Lear story as 'the' seminal creative starting point. However, her specific complaint that '[e]ach new theatrical, filmic or televisual re-presentation of *King Lear* is considered an adaptation of Shakespeare's play, not of either the "original" [legendary] stories or the previously published play text [*King Leir*]', is theoretically problematic insofar as it constructs all modern performances as forms of adaptation.[14] Her implicit position on what 'counts' as *King Lear*, as distinct from its adaptations, thus erases entirely distinctions between drama and forms of literature such as the novel (her own primary critical focus). According to Cardwell's analysis, a stage performance of *King Lear* would be no more the work of art than a stage performance of *Pride and Prejudice* since both adapt the conditions of one medium (literature) to another (performance arts). This bias towards understanding the work as embodied in its written or printed text is likewise evident in Fischlin and Fortier's introduction, where they present performance as a specialized form of translation: 'every drama text is an incomplete entity that must be "translated" by being put on stage. Adaptation is, therefore, only an extreme version of the reworking that takes place in any theatrical production … Theatre is always a form of reworking, in a sense the first step toward adaptation.'[15]

Hutcheon, by contrast, recognizes the 'definitional problem' associated with theatre when she argues that while 'every live staging of a printed play could theoretically be considered an adaptation in its performance', only some actually are. However, an extended consideration of this specific issue pushes beyond the scope of Hutcheon's wide-reaching study. She briefly glances at just two (I think contested) examples that she suggests might be considered adaptation – Peter Brook's 'radical' treatments of scripts in performance (precisely which scripts and performances Hutcheon has in mind are not specified) and what she calls the 'adaptation/production' in 2003 by Mabou Mines of Ibsen's *A Doll's House*, in which little people were cast in the male roles and average-height actors in the female roles – before returning to the more straightforward case of the adaptation of novels to stage and screen.[16] The challenge to adaptation studies thus remains: when speaking specifically of drama, what constitutes adaptation as distinct from production? How does this problem of identity inform the politics of adaptation, and the critical tools one brings to its analysis? *Shakespeare and the Problem of Adaptation* pursues drama's 'definitional problem' by insisting that drama, as distinct from the novel, is generically situated at the intersection of text and performance, so forestalling any ready identification of adaptation with performance. Somewhat unexpectedly, chasing down these issues as a first step towards a discussion of Shakespearean theatrical adaptation resulted in a study that is less entirely about adaptation than it is about the identity of Shakespeare's works and the intimately related *problem* of adaptation.

My argument is that the notion of the 'work', a term that has fallen out of theoretical favour partly as a result of post-structuralist challenges to the author and a swing away from what are often described as New Bibliographical editorial practices, continues to serve a practical function in both academic and generalist analyses of Shakespeare's drama. It is what enables one to speak of *King Lear* or *Pericles*, grouping under a generic title non-identical examples of text and performance that are somehow recognized as 'the same'. My stance, however, might be described as constructionist and pragmatic rather than idealist, showing points of contact with the theoretical positions of Stanley Fish and Richard Rorty. That is, I differ from critics who locate the work either in the author's mind or in a particular (often reconstructed or hypothesized) text by arguing that the work, far from functioning as an objective yardstick against which to measure the supposed accuracy of editions and stagings, whether current or historical, continually takes shape as a *consequence* of production. The criteria that are sufficient to mark out 'the work' – and so to separate it from adaptation, or what is 'not the work' – constantly shift over time, sometimes subtly, sometimes suddenly and drastically, in response to textual and theatrical production. Checks and limits on the work's evolving shape are provided informally by communities of users who accept, reject, or, more often, debate as genuine a new print edition or a particular theatrical enactment.

This endless cultural monitoring process is a bit like pulling oneself up by one's bootstraps since it depends on positing the work – a process without an origin – as an *a priori* category. It is only by actually believing or positing as a matter of theoretical expedience that the work always exists somewhere else, apart from and untouched by production, that one can assert a place from which to categorize and evaluate subsequent productions as potential instances *of* a particular work. To put this another way, authenticity in the context of Shakespearean text and performance is continually redefined over time by the activity and debates that take place at the work's constantly shifting edges. What might count as 'genuine' production can therefore be only provisionally known by recognizing adaptation. It is by marking instances and their reception, especially those instances of text and performance that seem in some way particularly controversial, that one arrives at a sense of where the line separating adaptation from 'genuine' production is located – at least for the moment – for a particular group of users. An important further implication of this argument is that it is potentially misleading to conceive of the work as a single or unified thing, even at one particular historical moment. Different constructions of the work may be found among diverse communities of users, separated, for example, by culture or geographical region, or even, as I discuss in Chapter 4 with reference to analogue and digital television broadcasting, within a particular (albeit perhaps only temporarily self-defining) community of users, such as BBC viewers.

The first chapter sets out this theoretical position in more detail, with the remaining chapters developing the argument in relation to specific instances of textual or theatrical production. Although any instance would potentially serve since the work is continually constructed through an endless process of locating adaptation, I explore in detail case studies that readily highlight in certain ways what is at stake with adaptation (and so, at least implicitly, with the identity of the work). Chapter 2, taking up the issues of identity raised by a conception of the work as process, compares two productions staged by the Royal Shakespeare Company around the turn of the twenty-first century in order to explore some of the contextual factors that might either prompt or hinder recognition of (what is thought to count as) the work. My examination of the Warchus *Hamlet* and the 2003 *All's Well that Ends Well*, directed by Greg Doran and starring Judi Dench, addresses important, in some ways even landmark, shows in order to investigate the range and type of innovations that could be introduced in a particular historical and institutional context before one began to hear complaints of adaptation and vandalism, terms commonly used to attack productions perceived to be incompatible with what some users believe they already know of the work. The terms in which the limits of the work are contested throw into relief the priorities and politics that constituencies of users at certain moments bring to bear on the work's contingent existence.

In effect, adaptation keeps emerging as a 'problem' for production since the work itself adapts over time. By classifying just *some* productions as adaptation, as a departure from the thing itself, communities of users generate through a negative logic the effect of conceptual stability. The work thus emerges in history as that which its adaptations are not, and becomes known (at times controversially) by means of the reception afforded its productions. While resisting a relativistic position which assumes, wrongly, that anything can mean anything, this book argues that there is no ideal iteration of any Shakespearean play towards which one can or should strive, either textually or theatrically. This is not to say that at any given moment it is impossible to identify texts and performances that are regarded as authentically Shakespearean; however, the production which today seems fully to capture or embody a supposed original – and this is true whether one speaks of text or performance – enjoys only a potentially temporary and limited currency. Precisely what constitutes authentic Shakespeare is a question that can never finally be resolved since there is no *a priori* category that texts and stagings are productions *of*. Far from concluding, then, that the arguments that continue to spring up around authentic and adaptive Shakespeare represent a critical or theoretical dead-end – that we should somehow move beyond or get past the authority or fidelity question – my point is that it is precisely through such processes of debate that users continue to define their particular ideological, institutional, or political investment in the work.[17]

This conception of the work has important consequences for the politics of Shakespearean appropriation, as Chapter 3 explores. How can production sustain a strategic adaptive distance from a work that is itself subject to change? An idea of the work as process might seem further to reinforce the importance of, and need for, strongly motivated interventions in the politics of the canon and its histories of reception. And yet this instability also poses a difficulty for acts of intervention in terms of gaining a purchase on the changing and permeable boundaries between work and adaptation, since writing 'back' to a master narrative depends, at least implicitly, on treating the work as a known quantity – so returning us to a model of identity in which the work, considered fixed, is always somewhere else. The difficulty here is the inverse predicament to the problems of identity explored in the earlier chapters: it is as hard to sustain a category of adaptation that is entirely independent of a fluid work as it is to make the boundaries of that work impervious to production. Somewhat paradoxically, since revision is one goal of appropriation, the work that modifies over time is difficult to counter in any predictable manner since it will not remain sealed off in/as the past; the site of adaptation keeps getting entangled in the work's ongoing development. The third chapter explores oppositional politics and the work as process in relation to the politics of history and appropriation through analysis of two Canadian stagings, Djanet Sears' *Harlem Duet* and Robert Lepage's *Elsinore*.

Because I am especially interested in cases where possible adaptation, to pick up Hutcheon's term, is *not* 'acknowledged' (or at least not by everyone), *Shakespeare and the Problem of Adaptation* focuses in the main on examples of textual and theatrical production – the two media one might argue are inherent to the dramatic work's form. Therefore for my purposes, 'production(s)' of the work, unless otherwise specified, refers interchangeably to both scripts and performances, not just theatrical stagings. That said, what is understood as the work cannot be entirely cordoned off from changing technologies, since those technologies eventually become naturalized as part of one's 'normal' experiences of the world. The fourth chapter therefore turns to Shakespeare on television in order to explore issues of media, specifically in relation to the ways in which digital innovations are shaping users' perceptions of Shakespeare's works. By looking beyond live theatre and film to consider television, this chapter seeks to isolate how a recognition of Shakespeare's work – both what one thinks it is and how one comes to know it – can become historically caught up in, and shaped by, new technologies. The discussion throughout this chapter centres on the BBC's *ShakespeaRe-Told* series broadcast in Britain in November 2005 with an optional interactive 'red button' supplement.

The conclusion turns to address in a more sustained way issues of adaptation as they bear on the editorial production of Shakespeare's works as reading texts. Through experiences of performance *and/or* text one comes to learn and form opinions about the dramatic work; it is this acquired and evolving set of assumptions which then functions, purely pragmatically, as the seemingly objective and fixed origin against which instances of production can be measured. The issue is therefore not how performance departs from or otherwise adapts text, but the shifting criteria by which *both* texts and performances are recognized – or not – as instances of a certain work. The final chapter thus reflects on some of the current intersections between textual studies, historicity, and editorial rationales, and considers how, when it comes to textual production (as opposed to theatrical production), appeals to the past shape attitudes towards what can be recognized as authentic textual instances of Shakespeare's works.

1 Surviving performance
Shakespeare's contested works

Let's begin then with an idea already heard in discussions of the Warchus production of *Hamlet*: the claim that the play has a fixed and secure existence apart from production. This assumption that there is a 'real' *Hamlet* against which production can be measured is actually less certain than it may at first seem. James McLaverty memorably captured the problem with a philosophical brainteaser about the nature of art: 'if the *Mona Lisa* is in the Louvre, where are *Hamlet* and *Lycidas*?'[1] McLaverty, of course, was rephrasing (and so popularizing) F. W. Bateson's defence of critical interpretation in face of claims by New Bibliographers to have developed mechanical means to resolve textual cruces once and for all.[2] Bateson's discussion of art and interpretation included no riddle, however, since to his mind *Hamlet*, like the *Mona Lisa*, has a form of artifactual existence:

> The fact that we can see a picture, whereas *Hamlet* is invisible, is because the picture's physical basis is spatial and not temporal; it does not affect the general similarity of their aesthetic status. *Hamlet* then is an object; but it is a man-made object and only usable by human beings, like the Constitution of the United States. If it has no Supreme Court, to which we can appeal over differences in its interpretation, the consensus of scholarship is an obvious approximate equivalent to such a Court.[3]

According to Bateson, there is an objective *Hamlet* that just 'is'. And yet since the work of literature as a thing of the mind exists apart from its printed copies and performances, the reader/spectator never has direct access to it: books and theatrical productions in this account function only as what he calls 'storage' containers. The literary original rests in speech – specifically, the 'oral drama of the [author's] mind in its definitive form'.[4] It is this Ideal state, according to Bateson, that should be the focus of editorial effort, and it is this Ideal state that informs one's experience of performance since it is the standard that 'enables us to say of a particular performance that it is "wrong-headed" or "one-sided"'.[5]

Bateson's analysis, for perhaps obvious reasons, stops short of a full examination of how precisely one might recover *Hamlet* as enacted in the author's mind. For him, one simply knows it, like one knows the *Mona Lisa*. McLaverty challenges Bateson's Idealist stance by focusing tightly on the particularity not of the Ideal object, but of the textual document. As a textual scholar McLaverty's concern is to develop a theoretical platform from which to argue for the ontological significance of what Jerome J. McGann would seven years later describe as the 'bibliographical coding' of the literary work.[6] As McLaverty's brilliant analysis of the type-setting and page layout of Pope's *Dunciad* Variorum makes clear, a major aspect of the signifying potential of the literary work rests in what Bateson dismisses as merely the work's means of 'storage'. According to McLaverty, far from existing in its definitive state in the author's head, the signifying potential of the literary work cannot be limited even to a particular sequence of letter-forms: it also consists of the visual effect of the page and the way that choices about layout and typeface take on meaning within a particular network of socio-historical circumstances. To divorce the literary work from its history of bibliographical production is for McLaverty to compromise both critical interpretation and – where it can be demonstrated that the author deliberately manipulates print conventions to particular effect – authorial intention. As he concludes, 'the existence of works of art as print and paper is not less but more important than bibliographers have generally taken it to be … I hope I have shown that the presentation of the text is open to exploitation by the author, that it can carry specific associations, and that a richer understanding of the relation of author, book trade, and public may lead to better interpretation of literary works'.[7]

McLaverty's argument that 'the physical appearance of books' is an essential part of the ontological condition of the work of literature is an early instance of what might now be called a sociology of text.[8] This strand of textual studies, perhaps most closely associated with the work of McGann and D. F. McKenzie, emphasizes the extent to which history and culture are embedded in the bibliographical document. To treat the work of literature as a particular sequence of letter-forms that can be disentangled from the physical documents in which the work first and subsequently appeared is to erase or at least marginalize the input of the very network of collaborating agents and practical constraints which gave it shape.[9] This argument applies even when – perhaps especially when – peculiarities such as erroneous errata sheets, variant speech prefixes, and seemingly incomplete stage directions, once familiar parts of the early modern reading experience, now make the document in its particularity seem alien to many modern readers. In such cases, the work of literature is inextricably caught up in a condition of indeterminacy that is inherent to its circumstances of print production, with the irregularities and contradictions of the text only smoothed away (for some scholars, falsely or misleadingly) through modern interventionist editorial practices.[10]

As studies by David Scott Kastan, Leah Marcus, and Randall McLeod have shown, a focus on the particularity of the unedited document can lead to powerful interpretative insights. Stephen Orgel has argued that, as an editor, his 'basic feeling … is that texts aren't ideas, they are artifacts', and he therefore 'want[s] to preserve as much as [he] can of their archeology'.[11] However, the full implications of materialist and socialized approaches to the text as an historical artifact remain the subject of debate.[12] What seems unclear, especially when one comes to act on the theory, is whether, and on what grounds, *any* aspect of the document may be considered inessential. If the position is that the work of literature is artifactual – that its authority lies in verifying its physical characteristics, the paper and ink of the unique document – how can it be reproduced?[13] How, if at all, does the text of a play differ from a painting? And what might this documentary emphasis mean for performance?

Identifying the dramatic work in text and performance

The identity of drama in text and performance is a vexed question, and has major implications for how one in turn recognizes adaptation. Part of the goal of this chapter is to depart from 'unediting' trends in Shakespeare studies in order to show that while a dramatic *text* might be considered an 'artifact' (to pick up Orgel's position and terminology), what directors, actors, and editors generate through print and performance is indeed something rather more like an idea. By this means I hope to suggest what is peculiar about drama and its perpetuation over time especially as it compares to non-dramatic literature, and in this way to explain why adaptation so often presents itself as an ongoing issue, or problem, haunting Shakespeare's plays.

To do this I want to step back to consider two classic statements of aesthetic theory, the first offered by Nelson Goodman and the second by Richard Wollheim. In *Languages of Art*, Goodman insists – in sharp contrast to McLaverty's and Orgel's positions – that books and paintings are *not* ontologically comparable, that books are not artifacts. Observing that while a painting can be forged, accurate copies of a literary or theatrical work 'are equally genuine instances of the work', Goodman distinguishes such forms of art in terms of their susceptibility to notation.[14] The identity of paintings, sculptures, and etchings is determined by their history of production: every detail of the work of art is constitutive of its identity, and no deviation is insignificant. Notation in such a context is impossible, and therefore '[t]he only way of ascertaining that the *Lucretia* before us is genuine is thus to establish the historical fact that it is the actual object made by Rembrandt'.[15] Such forms of art are described as 'autographic'. Literature, by contrast, the constitutive properties of which can be preserved in notation form, is categorized as non-autographic, or 'allographic'.

For Goodman, differences among handwritten or printed copies of a literary work in 'style and size of script or type, in color of ink, in kind of paper, in number and layout of pages, in condition, etc., do not matter':

> All that matters is what may be called *sameness of spelling*: exact corre-spondence as sequences of letters, spaces, and punctuation marks. Any sequence – even a forgery of the author's manuscript or of a given edition – that so corresponds to a correct copy is itself correct, and nothing is more the original work than is such a correct copy. And since whatever is not an original of the work must fail to meet such an explicit standard of correctness, there can be no deceptive imitation, no forgery, of that work. To verify the spelling or to spell correctly is all that is required to identify an instance of the work or to produce a new instance.[16]

Whereas any copy of the autographic work of art is a forgery, any accu-rately 'spelled' copy of the allographic work of art simply *is* the work of art. Goodman's theory has a certain common-sense currency. John Carey, for example, drawing on similar assumptions about what constitutes the work of art, explains that memorizing a poem is the equivalent of taking home from the Frick Vermeer's *Girl Interrupted at Her Music*; for Carey lit-erature is distinct from other arts because it can be made one's own simply by lodging the words accurately in one's mind.[17] The position that litera-ture is not what philosophers call an art-particular is likewise implicitly reinforced every time a new edition of one of Shakespeare's plays appears on the market.

And yet Goodman's philosophical claim to have 'emancipat[ed]' allo-graphic art from its history of production through notation rather than proclamation seems at best a partial achievement,[18] since his justification for putting to one side elements that are not susceptible to notation as contingent to the work of art depends on the circular reasoning that con-stitutive elements must be susceptible to notation. By departing from Goodman's schema in order to present particulars of the book that cannot be incorporated into a notational system as constitutive of the literary work, McLaverty in effect seeks to set literature outside of this binary categorization of autographic and allographic art.

The situation of drama, of course, is even more complex since plays bridge media and can be encountered as either text or performance. In Goodman's analysis, a literary work such as Joyce's *Ulysses* or Marianne Moore's 'Poetry' is identified with any 'correct' copy. The dramatic work, by contrast, is comprised of performances that comply with the script (the script being any 'correct' copy). Drama for Goodman is thus more akin to music, his primary example for the discussion of performance arts, than literature. Where the musical score is defined by a series of characters in a notational system (cues such as 'allegro', because not amenable to notation, are not part of the score), the dramatic script is defined by its dialogue (stage directions, which like tempo indications fail to meet the criteria for a notational system, are likewise contingent rather than constituent parts of the script). Any performance that exactly delivers the dialogue as scripted therefore constitutes another instance of the dramatic work.

Goodman's theory of notation is remarkable for the way it defines performance *as* the work of dramatic art, rather than treating it as a non-authorial 'add-on' or departure from the text. This is a conception of drama that admits of – even requires – non-authorial collaboration over time. The playwright's creative labour ends with the completion of the script,[19] but the work itself is located with the performance event. Crucially, however, what *counts* as a performance of the work is rigidly constrained. The identity of the work of art is preserved in Goodman's schema by admitting as genuine only those performances that exactly reproduce the script's dialogue. In other words, if one word is forgotten or improvised, or one speech omitted, the performance no longer complies with the script, and it is therefore not an instance of the work. With a knowledge of the notation system, one should be able to move from the correct script to the compliant performance, and from that performance be able once again to recover the correct script without any of these steps compromising the identity of the work.[20]

Such rigorous identification of the play with its notation leads to the counter-intuitive situation (one to which Goodman is not oblivious) in which art as performance is defined purely by accuracy. As he says of music: 'Since complete compliance with the score is the only requirement for a genuine instance of a work, the most miserable performance without actual mistakes does count as such an instance, while the most brilliant performance with a single wrong note does not.'[21] Music theorists have sharply resisted the identification of the work with any performance that complies with the score. As Jenefer Robinson explains, pace, phrasing, volume, and even the specific instrument on which the work is played are all elements that contribute to the work in performance, but 'none of these musical dimensions can be adequately captured by a notation'.[22] As I will discuss in a moment in relation to Shakespeare, a similar argument could be mounted perhaps even more readily for drama in relation to variables such as intonation, gesture, casting choices, set, and theatrical space.

Goodman's emphasis on accuracy of copying and compliance with the script has the benefit of clearly demarcated boundaries. By limiting the identity of the work to what can be rendered in notation form and then insisting that this notation must be fulfilled exactly, he renders forms of art such as drama and opera that are not art-particulars ontologically stable. More permissive definitions, while sometimes better in step with everyday practice, have trouble determining with any precision the parameters of the work of art, so making repetition of the work, over time and usually by means of collaborating artists, difficult. Anticipating the complaint that it is unreasonable to disallow a performance as being a performance of a scored work because of a single wrong note, Goodman allows that aesthetically the faulty brilliant performance may be considered preferable to the note-perfect, mundane rendition. However, he insists that ontologically the latter must be considered the only 'genuine' instance of the work:

> The innocent-seeming principle that performances differing by just one note are instances of the same work risks the consequence – in view of the transitivity of identity – that all performances whatsoever are of the same work. If we allow the least deviation, all assurance of work-preservation and score-preservation is lost; for by a series of one-note errors of omission, addition, and modification, we can go all the way from Beethoven's *Fifth Symphony* to *Three Blind Mice*.[23]

What is at stake, here as with other forms of allographic art, is the preservation of what Goodman considers the authoritative work.

Goodman's notational system is founded upon the assumption that the script/score exists in a single authentic form, presumably as it was composed or written by the author. Developments in textual theory since Goodman published *Languages of Art*, however, have shown how error and commonplace processes of revision make it difficult, if not impossible, to determine the precise shape of a script independently of critical judgement. Even the seemingly straightforward editorial goal to recover what the author wrote, powerfully formulated by W. W. Greg, raises complex interpretative and theoretical issues.[24] The problems derive not only from a willingness among historicist scholars such as McLaverty and Robinson to embrace a more inclusive, collaborative conception of the work of art, a position implicitly bolstered by late twentieth-century post-structuralist critiques of the author. The problems implicit in a pursuit of authorial intention are also practical. Should one print what one thinks the author *meant* to write but failed to put into words as the result, say, of a lapse in concentration (writing 'the the', for instance, instead of 'to the')? Does one preserve what the author actually wrote, or rather what one assumes she would have written if she had not been persuaded otherwise by a spouse, friend, or publisher? Are printing-house or playhouse changes 'authorial' if it seems they were tacitly approved by the author? Should authorial revisions be folded into the earliest complete text, or do subsequent alterations constitute a new conception, and so an independent version? At what moment in the development of the script – if ever – does the work fragment into multiple versions?[25]

The unstable textual condition of Shakespeare's drama is, of course, by now well established. Even if one sets aside as irregular cases such as *Hamlet* and *A Midsummer Night's Dream* where there is evidence of multiple versions, and so perhaps a revised conception; if one further ignores disparities in, for instance, spelling, layout, word choice, word order, and punctuation that can be traced between the earliest quarto and Folio editions of a single play; even if one chooses to disregard variants among copies of a single edition such as the 1623 Folio that arise from stop-press correction in the early modern printing house; then there would still be ongoing processes of editorial emendation, regularization, and modernization that intervene in and shape in significant ways the modern editions that readers encounter today. The possible response that the indeterminacy of the textual condition has been overstated – that apart from a few celebrated cases such as *Hamlet* and *King Lear* the texts are not all that different, and that therefore, as Michael D. Friedman puts it, 'our definition of "the text" need not be so rigid' – offers a common-sense approach to the problem.[26] However, it takes for granted the very issue around which there is a failure of consensus: how one determines in the first place adaptive production.

The crucial point here for my purposes is that in most, perhaps all, cases – even if one is working with a holograph manuscript, or a text that survives in only one published edition – Goodman's 'correct' script forever slips out of reach. But where then might one locate this object that is the dramatic work of art if not with performances regulated by strict fulfilment of the correct script, nor, as Bateson suggests, with the Ideal form as it exists in the author's mind? Richard Wollheim's type–token thesis, as developed in *Art and Its Objects*, provides an alternative model of the dramatic work that seems to accommodate some of the problems encountered in Goodman's theory of art. Rejecting the idea that works of literature and performance may be considered objects since it is impossible to point to the physical thing that is the work, Wollheim instead argues that '*Ulysses* and *Der Rosenkavalier* are types, my copy of *Ulysses* and tonight's performance of *Der Rosenkavalier* are tokens'.[27] What can be identified as the immediate or physical object is therefore merely a particular instance of the work of art.[28] The existence of the type of a work of art can be postulated in those circumstances 'where we can correlate a class of particulars with a piece of human invention'.[29]

For Wollheim, *any* property that is not purely a consequence of the token's material existence may be transmitted from a token to its type. This crucial detail distinguishes Wollheim from Bateson by preventing the type (i.e., the work of art) from being seen as an Ideal form that all its physical manifestations (fail to) replicate or fulfil.[30] Although Wollheim's type is immaterial, one has direct access to it since it is possible to speak of it as having physical properties: 'There is nothing that prevents us from saying that Donne's *Satires* are harsh on the ear, or that Dürer's engraving of St Anthony has a very differentiated texture, or that the conclusion of "Celeste Aida" is *pianissimo*.'[31] However, while any property belonging to the token *may* be transmitted to the type, in the case of performance arts not all of them *will* be so transmitted. This subtlety leads to the conclusion which is at the heart of Wollheim's aesthetic theory: in the special case of performance arts, the token (i.e., the performance) will inevitably have properties that are *not* shared with the type, that are 'in excess' of the type.[32] These properties make up the 'element of *interpretation*' which informs and shapes different performances of the work. It is this possibility, even likelihood, of dissimilarity among tokens in media such as drama and opera that is not accounted for in philosophical accounts such as Goodman's that attempt to reduce the preservation of the identity of the work of art to a purely mechanical exercise premised on accurate copying.[33]

In what follows, I will propose using a version of Wollheim's type–token thesis in order to account for the dramatic work's dual existence as text and performance, and as a means to distinguish between a work and its adaptations. As it stands, however, the difficulty with using Wollheim's model to establish the identity of the dramatic work is that it is impossible to discern which properties of the token are, as Wollheim puts it, 'transmitted' to the type, and which of them are in excess of the type. Or as he himself expresses this chicken-and-egg problem, 'there is no way of determining the properties that a token of a given type has necessarily, independently of determining the properties of that type'.[34] Since one cannot know what is essential to either the type or the token without a prior knowledge of the (Ideal?) work, one cannot apply the thesis to determine whether a particular token is 'genuine' (to return to Goodman's terminology), or even whether two or more particulars are tokens of the same type.

Wollheim seems to assume that the work of art, conceived as a type, is ultimately knowable, but he is unable to explain how one comes to a knowledge either of the work or, what is much the same thing, the necessary properties of type and tokens. When he finally arrives at the problem of locating potential shared identity among particular texts and performances – specifically, how to determine whether these instances should be understood as tokens of the same type – Wollheim suspends his analysis, merely acknowledging that such questions 'arise for instance sharply in connexion with translation'.[35] And, one might add, with adaptation.

Shakespearean performance and/as interpretation

Before introducing what I will call a model of pragmatic adaptation, I want to relate this foregoing account of the issues surrounding the identity of the dramatic work to some critical trends in Shakespeare performance studies. What does it mean to say that '*Hamlet* the play survives' a particular instance of production? Many of the arguments one continues to encounter decrying what Michael Bristol and Kathleen McLuskie, for example, describe as theatre's 'outlandish liberties' shuffle uneasily and sometimes inconsistently among the theoretical poles instanced in the work of Bateson, Goodman, and Wollheim.[36]

Complaints about theatrical non-adherence to the Shakespearean text are not hard to find. Thomas Clayton describes Jonathan Miller's production of *The Merchant of Venice* as 'reconstituted from the remains of Shakespeare's *Merchant* surviving amputation', while John Russell Brown objects that Peter Brook's landmark production of *A Midsummer Night's Dream* has 'left the text far behind'.[37] Not himself a Shakespearean, but similarly sceptical about the ways text is manipulated for theatrical production, D. C. Greetham asks if one can even 'imagine a "performance" (that is, edition) of a novel in which characters are simply omitted and their lines reassigned to other characters, as Laurence Olivier did with Rosencrantz and Guildenstern in his film of *Hamlet*'.[38] The answer to Greetham's question is clearly 'no', or 'only with difficulty'. But it is a curious exercise to propose. Why should one assume that the criteria for acceptable repetition in one type of art will apply to another? Production practices that are acceptable for the potentially endless circulation of literature in multiple editions, as Goodman, in particular, insists, in no way apply to an art-particular such as a painting which only exists (legitimately, at least) as a unique original. Greetham's rhetoric serves to predispose his reader to agree that the conventions governing drama permit performance to take exceptional, perhaps even unwarranted, freedoms with the work of art as defined specifically by its text.

As already shown, defining or locating what could be taken as the 'correct' text against which to measure performance is probably an insurmountable hurdle. But even if it *were* possible to identify 'the' script of *Much Ado About Nothing* or *Twelfth Night*, it seems unlikely that Goodman's notational system would serve in practice to dispel the problem of adaptation. On the one hand, his standards of compliance are too strict, disallowing as genuine any performance that fails to deliver every word of the script in its correct order. On the other hand, Goodman imposes no controls on such components of performance as intonation, physical stage business, or *mise-en-scène*. The interpretation offered by a 'genuine' performance, in Goodman's notational sense of the term compliance, could therefore easily fall beyond what Clayton, for example, considers 'the inferably integral meanings of the script' serving to define 'a hypothetical range of legitimate production':[39]

> Two examples given in the Performance Seminar at the International Shakespeare Conference in August 1986 clearly illustrate a line legitimately drawn between departure and extension: the weird sisters of *Macbeth* as 'three attractive young women in diaphanous robes' as opposed to a pregnant Lady Macduff. Can there be any doubt which better expresses the script? The second effect supplies a condition complementing the dialogue and stage directions. The first makes a wholesale reversal of script identities and appearances – in an adaptation, fine; in a production, distortive.

Or as Jay L. Halio explains it, even if the text is not cut or otherwise shaped, 'the visual aspects of a production … can so distract or distort that we find the connections between Shakespeare's original and the current production too distant – so far removed, in fact, that we are compelled to reject the production altogether'.[40] The theoretical position behind both of these arguments is that interpretation is inherent to the text. The text is thought to contain a possible – albeit potentially limitless – range of meanings which can then be enacted, even discovered, in performance. In effect, this builds into a less rigorous, 'common-sense' application of Goodman's thesis the interpretative component familiar from Wollheim's type–token thesis, while simultaneously pushing towards Bateson's Idealism insofar as the critic considers himself or herself able to discern in the text's correct word sequence a buried intention that can be either defied or obeyed.

The position is a difficult one. As we have seen, interpretation cannot be integrated into a notational system and therefore can play no part in Goodman's conception of the correct text or script. Wollheim, on the other hand, finds a place for interpretation but has little to say about texts, focusing instead on the work of art as a type with its tokens. Performance critics who invest in textual fidelity in effect posit the existence of a stable text which is then elevated to a status that closely resembles Wollheim's work of art as type. The text stands in the same relation to its non-identical performances as a type to its tokens, with the difference that the supposedly necessary properties of both text-as-type and performance are now somehow knowable, through appeal either to the text or to a common-sense response to it.

This leads to problems when Friedman, for example, argues that an 'authentic' performance may be defined as '*an enactment that expresses one version of the significance of a text that demonstrably falls within that text's range of meaning*', or when Richard Hornby insists '*that a script is realized* (or embedded) *in a performance via an interpretation, but that that interpretation is not something separate from the script but rather itself a function on* [sic] *it*'.[41] Friedman and Hornby fail to indicate how one can know the necessary properties of the text/script, a problem they perhaps unwittingly share with Wollheim's type–token theory, while nonetheless insisting that these properties are the criteria that determine authentic performance. As Goodman predicts, definitions that depart from a strict notational system have no certain means by which even to locate, much less regulate, the parameters of the work of art.[42] This is perhaps why a knowledge of the properties of the text-as-type is typically asserted in the form of rhetorical truth claims about the Idealist meaning of Shakespeare's text (see Clayton's examples of *Macbeth* in performance cited above) rather than justified on theoretical grounds. There is probably no other way to make the argument.

A second practical problem fidelity critics face in treating text as a form of type (or even archetype) is that it seems inevitably to fall into serious confusion when one considers drama's existence in two distinct media. It is precisely because Wollheim is careful *not* to identify type with text that his theory avoids logical inconsistency, with one and the same book – a copy, say, of *Richard III* – taken as a token when studied as literature in the classroom but as a type when carried into the rehearsal room. The difficulty here rests in constructing performance not on a par with text (or, as Wollheim would express the relation, as tokens in different media of the immaterial work of art as type) but as the text's (often illegitimate) offshoot.

There is no necessary reason, of course, why performance *must* be considered with text as integral to the dramatic work. The tendency among philosophers is to group literary drama alongside performance arts such as music and dance, or at least to consider how a script, a specialized form of literature, simultaneously functions in another art form as a 'score' for performance.[43] If the identity of drama is not constructed as bridging two distinct media, and what is essential to the work is limited to its text(s), then distinctions between drama and forms of literature such as the novel disappear. The position is not indefensible; it just makes different assumptions about the fundamental nature of drama. If this logic is pursued, performance of literary drama becomes *by definition* adaptation: a stage performance of *King Lear* is no more the work of art than a stage performance of *Bleak House* since both adapt the conditions of one medium (literature) to another (performance arts). This is the conclusion to which David McCandless is pushed, perhaps inadvertently, by the position that performance is interpretation not of the work, but of the text: 'all productions are necessarily adaptations in the sense that they adapt to the stage a specific interpretation of the text – always a distortion – rather than the text itself'.[44] It is impossible, of course, for 'the text itself' to appear on a stage because it exists as literature. The prior unspoken assumption that leads to an understanding of theatrical productions as 'necessarily adaptations' is the identification of the work of art with one idealized text, rather than with its (many) texts and performances.

It is perhaps in part to compensate for such difficulties that one often finds fidelity criticism shot through with appeals not just to the text or to the author's intention(s), but to moral probity. It is implied that honesty and a due respect for the truth on the part of producers should be enough to regulate performance and so enable the repetition and perpetuation of the dramatic work. Thus, a decision to transform 'old or otherwise alien scripts to new purposes and circumstances [is] hardly in itself a critical problem so long as the intention of adaptation is generally made clear as such'.[45] When, however, theatrical agents fail to make explicit such intentions, the perceived gap between text and performance becomes legible in terms of a discourse of fraudulent deception. As Friedman sets out the issue:

> Those who represent a production to the public ought to recognize that a theater event advertised as a performance of Shakespeare's *Measure for Measure* may reasonably be expected to demonstrate an authentic relationship to the text commonly known by that name. No theater company is under any compulsion to produce such a performance, but if the members of an ensemble have chosen to adapt the text rather than to perform it authentically, simple integrity demands that they characterize their production accurately as an adaptation.[46]

For commentators such as Clayton and Friedman the role of the scholar or interested spectator expands beyond a critical engagement with theatrical production to include bringing to notice and exposing as 'fakes' productions that they consider adaptations of Shakespeare that might otherwise be falsely passed off as performance. This seems very close to the anxiety that motivates a fear of forgery since the so-called adaptation, 'misrepresented' as production and so circulating undetected and unchallenged, debases the work's artistic and cultural currency. Where the integrity of paintings and sculptures is at continual risk from forgers, thieves, and vandals, the integrity of drama is presented as being no less at risk from theatrical adapters who misunderstand, fail to declare, or seek to conceal their true intentions.

At the end of a fascinating account of the intertwined fortunes of forgery and philology, Anthony Grafton concludes that although the tradition of criticism is often indebted to its 'criminal sibling' for its insights and methodologies, to lose sight of the gap between them, and so to accept the false for the true, is to undermine the foundations of civilization and morality:

> The forger seeks to protect himself and us from the critical power of our own past and that of other cultures. He offers us a refuge from the open-ended reflection on our ideals and institutions that a reading of powerful texts may stimulate. Above all, he is irresponsible; however good his ends and elegant his techniques, he lies. It seems inevitable, then, that a culture that tolerates forgery will debase its own intellectual currency, sometimes past redemption – as happened to Hellenistic Greek admirers of forged alien mysteries and modern German admirers of the literature of the Anti-Semitic International.[47]

The ability and desire to discern the cultural fake functions as the 'sign of health and virtue in a civilization'. A 'prevalence of forgery', by contrast, 'is a sign of illness and vice'.[48] The more canonical the author and dramatic work are, the more anxiety there is that one might inadvertently or carelessly accept false goods in place of the real thing. Because performance is perceived to have the unusual potential to slip *at any moment* into its criminal other, it is presented as requiring a special vigilance in what is figured as a never-ending effort to identify and secure the outer limits of what constitutes the author's work.

Textual production

Previous sections have already spelled out some of the problems of positing text as a foundation for performance. The more performance is demonized as the obvious potential source of surreptitious adaptation, the more text wrongly comes to seem apart from or impervious to production, an effect of inversely proportional authority that obscures the realization that textual production is subject to its own interventionist conventions.

For example, on the 'Drama – Shakespeare' shelf at my local bookstore a paperback copy of *Henry IV, Part 1* which promises to provide a 'clear modern version' of the work in 'plain everyday English' sits alongside other modern editions of Shakespeare's play. Guided by glowing testimonials from Sir Antony Sher and Dame Judi Dench printed on the back cover, students may buy this parallel-text edition in the 'Shakespeare Made Easy' series, only to meet with disapproval from their tutor or professor who explains that this is 'not' Shakespeare's play.[49] If this copy was wrongly catalogued by the sales assistant as 'Drama – Shakespeare' (is 'copy' a misnomer and should one call *Henry IV, Part 1* a new work?), where *should* this 'copy' of the play be shelved in the bookstore? The problem presented by this textual example concerns the relation to the work of instances of translation – an issue Wollheim, one recalls, identified as a peculiar challenge to the type–token thesis – compounded perhaps by a prevailing insistence among English speakers that the very essence of Shakespeare's works rests in their language.

A little further along the shelf are single-volume editions of *The Taming of the Shrew*, all of which reprint in an appendix the Sly scenes from the anonymous 1594 quarto *The Taming of a Shrew* (those same scenes one occasionally sees acted on stage in performances of Shakespeare's play).[50] Among the editions of *Othello* is *The First Quarto of Othello* – the dialogue is unfamiliar in certain key respects, but the back cover assures the reader that it is a copy of the play's 'earliest published version'.[51] Still further along the shelf, among the complete works collections, is a copy of the Oxford Shakespeare. This edition includes in its text of *Pericles* a scene which does not appear in the 1609 quarto (*Pericles* was not printed in the First Folio) and removes from its text of *Hamlet* the Prince's 'How all occasions' soliloquy with the exchange with the Captain that gives rise to it, printing these fifty-seven lines as part of an appendix called 'Additional Passages' (the same sort of appendix that marks the passages from *A Shrew* as both 'of' and 'not of' *The Shrew*). Greetham argues that performance is 'more susceptible to the [mis]quotation and misappropriation inherent in repetition and copying' than literature, but these instances of editions that, in their different ways, are copies of Shakespeare's plays might give one pause.[52] Original (in the sense of 'editorially invented') scenes are added, original (in the sense of 'authorially unrevised') speeches are omitted, original (in the sense of 'first') quartos are marketed as 'reveal[ing] how *Othello* was spoken in seventeenth-century performance', and different types of paratextual appendices, captured in the text's gravitational pull yet excluded from what the reader is encouraged to identify as 'the text itself', blur the supposedly crisp outline of the textual copy. The question for text, no less than it is with performance, is how one recognizes the work in the instance.

The problem of production, or rather the problem of the inaccurate or erroneous production, thus haunts textual no less than performance studies. What are one's criteria of accuracy? When is a copy accurate (enough)? This is perhaps the respect in which Joseph Grigely's discussion of the 'textual event' is most exciting. Grigely argues that a text can *never* be repeated. If every detail of a copy of the second quarto of *Romeo and Juliet*, from erratic punctuation to typeface to paper stock, is exactly replicated in 2008 – if somehow one could simply pick up where Thomas Creede's printers left off in 1599 – then according to Grigely the new printing will still be 'transposed ontologically by [its] historical context'.[53] Like Pierre Menard's *Quixote*, which is 'the same' as that of Cervantes and is yet a new work, this copy of *Romeo and Juliet* is of its own (twenty-first century) time.[54] Starting with the premise that no individual text can be 'more individual' than another, Grigely constructs the work of literature as consisting of an unfinished series of unique textual events characterized by 'acts of variance' rather than 'acts of compliance'.[55] A text – *any* text – is just another in a long string of texts by which an idea of the (necessarily unfinished) work endlessly comes into being. What interests me about the phenomenon Grigely calls textualterity are the points of contact it shares with a conception of the work as process. Grigely's position is particularly provocative, especially for textual scholars and editors, because it renders untenable accepted standards of textual authority. Bowdler's purged edition, to take a notorious example, is no more or less a text of Shakespeare's plays than is the First Folio – both are temporally located events in the work's series, each of them 'unique, and in its uniqueness, telling':

> Historically, textual criticism has tried to qualify moments of inscription according to their relative authority and establish a hierarchy of inscriptions according to authorial intent. It does not (from my point of view) matter whether these efforts succeed or not; indeed, there's no way to know. Nor does it matter whether the editions produced are judiciously emended texts, facsimile texts, scholarly texts, or condensed texts, for they all constitute further moments of inscription. This is where Derrida's point [about iteration] strikes home: a moment of inscription is no more than a moment of inscription ... [Bowdler's] often-cited maligning of Shakespeare is a historical argument about truth values, and such an argument cannot exist except by comparison with other moments of inscription.[56]

How performance might fit into this ontology of the work is not entirely clear. Grigely characterizes literary drama as primarily textual, as slightly more open-ended works of literature the peculiarities of which in terms of a dual existence as text and performance can be accommodated through a levelling account of textual authority; drama simply requires an extension of the basic principle of work as process. However, the way he characterizes the relations among work, text, and performance might seem more hierarchical than levelling:

> Nor is it necessary to exclude performances from this formulation. Where a series of performances is based on a specific text (what [Nelson] Goodman might call a score), and given
>
> $$W[ork] \rightarrow T[ext]_1, T_2, T_3, \ldots T_N$$
>
> then we might say that
>
> $$T[ext]_x \rightarrow P[erformance]_1, P_2, P_3, \ldots P_N.[57]$$

Grigely moves from this schema to the position that a performance is both *derivative* of text since a work generates an infinite number of texts, each of which in turn is able to generate an infinite number of performances, and is *itself* a 'text' that shapes one's idea of the work.[58] Performance even leads the way towards a conception of textualterity since 'we do not consider [pre-twentieth-century stage texts] to be adaptions [of Shakespeare] as long as they work within the genre of stage production'.[59] However, and as this chapter has been at pains to illustrate, this is much more than one can say. Certainly many Shakespeare scholars and students of theatre history would question his assertion that there exists an accepted convention that prevents the identification of adaptation in the theatre, as though the very fact of stage production secures by definition the integrity of Shakespeare's works. It is precisely because performance is conceived as bearing a second-order relation to the work – stage production is already an 'add-on', an adaptation of literature to another medium – that its status for Grigely seems uncontroversial.

These issues of textual and theatrical adaptation perhaps point to a more fundamental problem of origin. Grigely's theory of textualterity offers us brilliant insights in terms of the importance it sets on historical situation as contributing to the ontology of the work of literature. The way he finds difference among seeming identity by analysing the *timeliness of the text*, rather than the *timelessness of the work*, persuasively demonstrates the problems inherent in a conception of textuality that privileges object over process. And yet if every text is its own unique event – if there is 'no correct text, no final text, no original text, but only texts that are different, drifting in their like differences'[60] – then how does one link two texts to each other as related, or situate them, to adopt Grigely's own metaphor, as pearls on the string that is, for example, *Hamlet*? The differences between the texts are clear: what is no longer evident is what might connect them as the same. To come at it from another angle, on what grounds could one argue that any text on the *Hamlet* string could not just as easily be added as a pearl to the strings that are *Macbeth* or *Twelfth Night* – or *The Importance of Being Earnest*?

Grigely's unspoken assumption is that one brings to an encounter with texts an at least provisional idea of the identity of the work. This is what makes it possible in the first instance to distinguish texts as moments in the ongoing history of one work and not another. This, however, is to beg the very category that is under investigation. The insight that Grigely highlights as 'perhaps the most important aspect of textuality' is in this respect telling: '*a work of literature is ontologized by its texts*'.[61] Rephrasing the passage – 'a work of literature is ontologized by the texts of a work of literature' – makes more evident the circularity inherent in his use of the possessive case: unless one can already identify (something like) the work of literature, one cannot know the work of literature that the texts 'ontologize'. Again, this returns us to the problem of identity to which Goodman and Wollheim present such different answers: according to what principle(s) can Beethoven's *Fifth Symphony* be identified and perpetuated as a work of art that is distinct from *Three Blind Mice*? What is the reason why 'the various copies of *Ulysses* are all said to be copies of *Ulysses* and nothing else, why all the performances of *Der Rosenkavalier* are reckoned performances of that one opera'?[62] An 'uncentered alterity',[63] premised on non-identical textual events and the impossibility of repetition, can logically appeal to no external reference by means of which one could organize these discrete instances as a series, or as a 'work'.

Pragmatic adaptation

Discussions of text and performance in Shakespeare studies often arrive at something of a stand-off between those who argue that text should govern the acceptable limits of performance and those who argue that performance has its own independent status. Frequently the battle lines seem drawn along a purely ethical choice between equally unappealing alternatives: defying the text's instructions (so, by implication, denying the rights of the author) or constraining the creativity of theatrical producers. What has fallen out of this debate is an awareness that text, as Susan Wilsmore explains, has 'no independent existence'. To apply to theatre studies Wilsmore's insights into the ontology of literature, a text – no less than a performance – is always 'of' something else such as a novel or drama. '[A] work of art', by contrast, '*is* a poem, play, or novel.'[64] In textual studies, however, 'work' has come to seem something of a suspect term as new generations of textual scholars have challenged the circulation of 'texts that never were' and questioned the implicit (and often explicit) privileging of authorial intentions on the part of critical editors, an unease only further reinforced by Barthes' now famous statements about authorial canons and post-structuralist intertextuality in 'The Death of the Author' and 'From Work to Text'.[65] Editors of various stripes now prefer to speak of documents, texts, and versions, and to eschew a word like 'work' as smacking of the Idealist proclivities of an earlier age.

What this chapter has suggested, however, is that the work continues to have operative force in aesthetic theory, performance criticism, and textual studies. It is through recourse to an insubstantial idea of the work of art that stands apart from and bridges both text and performance that it is possible to explain how non-dramatic literature differs from drama. Instead of 'the text itself' coming to stand in place of the work, with performance assuming a second-order, adaptive relation as a performance of the text, performance and text are both, in their different ways, instances of the work. Moreover, it is only because one implicitly supposes the existence of the work that it is possible to draw relations of identity among non-identical instances of texts and performances in order to label some but not all of them *Hamlet* or *Twelfth Night*. This continued prevalence of the concept of the work (albeit rarely the actual word) among revisionist and materialist textual scholars alike can be obscured by the way the more neutral word 'play' or a title – *King Lear*, *Othello* – often does service for it. In the 'General Introduction' to the *Complete Works*, for example, the Oxford editors explain that they believe 'there are two distinct plays of *King Lear*, not merely two different texts of the same play'.[66] The distinction I believe they are drawing here is between a work that exists in two independently conceived versions that cannot be conflated, and a unified work that survives in slightly variant textual witnesses. Somewhat ambiguously, the idea of the 'work' is captured in the first half of the phrase by '*King Lear*' and in the latter half by the term 'play', a word which had moments earlier been synonymous with 'version'. David Scott Kastan, to take another example, rightly insists that 'physical texts' can tell us much that is lost in Idealist editions that present 'a work that never was', but he, too, falls back on the term 'play' to describe multiple, non-identical instances of the 'same' immaterial work in forms as various as manuscript, performance, and print.[67] In a terrific turn of phrase, Grigely explains how the word 'text' can conveniently point to everything and anything: 'almost without fail [it] sounds right, supplanting a vague uncertainty with a certain vagueness'.[68] The word 'play' is no less slippery. It sidesteps entirely debates in textual studies about versions and works, it can embrace either edition(s) or performance(s), or both, and most importantly, unlike 'text', it does not sound particularly theorized, yet remains available to theoretically inflected analysis.

It seems necessary, therefore, to redeem a term that is in danger of being entirely surrendered to Idealist criticism. Wilsmore describes the work as 'a normative structure embedded in the practices of a shared culture where values enter into the determination of the identity of the work of art', and argues that while it can be hard to identify, in 'normal contexts' we have no trouble determining it.[69] However, allegations of adaptation provide precisely the sort of abnormal circumstances that trouble recognition of the work, and at such moments the 'values' one brings to its determination are crucial. Wilsmore locates the work's essential properties through appeal to the artist, so returning us to the many theoretical problems associated with an intending author. I instead want to propose a more flexible account of the criteria by which one distinguishes one work from another, locating them not *prior* to the work's instances of production, for example in the mind of an artist, but *subsequent* to production, in users' perceptions of sameness and difference among the many variants found in distinct production instances. By formulating conceptual links among potentially unrelated and always non-identical instances of text and/or performance, a spectator who may or may not be a reader (and vice versa) constructs pattern(s) that he or she then provisionally identifies as one or more work(s).

This is where I depart from a vision of radical textual democracy, exemplified by Grigely's theory of textualterity, that dogmatically insists that because no text can be repeated, every text in its uniqueness is therefore no more or less an instance of the work than another. Any text, as Grigely argues, always carries with it its own historical context, but this insight does not disable one's ability in a present moment to draw distinctions and resemblances among instances. Indeed, it is only by means of this process – by evaluating the textual status of the first quarto of *King Lear*, or by deciding whether modern-dress productions or colour-blind casting should count as genuine or adaptive theatrical strategies – that one begins to emplot the work in history. Thus there is never, *pace* Grigely, a work without a centre. But neither is there an objective and knowable centre, as Bateson assumes, defined by the author's intentions.

In an important sense, Bateson belies his own insight into the pragmatic constructedness of the work of art. He likens a knowledge of *Hamlet* to the process of constitutional interpretation, yet insists that truth can be finally determined through appeal either to the Supreme Court or to the consensus of scholarship. To turn Bateson's analogy to a different purpose, I would argue that the dramatic work, no less than the constitution to which he compares it, cannot be known apart from the encounters between incompatible and contested ideological positions to which specific test cases give rise. As a result, the most one can say of the parameters of the work is that they are as flexible as they need to be to serve the changing purposes of its users. Work identity in such a model is responsive to textual-theatrical production, with users as varied as readers and spectators, no less than editors, publishers, and theatre practitioners, all of whom are influenced by their own particular historical and cultural circumstances, constructing competing ideas of the work's supposed essence, or constituent elements.

In denying a fixed or 'objective' work, my position is not that anything goes, or that any text or performance must be considered as genuine an instance of a particular work as the next – clearly, to take an extreme example of identity, one usually feels able in practice to distinguish between productions of *Hamlet* and *Macbeth*. Moreover, it is obvious that some readers and spectators will refuse to confer authority on *A Midsummer Night's Dream* as edited, for instance, by Thomas Bowdler as opposed to Peter Holland for the Oxford series, or as directed by Robert Lepage as opposed to Adrian Noble. Holland's and Noble's productions just seem to some users 'more' *A Midsummer Night's Dream* than the productions of Bowdler and Lepage. Valorizing or defending what some critics want to dismiss as an inauthentic textual or theatrical production is sometimes regarded sceptically as an irresponsible capitulation to dominant theoretical values, a form of postmodernist 'play' that opens culture to the sorts of dangers outlined by Grafton in relation to a too-willing acceptance of forgery. What I am trying to argue instead is that this problem of recognizing the work, and by extension its adaptations, is rather a necessary function of a form of art that circulates in two distinct media, performance and text, neither of which is controlled finally (or even arguably at first) by the author.

There will always be claims that some texts and performances of *Hamlet* are more authentic than others. However, once one abandons as impracticable Goodman's notational system, it is impossible, without recourse to wholly arbitrary assertions of boundaries and limits, to determine with certainty when one becomes its other, when a particular textual or theatrical instance is no longer a genuine instance of the work. How then can one distinguish the work from its adaptation? The simple answer is that without certain criteria to which one can appeal, one *cannot* absolutely separate the two. The more complex answer is that in such an indeterminate situation one constructs a provisional definition of the 'truth' of the work through ongoing debate. An individual instance 'counts' as the work if, and so long as, readers and spectators are willing to confer recognition on it as being a legitimate instance of, for instance, *Hamlet* or *A Midsummer Night's Dream*. Occasionally, as the result perhaps of professional calling, sense of duty, or temperament, one ventures to try to persuade others to share one's opinion. The pragmatic truth of the dramatic work of art – what is considered essential to an accurate, faithful, or authentic reproduction on the stage or page – is thus continually produced among communities of users through assertion and dissension, not legislated once and for all through appeal to an objective external authority. This is why, although there is no way logically to ensure that *King Lear* (to paraphrase Goodman) will not be transformed into *Dick Wittington*, this event has yet to happen. *King Lear* has not mutated into a Christmas pantomime – although it did for a while survive on stage as a tragicomedy – because the accepted boundaries of the work are monitored and regulated by interpretative communities that continually draw distinctions between work and adaptation.

The distinction I am seeking to draw here between provisional and absolute truths comes into contact with Richard Rorty's neo-pragmatic work on belief systems. The supposed limits of the dramatic work function as though they are true if they seem to account for what at that moment are considered important, even essential, criteria. Because the work is pragmatically determined according to use, it can be modified – or not – to accommodate better the different needs of successive ages and contemporaneous cultures. Border skirmishes about Shakespeare's works are thus significant, because they signal the presence of a form of cultural politics. Arguments about whether or not forms of corruption or adaptation are taking place are a sign of competing sides vying for the power to define, for the moment, that cultural construction that will 'count' or be valued as authentic Shakespeare – and the more canonical the work, the more hotly disputed is the debate about its authentic instances. Not surprisingly, then, instances of text and performance located either well within or well beyond currently accepted boundaries of the work rarely emerge as contested sites. However, as a textual or theatrical production approaches those cross-over points that for the present moment distinguish work from adaptation, debates about fraudulence, corruption, and the survival of the play increase proportionately. By marking where a failure of consensus occurs and considering the terms in which the conflict is represented, one can discern something like the present and evolving limits of a particular dramatic work.

2 Defining the work through production, or what adaptation is not

In the previous chapter I argued that the dramatic work, whether encountered as text or performance, is a dynamic process. This process begins with a stretch of creative activity, one or more events in the course of which might be arbitrarily posited as the moment when the work comes into existence (i.e., when a playwright hands over a manuscript, when a printed text is published, when actors deliver a first performance).[1] This creative activity might be textual or, in the case, say, of improvised or workshopped theatre where the written form is introduced late in the course of things and sometimes only as a derivative documentary record of the theatrical event, it might be a performance or rehearsal.[2] In practice, however, these two seemingly distinct starting points often become inseparably blurred since playwrights rarely maintain fully independent artistic control over theatrical production, or in many situations even over textual production. Such texts and/or performances are then available for subsequent (inevitably non-identical) repetition in either medium. The identity of the *work* of dramatic art, by contrast, is not limited by a supposed originary moment of publication, either theatrical or textual, but continually constructed in response to production by users as varied as theatrical practitioners, spectators and readers, and publishers and editors. One can see a performance or read an edition or script, but a perception of that production as an instance of something else, or of two or more such productions as instances of the same and not separate work(s), depends on a process of narrative emplotment.

The dramatic work is therefore the interpretative *consequence*, rather than origin, of textual and theatrical production. An encounter with an instance of dramatic production prompts one either to find a place for it within an already-existing conception of a dramatic work (or to *make* a place for it, if necessary, by adjusting one's expectations of the work), or to identify it as a first encounter with what seems, in one's own experience and according to one's own historically and culturally contingent criteria, a new work.

One therefore always has a pretty good sense whether a particular production is *Hamlet* or not, for it is only by means of such assertions that the work can come into existence at all. And to the extent that a consensus of opinion can be at least provisionally arrived at concerning the properties that seem essential to repetition of the work in the textual-theatrical instance, the work will achieve relative stability. On some level, of course, there is always an awareness that the direction of consensus-building might potentially be counter to one's own opinions about what Wollheim might call the 'necessary' properties of the work (hence anxieties about so-called adaptations of a work 'passing' as performance). This perhaps explains the persistence of appeals to the text as the origin of the work in face of the complex theoretical and practical complexities confronted by textual scholars and editors; holding a book provides a comforting, if false, perception of objective fixity, a seeming foundation for one's own beliefs about the work. Certain properties of the work can seem essential – non-standardized spelling and punctuation, the inclusion in *Hamlet* of a scene on the battlements or a fourth act soliloquy, a male actor in the role of King Lear (or Cordelia) – but any of these 'necessary' properties could be challenged or disputed in production, in turn potentially generating further modifications to the popular consensus about the nature of the work. To take an example of this process, the contributors to *The Division of the Kingdoms* along with the editors of the Oxford *Complete Works* edition presented *King Lear* in the 1980s as surviving in pre-theatrical and post-theatrical versions; two decades later, bolstered by narratives about Shakespeare's literary intentions that seem revisionist in a critical climate that prioritizes 'Shakespeare, Man of the Theatre', arguments are once again being strongly advanced in favour of understanding *King Lear* as an artistic unity.[3] These sorts of shifts are not only unsurprising, they are inevitable; the only thing that is remarkable about the watershed moment represented by the 1986 Oxford edition is how suddenly critical orthodoxies seemed to alter in response to its publication.[4]

What should be emphasized is that it is only by positing the work as prior to production – by supposing that the work is external to, or untouched by, production – that one is enabled to evaluate at all a particular instance of textual or theatrical repetition. As noted earlier in response to Grigely's important contribution to theories of art, without recourse either to a real belief or to a pragmatic willingness to accept that a knowable work is just 'there' one would lack the grounds from which to articulate what it is about non-identical instances that causes one to recognize them in the first place as productions of the same work. Thus even though the work is not the origin but the effect of production, it functions in the manner of a 'type', generating the perception of essential criteria that allows one to assess in texts and performances degrees of difference and similarity, and perhaps even to argue, where the differences seem too great, that the play in its essence exists *apart from* these instances. It is this pragmatic construction of the work that is responsive to textual-theatrical production, finally to return to the question concerning the whereabouts of *Hamlet* posed at the beginning of the previous chapter, that 'survives' performance – potentially it might survive, however, in an altered form.

In this chapter I will study two Royal Shakespeare Company (RSC) stagings that played in Stratford and London within five years of each other: the 1997 production of *Hamlet* directed by Matthew Warchus and starring Alex Jennings at the Royal Shakespeare Theatre (RST), and the 2003 production of *All's Well that Ends Well* directed by Gregory Doran and starring Judi Dench at the Swan Theatre. These two stagings offer useful points of contrast in terms of a practical application of this theoretical analysis of work identity and the intimately related problem of adaptation. Both shows were in their different ways popular with audiences. However, while the former created among some spectators a strong perception that there was an essential work somewhere else that was not being fully realized in this instance of production (so leading to allegations of adaptive direction), the latter was celebrated as the work itself embodied in, or even discovered through, performance. The Doran *All's Well* projected an illusion of work stability as the reassuring effect of performance by seeming deliberately to turn away from a very specific form of adaptive practice at a heightened moment in the RSC's institutional history. By contrast, the self-consciously innovative Warchus *Hamlet* challenged in key ways expectations of the work, so prompting a debate about the essence of *Hamlet* that serves no less effectively than the Doran instance to highlight how critical assessment of the particular instance *produces*, rather than meets or fails to meet, the criteria of identity by which the work is defined.

Recognizing *Hamlet*

Speaking of directing *Hamlet* for the stage, Trevor Nunn explains that 'the cutting is virtually the production. What you decide to leave in is your version of the play.'[5] For Nunn, how one shapes the text(s) of *Hamlet* is the crucial factor when it comes to performance – more important, say, than concept, lighting design, or casting. It creates a version over which the director can assume a proprietary interest (it is 'your version'), and yet it is not a new work, or even an adaptation. The copy one prepares is deliberately different from the copy one works from, both of which will be very different from the anticipated theatrical production (a copy in another medium), yet all of these repetitions share enough in common to allow one to recognize them, in their variety, as *Hamlet*.

A crisis of recognition is commonly provoked either as the result of the sheer number of textual and/or visual innovations or as the effect of a single striking innovation. Peter Hall, complaining that concerns about expense force directors to cut 'like barbarians', explains that he once shortened a show's running time by 'chipping within speeches', making the type of cuts that Stanley Wells describes as 'practical rather than interpretative'.[6] Hall's goal is to trim the text in such a way that elided lines are not likely overly to disturb an audience's expectations of the work. However, what renders a particular cut visible and so potentially worthy of comment as an 'interpretative' rather than 'practical' choice is not easy to determine. Warchus, trying to downplay the cuts he made to *Hamlet*, mentions in an interview that in a previous RSC season he cut one thousand lines from Jonson's *Devil Is an Ass*, and 'absolutely nobody noticed'.[7] Doran, in the production discussed later in this chapter, cut an entire scene from the text of *All's Well* without attracting any of the controversy caused by Warchus's decision to cut from *Hamlet* the opening scene on the battlements.[8] Sometimes a certain type of cut matters, perhaps even prompting concerns or queries about adaptation; however, in another work, or at a different moment in the same work's performance history, a similar or even identical cut passes unremarked. What makes the Warchus production such an interesting site to explore Shakespeare's works and the problem of adaptation is thus not solely what the director brought to the show, but what audiences took away from it. It was precisely the dynamic between the two that led to a perception that this show stood 'a goodish way along the road that leads from "version" to "adaptation"'.[9]

The extent to which this production challenged ready identification as an instance of *Hamlet* is suggested by the striking diversity and extremity of opinion one finds in the reviews. Some think this 'newly minted' staging taps into a 'genuine sense of modern spiritual anguish' that makes 'the most hardened Hamlet-watcher feel he or she is seeing the play for the first time'.[10] Not everyone, however, agreed. Complaints about the director's 'bravado' reach their fullest expression in John Peter's blistering attack on the 'special arrogance' that would prompt such 'butchery'.[11] Adapting to new circumstances a line from John F. Kennedy's inaugural address at the height of the Cold War, Peter puts the heightened rhetoric of a threatened national security to the service of Shakespeare's artistic integrity: 'This is not a question of Shakespeare-worship, or the sanctity of the text: it is a question of what the play is about and how it works. It is not sissy to be humble before a classic. Ask not what Shakespeare can do for you; ask what you can do for Shakespeare.' The implicit suggestion seems to be that an undisciplined or perhaps just thoughtless individualism endangers a greater good (whether one understands that to be the freedom of the Western world, or the survival of canonical drama). But even a moderate such as Robert Gore-Langton, who praises Warchus as a 'brilliantly stylish' director who 'bravely rejects the Stratford house style', likewise feels obliged to warn traditionalists to stay away, reflecting that 'when you think about it, [this treatment of *Hamlet* is] a damn cheek'.[12] A recognition of its excesses is thus no less evident in those who see merits in the show than in the 'purists' with whose anticipated objections the former seem to have sympathy.[13] Many are willing to call it good theatre, but there remains an uncertainty about whether it is 'really' *Hamlet.*

Especially controversial was the decision to cut the opening scene on the battlements, along with Fortinbras, any threat of military invasion, and the 'How all occasions' soliloquy which is printed in the second quarto and sometimes included in editions as part of the fourth act.[14] Attention is shifted from the public world of Denmark to what some critics described as an Ibsen-like preoccupation with the domestic world of the prince, a naturalistic treatment of family enhanced by the modern dress setting and a 'low-key and conversational' delivery of verse.[15] The production's emphasis on family relations rather than state politics is signalled from the outset by an opening tableau in which Jennings, dressed in a black suit and holding an urn, stares out at the audience while he listens to the booming voice of an unseen Claudius narrate the events that led to his marriage to his brother's widow. On a screen behind him is projected a black and white film of a boy playing in the snow with his parents; whether this is an actual home movie or Hamlet reliving in his mind's eye memories of childhood is unclear, and probably not important. The last image of the ninety-second film, as Hamlet pours out his father's ashes, is a close-up of husband and wife laughing in each other's arms.

This tableau is interrupted by an explosion of fireworks, and the screen pulls away to relocate the action at a modern wedding reception complete with lights and balloons, a wine table, and a live band. As couples dance and guests circulate in evening gowns and dinner jackets, a roving spot picks out key moments of interaction, such as Hamlet handing a letter to Ophelia or taking Polaroid photographs of his mother and Claudius. Heavily cut passages of dialogue from the first four scenes are rearranged and spliced into this 'wedding feast Shakespeare never wrote', creating of separate episodes one long sustained scene.[16] The effect is of a restless, swirling action in which characters briefly intercept each other, the action seeming almost filmically to 'cut' from one exchange to another. Claudius's office, in a manner reminiscent of *The Godfather*, is established as a private enclave within the space of the party by means of a grille that

slides in place to separate a small downstage area from the reception
continuing upstage; as Hamlet finishes his first soliloquy (the speech that
usually begins 'O, that this too too solid flesh would melt'), the grille slides
away, the furniture descends on the trap, and the audience is returned to
the public space, where Laertes encounters his sister. Polonius joins them
to bid farewell to Laertes and ushers Ophelia away from an approaching
Hamlet, who instead encounters Horatio who tells him the news of the
Ghost's sighting. As Hamlet comments on the time, the light design
changes to a grey dimness, all of the guests apart from Hamlet and Horatio begin to move in slow motion, and the Ghost of Hamlet, dressed in
formal wear, walks towards his son. As the beckoning Ghost departs
upstage, the lights return to normal and the other actors snap out of what
the promptbook calls 'Treacletime'.[17] Ophelia, registering Hamlet's odd
behaviour and making towards him, is intercepted by her father, who
emphasizes that he would not have her 'slander any moment leisure / As to
give words or talk with the Lord Hamlet', and the scene ends with her
promise to obey.

The structure of this sequence, with its fluid staging and heavily edited,
intercut dialogue, owes an evident debt to story-telling techniques familiar
to film, and the production script includes sometimes elaborate accounts of
non-verbal action after the manner of a screenplay. The decisions to open
with Hamlet holding his father's remains both in his hands and in his
memory, and to return to the home-movie footage in the play's closing
moments as an epilogue to the tragic action, create a powerful sense of an
anguished psyche. Further explanation of his mental strain and extreme
sense of isolation is offered by an inset dumbshow placed after his
encounter with the Ghost in which Ophelia returns to Hamlet his gifts. As
the promptbook describes the 'Night of Madness':

> We see OPHELIA in her room fastening a box of papers. She weeps.
> They are given to a servant who delivers them to HAMLET who is
> with HORATIO. It is night. HAMLET opens the box. Letters and
> small objects cascade onto the floor. With disbelief he recognises the
> love letters and gifts he has sent to OPHELIA. He runs to her room.
> He knocks and calls her name repeatedly, but there is no reply. He
> cries out in great distress. Inside the room OPHELIA sits on the floor,
> her hands over her ears, sobbing.[18]

The scene's simultaneous staging of action in separate bedrooms along
with an exclusive reliance on visual narration is another device perhaps
more typical of film and television than theatre – Branagh, for example,
frequently introduces this kind of device into his film productions to inform

viewers of a significant backstory, whether that is of Hal's troubled friendship with Falstaff, or Ophelia's sexual relations with Hamlet.[19] The exchange ends with Hamlet upstage centre, screaming as the walls close in on him from either side. The emotional intensity of this interpolated scene prepares for Hamlet's retreat a few scenes later to a cramped attic, where, surrounded by the boxed remnants of a past life, he contemplates suicide. Instead of carrying a dagger, this very modern Hamlet pulls out of a brown paper bag a gun, pointing it at the audience before turning it to his head. However, private space, like memories, can be intruded on, and Hamlet is forced to hide the gun as first Rosencrantz and Guildenstern, then Polonius and the troupe of travelling players climb up through the trap to fill a room that seems no longer able to offer a haven from the court.

The placement here of the 'To be or not to be' soliloquy does not precisely correspond to any of the three early texts, but it seems at least partly indebted to the narrative shape of the first quarto (Q1) insofar as it falls before rather than after the Player King's speech and Hamlet's sudden inspiration to trap the King at a play. Also from the first quarto is an exchange between Gertrude and Horatio describing Hamlet's return from his voyage to England that is rarely seen in performance. After Ophelia exits the stage mad, followed by her brother and the King, Horatio approaches Gertrude to tell her that her son has returned to Denmark. He then reads to her the contents of the letter as printed in the second quarto (Q2) and Folio (F) texts. Thus although Warchus does not make Gertrude privy to Claudius's plot to murder her son (Horatio's Q1 summary of the letter makes the King's treachery explicit, whereas the Q2/F letter only promises to reveal in person news that 'will make thee dumb'), he gives the Queen more agency by allowing her a scene in which she receives information independently of the King. This effect of a strong and capable wife and mother is reinforced by decisions elsewhere to augment her part with lines usually spoken by Claudius. Most notably, she dominates the early scene in which Rosencrantz and Guildenstern are formally welcomed to court, the ineffectual King interrupting his prayers only long enough to get their names wrong; later, when Ophelia retches during her mad scene, Gertrude passes Claudius a scarf to wipe up the mess.

What one might typically think of as *Hamlet* is thus not only cut and rearranged, incorporating material from all three extant early texts, but also supplemented with business as diverse as a home movie and the enactment of Ophelia's rejection of Hamlet. Although Warchus explains that he found appealing 'something short and fresh, fast and furious', the production still ran three and a quarter hours with interval.[20] The issue is thus not (or not only) the show's abbreviated running time, but the way Warchus shaped a production so noticeably at odds in certain key respects with the *Hamlet* to which many spectators were accustomed. To take the decision to omit the first eight lines of the first soliloquy as a small but telling example, the cut makes good narrative sense in the context of the action since Hamlet's bitter opening line in this production – 'That it should come to this' – is prompted specifically by the sight of his mother and Claudius leaving the inner office to return to their wedding reception. Starting a well-known speech at an unexpected point has the additional practical benefit of a slight jarring effect that captures the attention of even seasoned spectators, encouraging them to hear Hamlet's words as though for the first time. But by insisting in rehearsal, at least as Jennings tells it, that the famous phrase 'O, that this too too solid flesh would melt' would not feature in the production, Warchus seems to enter deliberately into – or at least not shy away from – a dispute about what audiences can, or will, recognize as *Hamlet*.[21] Warchus's cuts to even famous lines, by sharp contrast to Hall's account of 'chipping' within speeches, are conspicuous – and, insofar as such lines are considered by some spectators among the necessary properties of the play, inflammatory. I would disagree with John Gross, however, that this is Warchus self-consciously 'establish[ing] his credentials as an Innovator'.[22] His position, as he explains it, is that great dramatic works are done a disservice if they are allowed to become as familiar as 'nursery rhymes'.[23] Although it may seem to some a paradox, his directorial choices are designed to *preserve* the integrity of the work – to prevent *Hamlet*, in a provocative reversal of Goodman, from being transformed into *Three Blind Mice*.

Certainly there is no sense in the programme that this show self-identifies as adaptation. Credits for 'Children', 'Party Guests', and a 'Film sequence', along with a description of Polonius in the plot summary as 'an old family friend', might alert some to a production that is somewhat out of the ordinary.[24] However, a note that the text 'has been specially cut and partially restructured by the director with reference to the First and Second Quartos and the Folio' asserts the production's authoritative, if eclectic, textual credentials.[25] A two-page spread overleaf entitled 'Hamlet: The Historie [*sic*] of a Text', which includes a scholarly essay by Neil Taylor, a long quotation from Philip Edwards, and the text of the 'To be or not to be' speech as printed in the first and second quartos, makes the point that 'study of the early texts of *Hamlet* is the study of a play in motion'.[26] '[I]s there a fixed entity which we could call Shakespeare's *Hamlet*?', Taylor continues, concluding that since texts continue to 'proliferat[e]' by means of editorial and theatrical interpretation, '[t]he answer has to be no'. The quotation from Edwards, cited from his New Cambridge edition of *Hamlet*, explains differences among the three texts printed in the early seventeenth century as 'representations of different stages in the play's development', and Edwards suggests that 'our task' is 'to choose the moment at which we would try to arrest the movement of the play and say "This is the *Hamlet* we want"; or even, if we dare, "This is the *Hamlet* that Shakespeare most wanted"'.[27] The combined force of the two analyses is to present a strong argument in favour of understanding *Hamlet* as an evolving process. The arrangement of the extract from Edwards as a narrow ribbon of text running the length of the page just to the right of Taylor's essay makes his ambition to identify one version of the play with Shakespeare the last thing a reader comes to before an examination of two markedly variant versions of Hamlet's most famous soliloquy. Although Edwards is speaking specifically of a choice among the early quartos and Folio, the rhetorical and visual effect of the two-page spread is to suggest that one might choose to 'arrest the movement of the play' at *tonight's* performance, that we might even 'dare' to call this, its most recent theatrical production, 'the *Hamlet* that Shakespeare most wanted'.

The programme thus primes audiences to see and hear a *Hamlet* which may not be familiar in all its parts, but which is still as authoritative as, and for some spectators even preferable to, other productions. The irony, of course, is that by presenting textual adjustments as a discussion point the programme betrays its own doubts about the status of this production, generating the very questions of authority it seeks to dispel. It is only because those involved with the production have a perception of it as unusual or edgy that such care is taken in the programme to insist that this is 'really' *Hamlet* – if the show did not already seem a potential problem, there would be no need to rally academic commentary to address the status of the text. There is little surprise, then, that some spectators should refuse to grant the production the authoritative status the programme seems so anxiously to defend. 'Directors will always find tame scholars to endorse such efforts', Gross scathingly notes. 'There is one in the Stratford programme, pointing out that "there isn't a fixed entity that we can call Shakespeare's *Hamlet*". Of course there isn't. There isn't even – can't be – a definitive text. Our perspective on the play is bound to change from generation to generation. But Everything Flows doesn't mean the same thing as Anything Goes.'[28] Gross's complaint gives popular expression to my theoretical point about the work's pragmatic, fluid existence: without reference to a definitive text, one still feels confident at any given moment to evaluate whether particular productions should be included among textual-theatrical instances of *Hamlet*. It is patently not the case that 'Anything Goes' since not *every* instance of production will be considered *Hamlet*. The company, lacking the grounds on which to prove that this must *necessarily* be accepted as a production of *Hamlet*, is on exactly the same footing as critics who attack the production as a travesty or adaptation of the 'real' thing. Gross and Warchus simply disagree about what will constitute (for the moment) the work's necessary properties. The most either party can do to pursue the dispute is seek to persuade a wider public of the legitimacy of his position using the vehicles for argument (a newspaper column, a theatre programme) available to him. Warchus, of course, is right when he insists that there was nothing unusual about his handling of the text for performance. What seems especially remarkable is that an 'issue' was made of his text even though many of his specific choices had frequently been anticipated by earlier productions, or were consistent with long-standing stage traditions. The uproar caused by the excision of Fortinbras, for example, seems particularly strange, since this was a standard convention of performance throughout the nineteenth century; Forbes-Robertson's decision in 1897 to bring on Fortinbras in the final scene was considered a major innovation, and it is one that was not adopted, for example, by Olivier.[29] Robert Hapgood notes that until the middle of the twentieth century '*Hamlet* had sailed serenely past the sort of involvements with contemporary politics experienced by other Shakespearian plays', and, according to Billington, interest in *Hamlet*'s national and international politics began to prevail in British theatres only as late as the 1980s.[30] Thus the widespread claim that Warchus, in choosing to exclude Fortinbras and Norway, has 'reduce[d] "Hamlet" to an Ibsen play, albeit the greatest one ever written', or transformed 'Elsinore [into] a rather large back porch' in a 'sentimental American father–son drama' seems a striking case of theatrical-critical amnesia.[31] Even the oft-remarked decision to cut Shakespeare's tense opening scene was nothing new. Richard Eyre, to cite but one contemporary instance, cut both battlements and Ghost in an acclaimed production at the Royal Court in 1980 in which a possessed Hamlet (played by Jonathan Pryce) seemed to belch up the dead man's words.[32] J. C. Trewin, writing of this production in the context of a retrospective look at *Five and Eighty Hamlets*, notes that by the last quarter of the twentieth century '[t]he loss of the great opening had become commonplace'.[33]

It is not inconceivable, therefore, that Warchus's *Hamlet* might have been received without outcry. However, without the kind of necessary criteria of identity that is provided by Goodman's notational system or invoked by Wollheim's type–token thesis, work recognition in practice depends in large part on the contextual influence of historical, national, and even institutional circumstances. In this light, it was probably inevitable that a shortened text would come under sharp scrutiny since recent publicity had forged a strong link between theatrical authority and full-text presentation. The previous RSC production of *Hamlet*, directed by Adrian Noble and starring Kenneth Branagh, was based on a text – popularly known as the 'eternity cut' – that is a conflation of the second quarto and Folio texts. In sharp contrast to the Warchus programme, a short statement about the variant texts in the 1992 programme resolved textual authority into a clear, reassuringly matter-of-fact, hierarchical order: the first quarto is 'a pirated edition transcribed from performance', while the Folio text is a revised and shortened version of the second quarto which is in turn 'thought to be a genuine text revised by Shakespeare himself'.[34] The choice in 1992 to play an editorially conflated text, and to advertise it as the complete, full-text *Hamlet*, 'promoted the impression that here was a definitive version of this chameleon play'.[35] The authority of this production was further enhanced by the acknowledgement in the programme that '[s]pecially bound rehearsal copies were provided for the company's use by Cambridge University Press'.[36]

Conflation, however, is just another form of textual construction. To return to Nunn's point that what one chooses to leave in is one's own version of the play, even the 'eternity cut' (as the term 'cut' implies) cannot include everything, since the director-as-editor is inevitably forced to choose among variant textual versions of the 'same' scene or passage. But the perception that 'more' Shakespeare leads to 'more authentic' Shakespeare had only grown in the five years between 1992 and 1997, prompting a heightened awareness of textual decisions even before the Warchus production opened in May. The film version, directed by and starring Branagh and running over four hours like the stage production that inspired it, was released in the United States at Christmas 1996 in time to be nominated in March 1997 for best adapted script at the Academy Awards. So although Warchus told reporters curious about rumours of cuts not to make 'a big issue' out of his treatment of the text, emphasizing (with Nunn) that 'everyone who has ever staged *Hamlet* has cut it in some way', it was never likely in such a context that the extent and type of shaping he undertook could be made without inviting controversy.[37]

The interpretative balance for some spectators was simply out of kilter: there was too much Warchus and not enough Shakespeare.[38] This perception of an interpretative surfeit is yet again revealing of the theoretical problems inherent to 'recipe' or 'blueprint' models of the work indebted to Wollheim's type–token thesis.[39] The premise is that tokens of a type have certain 'necessary' properties, but that each token, precisely because it offers a new interpretation, will also inevitably have properties in excess of its type. Without prior knowledge of the essential properties – something one cannot achieve short of positing an Idealist conception of the type, ultimately located in the mind of the author – one cannot determine when precisely the introduction of interpretative properties such as added business, deleted words, or scene substitution compromises the work in its instance to create a token of another type altogether. This is not to imply that transformation can never be identified, only to say that the precise moment when a production no longer seems an instance of a particular work is a matter of opinion. The controversy surrounding the Warchus staging clearly signals that for some reason, for at least some spectators, the show generated a crisis of recognition. In the dialogue and polemic that ensued about Shakespeare's work and why this should not be considered a legitimate instance of it, one is able to trace the specific ways in which an implicit consensus about the shape of *Hamlet* was felt to be breached – or to look at it from an alternative perspective, one can begin to locate in such criticism what was thought at that moment most to threaten the continued survival of *Hamlet* as a work of art.

Film's influence on the production registered as especially problematic, with projected images, scenes of extended non-verbal action, and the narrative fluidity of the wedding reception seeming to blur cinema and live theatre as distinct media. Lloyd Rose, writing at the time of the show's American transfer and finding in the production specific allusions to films and film genres, calls it 'radically inclusive': '[T]his "Hamlet" takes place in The Movies – gangster films, swank musicals, female sob stories, even horror films, a world of props and manners we instantly recognize. As this common cultural reference for the audience fuses with the play, the production expands into the Eisenhower Theater like an explosion in slow motion.'[40] Inclusion and accessibility, however, are not necessarily positive attributes. In the context of a theatrical staging that 'aspires to being a film rather than a play', and a director who 'seems to think he is patching up a film script for Hollywood, not staging Shakespeare in his home town', a perception of popularism can make major interpretative sticking-points of otherwise commonplace directorial choices.[41] More precisely, it seemed to make Warchus's emphasis on the domestic family situation to the exclusion of international or state politics potentially legible as typical of a supposed late twentieth-century tendency to 'dumb down' Shakespeare.

The 'problem' of popularism was a hot topic in Britain throughout the spring of 1997, sparked off by the media sensation surrounding the release of Baz Luhrmann's *William Shakespeare's Romeo + Juliet*. Overlooked at the Oscars in March of that year, the film was critically savaged as a gimmicky, badly spoken picture that panders to the shallow inclinations of a postmodern generation better equipped to spot pop culture references than to evaluate high culture art.[42] And yet Luhrmann's fast-paced, visually extravagant film, with its high-energy soundtrack and playful anachronisms, was a massive and unexpected box office success in both the United States and Britain. Released in Britain just five weeks before *Hamlet* opened at the RSC, and praised by Warchus as 'a visionary, inspired piece of work', it was perhaps inevitable that the heightened polemic generated by *Romeo + Juliet* should spill over to attach itself to *Hamlet*.[43] Billington's prediction that Jennings' performance 'could become as much an emblem of the times as David Warner's student-scarved version was in the sixties' thus seems particularly apt, Georgina Brown likewise concluding her enthusiastic review by claiming that '[t]his is a *Hamlet* of our time for our time'.[44] Depending on one's perspective, such praise can be read as evidence of what is both right and wrong about the production. Seeming to speak so clearly to, and for, a film and television literate audience, the production provides the occasion for debate about the values and aesthetics of classical theatre at the end of the millennium. The way Shakespeare suddenly seems 'of our time' rather than 'for all time' may be the source of the trouble, this *Hamlet* just standing as an acute modern example of perceived cultural failings.

Hamlet, the flagship production of a flagship theatrical company, thus becomes the site for a struggle over the ownership and meaning of Shakespeare. 'How much', as an opinion piece in the *New York Times* characterized the debate, 'should [the RSC] popularize – or Luhrmannize – Shakespeare to appeal to MTV-fed audiences?'[45] The possible popularity of the stage production becomes an irrelevant measure of the show's true worth; indeed, popularity among the *wrong* audiences could be taken as evidence that the production has certainly missed the mark in terms of the work's artistic complexity. This is 'a little *Hamlet* for little minds', Alastair Macaulay concludes, filled with "90s sightbites delivered at compelling pace, fit for an impatient generation'.[46] In other words, like Luhrmann's treatment of *Romeo and Juliet*, this is 'Shakespeare Lite', the theatrical answer to the 'Shakespeare Made Easy' editorial series. Since the traditional hallmark of high art is supposedly its *in*accessibility, the uneasy feeling grows that this is perhaps not Shakespeare's work after all. This is the real force of complaints that Warchus has transformed *Hamlet* into American family drama, and classical theatre into popularist film: the process posited by Goodman whereby great canonical works can be altered by a series of tiny substitutions, omissions, and alterations into easily consumed popular art seems already under way. What is worse, some spectators not only seem willing to accept in place of the real thing what some consider a fake, they even seem to prefer it.

At a roundtable discussion hosted by the RSC to address a *Guardian* report by Lyn Wardner in which Warchus is quoted as calling for a ten-year moratorium on performing Shakespeare, Stephen Poliakoff argued that the desire to make the plays exciting by 're-shaping Shakespeare into something he is not' is the sign of '*fin de siècle ennui*'.[47] This diagnosis reiterates Gardner's original speculation that Warchus is 'tired', suffering the sort of deep-seated 'weariness' that comes from being a hot director in constant demand.[48] It is wrong, Poliakoff continues, 'to twist Shakespeare into becoming a "new play" ... The plays can be done in many new ways but we shouldn't be making him into "new work": we should have faith in new audiences changing the context of his plays by themselves.' The problem, as we have seen, is that works themselves inevitably alter in face of changing contexts. But for Poliakoff, the greatest challenge to the perpetuation in performance of authentic Shakespeare is a loss of 'faith', a late-millennial exhaustion or vaguely defined postmodern cynicism that prompts a restless, shallow search for novelty. A debate about genuine production is thus reconfigured as an indictment of the moral values of a jaded age that prefers out of boredom or inadequacy to consume a corrupt or fraudulent form in place of the real thing, a values-based discussion of the problem of adaptation that recalls Grafton's reservations about forgery and cultures willing to tolerate its circulation.

Is Warchus's *Hamlet* an instance of Shakespeare's work or an instance of some other work, perhaps an adaptation? A timely interpretation or (if it is not the same thing) evidence of a pervasive 'Shakespeare fatigue'?[49] The urgency with which the debate was pursued on all sides suggests that the production could at least potentially be considered to fall within the boundaries that defined *Hamlet* – but at that moment in the work's history not by everyone. Ultimately, however, the controversy surrounding this production functioned not to legislate once and for all whether this *Hamlet* can be taken as an authentic instance of the work but rather, and especially for those who might consider it to approach the category of adaptation, such debate serves the pragmatic effect of bringing into existence a perception of a stable, pristine work somewhere else, somewhere beyond this particular instance of production. And thus *Hamlet* once again survives (this) performance, the defining limits of the work seeming to everyone who makes recourse to such a concept to be 'necessarily' as broad or as narrow as new interpretation requires, and popular cultural consensus – or its failure – will allow.

Recognizing the Royal Shakespeare Company

As the Warchus example suggests, debates *en vogue* among particular interpretative communities can impact on work recognition, suspicions, for example, of an apparent 'Americanization' of British culture or of a supposed postmodern detachment from activist politics seeming to heighten the perception of adaptive production. This section, no less interested in contexts of reception, adopts a slightly different strategy by taking as its focus a staging that few, if any, would describe as adaptation – Gregory

Doran's 2003 staging of *All's Well that Ends Well*. This production was not only widely hailed as an instance of classical performance at its very best, but it was praised by critics for allowing audiences to see and appreciate more fully what had apparently been there in the text all along. John Gross pays the director the backhanded compliment of 'not getting in the way', and so 'let[ting] Shakespeare's words speak for themselves'.[50] Charles Spencer, describing the show as 'miraculous' and 'the Shakespeare production of one's dreams', makes even greater claims for it as a landmark event with the announcement that 'A neglected masterpiece has been triumphantly reclaimed'.[51] My goal here is to press at this assumption that authority necessarily or in a straightforward manner derives simply from being 'true' to the text by exploring in some detail the factors that led to the conferral of authority on this production. My argument is that in this particular case what was recognized as authentic Shakespeare resulted in part from what could be recognized at this moment in the company's fortunes as an authentic Royal Shakespeare Company.

All's Well that Ends Well opened on 11 December 2003 at the Swan Theatre in Stratford-upon-Avon and transferred two months later to the Gielgud Theatre, London. The advance publicity for the show caused an immediate sensation because it was to mark the return after twenty-five years to the Stratford stage of Judi Dench in the role of the Countess of Rossillion.[52] The production, as though to acknowledge that Dench's presence was itself an event, opened on a picture of quiet reflection as the Countess entered alone to walk slowly downstage, her private musings underscored with the lonely notes of a solitary cello. Although she was followed moments later by a busy household readying itself for Bertram's departure for the French court, this early, almost Chekhovian, sense of things winding down permeated the action set in Rossillion, and coloured more generally Doran's interpretation of the play. An autumnal coldness was suggested by a lighting design that fluctuated between a high, watery light cast onto the floor at Rossillion as though streaming through tall latticed windows, and the intimate candlelight which etched out the interior spaces of Paris and Florence.

As Michael Billington among others commented, Stephen Brimson Lewis's wintry design was 'stunningly beautiful',[53] and paired with music by Paul Englishby and lighting by Paul Pyant it could evoke variously a sense of bereaved loss and haunting magic. The spare set, with its textured grey stone flooring and opaque smoked glass backdrop, was elegantly flexible. A low afternoon sun seemed to shine through the glass in the opening scene, revealing in silhouette grey trees carved into its surface; after the intermission, lighting and sound effects in combination with simple hand-held props transformed the roar of a smoke-choked battlefield (Act 3.3) to the stillness of a misty morning on a country estate (Act 3.4).

All's Well, with its supernatural overtones and troubling portrayal of marital entrapment and betrayal, has traditionally been a play neither well liked nor frequently staged. Bertram's poor judgement in seducing Diana, as he believes, and then publicly denying both his suit and her claim to him in marriage make him seem an increasingly unattractive protagonist, while on the other side one feels no less uneasy about the calculated way Helena first wins and then retains, through a bed trick, a reluctant husband as a gift or prize from the King of France. The reviewers disagreed about whether Doran found a solution to this most problematic of problem plays, Spencer likening the production's mixture of 'sunlight and shadows' to the bittersweet tensions typical of modern stage treatments of *Twelfth Night*, others highlighting the unresolved ambiguity of a final stage picture where the lights fall on Helena and Bertram standing motionless at a distance from one another, a tableau that deferred indefinitely the comic resolution promised by the play's title.[54]

Past directors have often addressed a difficult storyline by cutting it – Tyrone Guthrie, for example, excised the bitter clown, Lavatch, and the early discussion of virginity between Parolles and Helena was for years omitted as indecorous.[55] Doran likewise made conspicuous rearrangements and cuts to dialogue and scenes, as well as 'chipping within speeches' as recommended by Hall. The most sustained cuts were the partial curtailment of Lafeu's discovery of Parolles as a fool in 2.3 (about fifteen lines prior to Lafeu's first exit were cut), the elision in its entirety of the short scene featuring the Duke of Florence (3.1), a rearranged and so slightly less malicious account of the Dumaine brothers by Parolles during his supposed capture by the enemy (4.3), and the omission of the King's epilogue to allow attention to linger on Helena and Bertram. In total, Doran cut about 340 lines, or just over ten per cent of the Folio text.

However, rather than simply cut away the troubling and inaccessible emotional register of *All's Well*, Doran cushioned its impact by balancing the ethical complexities of the marriage plot against the values and experience of a central core of characters – the King, the Countess, Lafeu, and the clown, Lavatch (cast in this production as being of an age with his mistress) – stretching from Rossillion to the French court. One sensed in these performances a shared impulse to care for and protect from pain family and friends, an ethic that had yet to be instilled in the likes of Bertram and Parolles. Lavatch, upon his return to Rossillion from the French court and, as a note in the promptbook explains, 'Not really wanting to deliver [Bertram's] letter', banters with the Countess in an effort to delay passing over her son's bitter rejection of his wife;[56] the King in the play's closing moments gently draws an uncertain Countess away from the young married couple; and even the humiliated Parolles is eventually brought back within the shelter of the community by an amused and judicious Lafeu. The Swan Theatre, visually dominated by the welcoming blonde pine of its tiered galleries and with a thrust stage that encourages an immediacy of exchange between performers and audience, is known for the sense of intimacy it lends productions. Directors sometimes seek ways, in Colin Chambers' words, to 'roughen up' this 'feel good' space.[57] Doran's spare but rich production, by contrast, used the theatre's inherent architectural warmth as another form of buffer to protect the action and the audience from the play's sharper edges.

What various critics described as the production's 'humane' tone proved especially supportive of Helena.[58] Because this older, wiser generation that constitutes the moral backbone of the production speaks well of Helena and takes her part, potential reservations about an enforced marriage are sidestepped, with the 'problem' coming to rest entirely with the 'rash and unbridled boy', Bertram.[59] The perception of a cross-generational bond between Helena and the Countess, in particular, was reinforced by moments of intense emotional contact, Doran affording special attention to the speech in which the Countess, learning of Helena's love for Bertram, cries: 'Even so it was with me when I was young', reprinting its opening lines in enlarged text in the programme.[60] This contact between the two women is also made physical, the Countess embracing Helena at key points throughout the action. This repeated gesture of warm affection prepared the ground for what was perhaps the most affecting, yet understated, moment in the production, when the Countess filled the silence with which she meets Helena in the final scene with a simple movement, gently extending her hands towards her daughter-in-law, as though inviting her embrace. The trajectory of the action, both emotionally and in terms of the play's geography, was thus to return the prodigal Bertram to the production's well-defined moral centre.

This production of *All's Well* was not just popular with its audiences; it was also judged to have attained a standard of technical excellence rarely encountered in classical theatrical performance. John Peter announced that Doran 'is heir to the great tradition built up by John Barton, Peter Hall, and Peter Brook. Its elements are: swift, clear, unfussy action; simple, uncluttered presentation; relentless attention to character, psychology and the secret of the text; and clear, luminous speech, crystal words that observe and explore the meaning and drive the action.'[61] Guy Henry's comic inventiveness in the role of Parolles, a performance deepened through his self-knowing dignity after his humiliation at the hands of the Dumaine brothers, was singled out by many critics for praise.[62] Undoubtedly, however, it was the performance of Judi Dench as the Countess that dominated the show. Spencer described the sensation of watching Dench as 'realis[ing] you are encountering something rarely experienced in either life or art – perfection', while Billington described her performance as a 'masterclass in classical acting'.[63]

Doran considers the Countess 'the very beating heart of the play',[64] a perspective that was picked up by publicity which featured a pensive Dame Judi in medium close-up staring sidelong out of the picture (see Figure 1). The importance of Dench's involvement in the production can be further registered by comparing review headlines such as 'All rise for Dame Judi' and 'There is nothing like a dame' to the accompanying photographs, which in all but one case were of Dench's Countess.[65] Whether one thinks of the publicity, the reviews, or of her early solitary

Figure 1 Publicity image of Judi Dench, *All's Well that Ends Well* (2003).
Source: Image © Alastair Thain. Reproduced by kind permission of Alastair Thain and the Royal Shakespeare Company.

entrance onto the Swan stage, the production was in large part defined by the presence of Judi Dench. Complaining that Doran's interpretation of action and character is needlessly complicated, Benedict Nightingale tellingly concludes his four-star review with the opinion: 'Myself, I'll remember Gregory Doran's lucid, sensitive production mainly for Dame Judi.'[66]

The excitement generated by Dench's involvement stemmed from a number of factors, which individual spectators would no doubt prioritize differently. She is a Hollywood star with a high-recognition name a theatre company can bank on, known to some audiences as M in recent Bond films, Queen Victoria in *Mrs Brown*, and perhaps most famously as Queen Elizabeth I in *Shakespeare in Love*, a nine-minute performance for which she won an Oscar in 1998. She is also known in Britain for her long-running part opposite Geoffrey Palmer in the television situation comedy *As Time Goes By*, and her popularity as an actor was signalled when she 'beat the Queen into second place' in a poll in 2002 – the Jubilee year – to find 'the most respected and liked British public figure'. As Matt Wolf put it in an interview with Dench conducted a month before *All's Well* opened in Stratford: 'Since her Oscar-winning cameo ... Dench has *become* royalty ... and her name on the cast list is a coup for the RSC, which is in desperate need of stardust.'[67]

But the lens through which Dench's performance as the Countess was viewed was shaped not solely by the glamour of her name. As Spencer's and Billington's reviews make clear, Dench's reputation as an actor is built on an excellence founded on solid classical training honed at an early stage in her career at the Royal Shakespeare Company. To this extent, the buzz that surrounded Dench's return to the company was generated by the sense that she provided a direct link back to the principles and ethos of its founding years. She was acclaimed as Lady Macbeth in 1977 (directed by Trevor Nunn) but had been associated with the troupe much longer, performing Anya in *The Cherry Orchard* at Stratford and London in 1961 – the second year of Peter Hall's tenure as Artistic Director, and the year the company based in Stratford became known by royal charter as the Royal Shakespeare Company.

Dench's long association with Stratford was a key part of the story of her return to the Warwickshire stage for a media that was keen to situate Dench firmly within, rather than at a distance from, the local community. Articles published in local papers repeatedly mention the powerful personal memories the town holds for her, the home she made for twelve years with her husband Michael Williams with two sets of parents and a young daughter at Charlecote (a village just outside Stratford), and the sense of belonging she felt upon returning to Stratford and to the RSC: 'I've never had a welcome, *never* had a welcome like I've had back here ... Walking along the street I have to allow double the time to do a job, just to go, because I'm stopped either by people I knew 25 years ago or by new people who say, "How terrific that you've come back to Stratford, pleased to see you" and all that, so I feel very, very welcome.'[68] This sense of community is something to which Dench is obviously committed, taking time out in January 2004 during the *All's Well* run to reopen Stratford's local library.[69] The local and professional communities come to seem for Dench forms of extended family, and, as she explains it, it was these complex associations of family that persuaded her that she should return to perform in Stratford: 'I was in two minds', Dench explains, 'and Finty [her daughter] said: "You know you ought to do this, nearly all my childhood was in Stratford. And it was so happy and Sammy [Dench's grandchild] ought to know about that."'[70]

In lots of ways, then, Dench was perhaps uniquely positioned in 2003 to be perceived by a wide range of constituencies – the Stratford community and local press, the group of actors with whom she performed, the company's national and international audience base, and the national arts press – as the *grande dame* of RSC theatre, the embodiment of a legacy dating back over forty years. And her return to the company came at just the moment when each of these constituencies was struggling to understand precisely what that legacy entailed following the decade-long tenure of former Artistic Director Adrian Noble. In May 2001 Noble made the shock announcement that the RSC would no longer transfer Stratford productions to the Barbican Theatre in London.[71] The Barbican is a notoriously unwelcoming complex for both actors and spectators – rehearsal and dressing rooms are windowless, transportation is awkward, there is no passing trade and few restaurants in its immediate vicinity to service audiences before or after shows, and the structure of the building, with its seemingly endless series of foyers, is alienating. Moreover, the second of its two theatrical spaces is too small to accommodate Swan productions, with the result that shows had to be either scaled down or else scaled up for the main stage. Instead of using the Barbican, the company would enjoy a peripatetic London residency, finding the theatre that would best accommodate each particular production.

This announcement was accompanied by a major revision to the contractual requirements of actors, in effect further extending changes to the structure of the company and its season initiated by Noble in the 1990s in order to allow actors to take up shorter-term contracts. Prior to 1996, a company of actors would be contracted for a two-year term. In Stratford they would perform in repertory from March to January before transferring, via a short residency in Newcastle, for a London season that likewise ran from March to January. In 1996 the Stratford season was shifted to run from November to August, touring between Stratford and London was extended, and the Barbican residency was shortened to six months.

In 1998 Noble introduced the concept of two Stratford seasons: a Winter Season that would run from October to February, and a Summer Festival Season that would run from March to October before transferring to London via Newcastle. On this model, the summer block was shaped on the familiar RSC structure of cross-casting actors in shows mounted in the three Stratford theatres followed by a short tour and a London transfer. The winter block, by contrast, was to open with two short, straight runs, one in the RST and a second in the Swan. When these shows ended, two new companies would be introduced, performing two shows each, neither of which was cross-cast between the theatres. Productions in the Winter Season might tour, transfer to London, or simply close after the Stratford run. The benefit of this restructuring was that it released actors from the requirement to commit to a sixteen to eighteen month contract, and the hope was to reinvigorate the company's work, in part by attracting to the RSC actors who might otherwise choose to keep themselves available (and based in London) for opportunities in film and television.[72]

What Noble undertook in 2001 was in effect to model the Summer Festival Season on the recently introduced Winter Season, with smaller, entirely separate companies running in parallel on different projects. The Other Place – Stratford's small studio space – was closed to public performance and turned over to an actor training academy led by Declan Donnellan. Elsewhere, one group of actors played *Antony and Cleopatra* and *Much Ado about Nothing* at the RST, another mounted in the Swan the so-called 'Jacobethan' season of five rarely performed plays from the reigns of Elizabeth I and James I, and a third performed three of Shakespeare's late plays at the Roundhouse in London; the first project transferred into the West End, eventually followed by the Jacobethan season underwritten by theatre impresarios Thelma Holt and Bill Kenwright, and the third project transferred to Stratford. The following year, however, the RSC had trouble finding London homes for its productions, with West End producers reluctant to take on a financially high risk transfer – despite being critically acclaimed, the Jacobethan productions lost a reported £1 million.[73] It thus seemed that 2003 would mark the first time since its inception in 1961 that the Summer Season would fail to transfer from Stratford to London. This unwelcome landmark event was avoided when Holt and Kenwright stepped in again to bring Doran's productions of *The Taming of the Shrew* and John Fletcher's *Tamer Tamed* to the Queen's Theatre on Shaftesbury Avenue; this only partial recovery of the season, however, was met with anger from both actors and audiences, who saw the other shows in the repertory close after their Stratford runs.[74]

Noble's goal in 2001 seems to have been the same as it was in 1996 and 1998: to build flexibility into an inherited company structure, to streamline its operations, and to sustain through innovation Peter Hall's original vision of a world-class repertory ensemble. 'Project Fleet', as the reforms were eventually titled (as in 'fleet of foot', picking up on Noble's ambition to achieve what he described as a 'more nimble … fitter' company),[75] was immediately attacked as 'cultural vandalism' by theatre unions representing workers in Stratford and London facing redundancy as a result of the plans to restructure.[76] The national press, on the other hand, at least at first, seemed cautiously to welcome the plans, accepting, albeit with reservations, the 'pragmatic necessity' for change.[77] However, this wait-and-see attitude deteriorated over the ensuing months, along with confidence in Noble's leadership. When plans were announced in October 2001 to demolish Stratford's Royal Shakespeare Theatre – a Grade II* listed building dating to 1932, designed by the female architectural pioneer Elisabeth Scott – and to replace it with a Theatre Village, the RSC's senior management became increasingly mired in a public relations disaster.[78]

The perception was that in terms of its physical theatres, company structure, and founding ethos the RSC was cutting itself off from its own illustrious heritage, sacrificing staff and patron loyalty in pursuit of a destabilizing vision of radical change. English Heritage insisted the RST should be renovated rather than knocked down; the unions threatened strike action; local Stratford interest groups picketed the theatre; Prince Charles invited Noble and his Managing Director, Christopher Foy, to discuss their plans with him at Highgrove; there were a number of highly visible resignations, and the London audience base declined as a result of confusion about when and where to find RSC productions in the capital. In the short term, at least, the reforms were costly and seemed to belie claims that they heralded a tighter financial operation. The RSC not only lost an annual £3 million subsidy from the City of London as a result of leaving the Barbican but had to compensate the City for vacating the space before the end of their contract, and the move in 2002 to the London Roundhouse, a space requiring expensive refurbishment, failed to draw the anticipated audiences.[79]

Perhaps even more critically in terms of increasingly elusive public support for the changes, the desire to make the RSC attractive to actors became interpreted as a bid to secure big-name Hollywood stars, and the proposed Theatre Village, a label that summons up what was in the circumstances an unfortunate vision of Disney-style entertainment, met with suspicion and hostility. Attention focused increasingly on Noble's self-professed determination to expand the company's commercial operations into an international market and to exploit the RSC as a 'global brand', wooing the American dollar, in particular, through the services of Andrew 'The Jackal' Wylie, a New York literary agent, and through the formation of lucrative partnerships with theatres and universities in the United States.[80] This reorientation towards an American market became especially visible in 2003, when it seemed that Doran's acclaimed 'Shrew' productions would be seen at the Kennedy Centre in Washington, DC, but not in London.

Project Fleet set in motion a bitter and highly publicized struggle to define what the RSC would, or should, embody for a new millennium.[81] This debate led to a massive crisis of institutional recognition that prompted government funding bodies and the press to challenge the company's right to exist at all as a heavily subsidized organization. In January 2002, eight months after Noble's announcement of the restructuring, RSC management was called before a Commons Select Committee to explain its plans for redeveloping the Stratford theatres (an initiative dependent on receiving the £50 million earmarked for it by the government). At that meeting Debra Shipley, Labour MP for Stourbridge, posed the perennial question about public funding for the arts, arguing that the RSC is irrelevant not only to 'the poor end' of Stratford, but also to her own economically deprived constituency, and demanding of Noble, '[W]hy should you get all the money?'[82]

The money for a Stratford refit was ultimately approved by the Commons committee, but the question of subsidy – and how the RSC might in the future justify its subsidies – had been put on the table.[83] Commentators argued ever more insistently that Noble's proposed restructuring abandoned the original vision on which the RSC's continued excellence depends, in effect reinventing the company as a brand name emptied out of substance.[84] Peter questioned whether the RSC is now 'a subsidised theatre, [which is] a cultural asset to the nation, or a global business subsidised by the state? Cohesion, company work and ensemble acting make the RSC what it is; that is what its subsidy is for.'[85] Arguing that 'Hall's primary vision is in danger of being eroded', Billington agreed that 'the RSC is an ensemble or it is nothing'.[86] And Sheridan Morley, calling for Noble's resignation, further suggested that: 'This might well indeed be the moment to close [the RSC] down altogether, since it would now be impossible to claim that the RSC is still fulfilling its own, or any, useful purpose whatsoever.'[87]

Since the mid-1990s Noble had been slowly redefining the idea of ensemble at the heart of the RSC, disconnecting it from the system of rolling two-year contracts he inherited when he took over as Artistic Director. Although his leadership up until the spring 2001 announcement was at times controversial, it was possible still to interpret it as not only financially and artistically successful but also compatible with the mandate to remain 'at heart an ensemble company' despite 'continual change'.[88] Looking back in March 2002 on Noble's decade-long career prior to Project Fleet, James Morrison noted that he 'was widely regarded as one of [the company's] most successful directors'.[89] Billington, writing in the same month and criticizing as 'dismal' the work that has been produced since the launch of Project Fleet, tellingly describes the current Barbican season – 'conceived on the old principles' – as excellent.[90] Although his revisions of 1996 and 1998 were at first disruptive, Noble's adaptations still had the potential to be recognized as genuine RSC.

The RSC's millennial project, 'This England', was perhaps the moment when Noble could point confidently to a high-profile project – instantly recognizable in its ambition, Shakespearean remit, and award-winning excellence as thoroughly 'RSC' – that had been achieved within a partially adapted schedule. As Noble reminded his media critics and their readers in February 2001, perhaps somewhat defensively: 'You guys moaned, but my changes are sound.'[91] Crucially for Noble in terms of his subsequent decisions about how best to organize the company's future work, this 'crazy, impossible' staging of the English history cycle was accomplished only because they 'chucked out the RSC rule book', prioritizing the project over the traditional structure of the season: 'Rather than fitting the ideas of actors and directors around a schedule first framed in the Sixties, we let the artistic ideas shape it. And it was on that desperately simple principle – that artistic organizations need to be built to support art, not the other way round – that we reshaped the RSC.'[92]

'This England' consisted of productions of the two tetralogies, and it staged in order of the chronological reign of English kings a history that began with *Richard II* and ended with *Richard III*. The sequence made use of all three of Stratford's spaces, with *Richard II* opening in The Other Place on 29 March 2000, followed by the two parts of *Henry IV* in the Swan in April and June, and *Henry V* at the end of August in the Royal Shakespeare Theatre. This tetralogy then transferred to Newcastle for the month of November and opened at the Barbican at staggered intervals between December 2000 and March 2001. The 2000 Summer Festival Season thus offered in its broad shape the familiar RSC model of an accumulating repertory of productions with actors cross-cast among plays and theatres. The logic for the casting was the identification of actor and character in successive plays (Sam West, for example, starred as Richard II, the only part he took in the season, but David Troughton played Bolingbroke at The Other Place and Henry IV in the Swan productions, while William Houston played both Prince Hal and Henry V).

It was in the next stage of the project that the break with conventional RSC practice became apparent. Instead of waiting until the following spring for the company to renew itself, spectators saw the second tetralogy of plays open in the Swan with all three parts of *Henry VI* on 13 December 2000. As with the summer productions, these shows were cross-cast according to character and played in repertory. *Richard III* completed the story of 'This England' when it opened, again in the Swan, on 14 February 2001. Stratford theatregoers thus saw both tetralogies over the course of a continuous eleven-month period, a collaboration of actors, directors, and backstage staff that was enabled by the 'two seasons' structure set in place by Noble in 1998. The *Henry VI* and *Richard III* productions then toured for a week in March to Ann Arbor, an event which launched a long-term commercial partnership between the University of Michigan and the RSC. The *Henry VI/Richard III* tetralogy opened at the Young Vic over nine days (27 March to 4 April), while the earlier half of the cycle was still in repertory at the Barbican. 'This England' thus developed to its climax and completion when in April 2001 theatregoers in London were able to see the cycle in its entirety from *Richard II* through to *Richard III*.

The project was ground-breaking not just in its scope and achievement, but in the way it demonstrated the potential of a revised conception of the RSC ensemble. Although thematic continuity emphasized by the over-arching title 'This England' made the Winter Season seem an extension of the Summer Festival Season, the company of actors assembled under the directorship of Michael Boyd to perform the *Henry VI/Richard III* tetralogy in fact came together for an intensive rehearsal-performance period of just over eight months.[93] In effect, this was a limited-term project mounted on a single Stratford stage, yet it was nonetheless recognized by its audiences as an authentic ensemble effort in keeping with the principles and ethos of the RSC tradition.[94] It is the very absence of controversy around the circumstances in which this second tetralogy was realized which suggests that it was not perceived to threaten an RSC identity. Indeed, if anything it was seen to clarify and reinforce company identity, as this strand of the 'This England' project – rewarded with an Olivier Award in 2002 – drew on no big-name actors. Instead of relying on established stars of British theatre, Boyd, like Peter Hall before him, discovered and nurtured the stars of tomorrow.

What is remarkable then is the extent to which Noble, within months of the 'This England' triumph, failed utterly to persuade the British public that further changes to the RSC structure to accommodate more such limited-term projects would reinvent, rather than dismantle, the RSC's tradition of repertory ensemble performance. There were a number of factors that led to this inability to recognize in Project Fleet the original RSC, not least the abandonment within six months of the Barbican, The Other Place, and the Royal Shakespeare Theatre. Noble sought to define the company through its work not its buildings, but buildings by their very monumental fixity lend at moments of change a useful and ready sense of continuity. The timing of decisions about the remodelling of the RST was forced on management by the availability and distribution of Lottery money, and changes to the company's use of The Other Place were prompted by financial practicalities.[95] The sudden withdrawal from the Barbican, however, seems to have been a proactive initiative, a creative idea driven in part by the success of the *Henry VI/Richard III* season. The management problem facing Noble early in 2001 was that there could be little opportunity for further structural experimentation within the Summer Festival Season so long as there was an imperative to fill the Barbican theatres for six months of every year with a block of Stratford shows. A turn to more project-led initiatives depended on a timetabling flexibility that could not be achieved within the terms of the RSC's rental contract with the City of London. The obvious answer, therefore, was to end that contract. But this expensive and highly publicized venture quickly came to seem less a reinvention of past traditions than a drastic departure from them.

Another factor contributing to a failure of recognition of the old in the new was Noble's avowed entrepreneurialism. By explicitly rejecting as no longer relevant 'culture [with] a capital C', by aggressively marketing stage productions as 'product' and the RSC as a 'global brand', and by seeming to turn to the United States for both financial backing and corporate know-how, Noble set about reinventing not only the shape of the season but also the ethos within which the company would in future make theatre.[96] The terms in which the broadside and academic press reported and commented on the details of Project Fleet make it clear that this culture shift was being read as a political and ideological departure from the company's broadly leftist origins. Michael Dobson, writing in *Shakespeare Survey*, likens Project Fleet to the damaging reforms to higher education instituted under Margaret Thatcher; *The Economist*, directed at a very different elite international readership and alluding to Tony Blair's New Labour economic platform, welcomes 'what sounds a lot like a Third Way for Shakespeare'; while Billington, reflecting almost in the elegiac mode on something already gone, asks whether 'in a world of flash and dazzle' a moving radicalism perhaps lies in the 'life values as well as art' that bind together a company.[97] Two years later, again in the context of the threat posed by Project Fleet, Billington approvingly quotes Harold Wilson to the effect that 'the Labour party is "a moral crusade or it is nothing"' – a telling point of comparison that implicitly reads the RSC mission through the competing 'life values' of Old and New Labour.[98] The problem was not a naive objection in principle to the mingling of commerce and art, but reservations about the practical and ideological consequences of the RSC trying to reinvent itself as a commercial competitor in a global market. Attacking such an idea as 'ignorant, arrogant management speak', John Peter insists on the differences between subsidized theatre and the market economy: 'The RSC does not compete with the National or the Royal Exchange, in Manchester, still less with the Comédie Française or the Lincoln Center, in the way Unilever competes with ICI. It has a specific artistic agenda, dominated by Shakespeare and the English classics. It is not a plc. Taxpayers are not investors.'[99]

The debate became increasingly focused on competing definitions of ensemble, critics of reform finding in Boyd's productions of the *Henry VI/ Richard III* cycle 'the last flowering of the RSC as we thought we knew it', advocates of reform interpreting the same tetralogy as 'the model for how [Noble] wants ensemble to be shaped in the future – tighter-knit and more hard-working, albeit over a shorter period of time'.[100] Writing in October 2001 about the forthcoming 2002 season, Noble situates his proposed changes within a changing theatrical world while simultaneously claiming for his conception of the ensemble continuity with the past:

> Next year, three companies of actors will each present very different, but *equally authentic versions* of the repertoire ensemble. [my emphasis] One company will tackle two Shakespeare plays, another will explore three of his late plays by performing them in promenade, and the third company will examine the principles of Elizabethan and Jacobean acting by performing six plays of the period in repertoire.
>
> This is certainly not abandoning the repertoire ensemble. Crucially, it creates an ensemble of actors working on a specific idea. There is a lot of nostalgia for the way the current ensemble operates at the RSC. Yet in the current Stratford season, six leading actors are only contracted for one show. For many, it's the only way that working for the RSC is possible.[101]

It was by no means a foregone conclusion that this interpretation of the ensemble would not find popular support. In September 2001 Spencer was persuaded that: 'None of this sounds like a diminution of the company's core principles of exploring the classics and cross-casting'; he looks forward to the RSC 'regain[ing] a quality it has often lacked in the past – excitement'.[102] Looking back in 2002 on recent past practice, Stanley Wells cites Kenneth Branagh's *Hamlet* (1993), Declan Donnellan's *School for*

Scandal (1998), and Derek Jacobi's *Macbeth* (1994) as instances of the flexible interpretation of ensemble: none of these shows was cross-cast or mounted in repertory, yet '[n]o one has denied that they were still RSC productions'.[103]

Too few people, however, could find a correspondence between the restructured company and their conception of the RSC ensemble. The omission in 2001 of the word 'ensemble' from the discussion of the company's mission at the front of RSC programmes was interpreted by many as a turn away from a founding principle of the company.[104] Crucially, although 'ensemble' sounds like a technical term, it has long resisted precision of use; it is more often recognized in practice than defined in theory. For some, it depends on giving actors time to learn and grow together as a cohesive unit; for others, the intensity of work, not length of contract, is the defining factor. Some argue that it should have a permanent membership in the tradition of the Berliner Ensemble, while for Peter Hall, writing in 1995, ensemble needs change: 'if you elevate ensemble into the concept of a permanent company then you have dogma, and that's death. Literally death.'[105] In Hall's view, ensemble 'can be created from scratch' and depends not on time but on a 'spirit of sharing, and support, and understanding of a common goal', particularly as that makes possible a coherent approach to the 'technical problem' of Shakespeare's verse.[106] However one defines ensemble and seeks to foster the circumstances that might allow it to come together, its realization seems ultimately to depend on shared beliefs and the pursuit of a common goal. Typically, its existence is discerned by its audiences through a perception of company coherence, onstage collaboration, and performance excellence. The fundamental problem with Noble's bold reinvention of the company for a new millennium is that one inspires, rather than legislates, a spirit of ensemble. Failing in the first instance to generate this sense of community, and then subsequently unable to attach itself to the ethos through which the RSC had traditionally defined itself, the plan for change finally came to seem no longer self-identical with the institution. It became perceived as its own thing, an inauthentic *adaptation* of the original, complete with its own name and founding genius – no longer Peter Hall's RSC, but Adrian Noble's Project Fleet.

Whether the plans were misguided in principle, badly executed, or overly ambitious in scope, Noble's argument that his model offered 'authentic versions of the repertoire ensemble' claimed a legitimacy that Project Fleet was ultimately denied. By March 2002 the RSC in its current form was no longer considered 'genuine' – a telling choice of word that echoes the term frequently used by critics and scholars to distinguish authentic from adaptive production of Shakespeare's works. 'How to make the RSC a genuine *company* again?', Nightingale wonders, Billington in a similar vein asking: 'Is it a genuine company? Or is it simply an umbrella organization trading on a brand-name and housing a number of discrete, increasingly isolated projects?'[107] Towards the end of that same month, Sir Donald Sinden and Sir Michael Gambon publicly attacked plans to demolish the RST. On 18 April *The Stage* published a letter written by Dame Judi Dench in response to a document circulated by concerned Stratford citizens, in which she writes: 'I applaud your submission to the RSC governors, and you have my wholehearted support. I am deeply worried about what is happening as I know are so many people in the profession.'[108]

Noble resigned one week later, followed eventually by his Managing Director, Christopher Foy, and Chairman of the Board of Governors Lord Alexander of Weedon, men closely associated with the Project Fleet initiative. However, the perception that the RSC lacked a strong sense of what Morley called 'purpose' lingered on. A year later the Arts Council seems to penalize this lack of vision by awarding the RSC what Dalya Alberge writing for *The Times* described as a 'paltry grant' by comparison to the National Theatre and Donmar.[109] Then in November 2003, a year and a half after Noble's resignation, and in response to the news that the RSC could not afford to transfer its season to London, the new Artistic Director, Michael Boyd, was summoned to give evidence before the London Assembly Culture Committee. In the words of the committee's chair, Meg Hillier: 'This is a risk for the RSC. They are on trial and have got to get through this to prove it's worth £13m a year [in Arts Council funding] when there are other important cultural institutions also in need.'[110] It is significant that rumours began to circulate at this time that the company was in danger of losing not just its funding but its royal charter – they were ungrounded but point insistently to a perception of a company lacking a *raison d'être* and on the brink of collapse.[111]

Once the question of purpose had been asked, it seemed difficult to *stop* asking it until some kind of answer could be found. Noble's vision for the company was rejected as entrepreneurial, commercial, and incompatible with Hall's founding principles. Now that he was gone, what options were available? The eleven months between the announcement of Project Fleet and Noble's resignation focused widespread attention on issues that the RSC and its audiences had been struggling with for a decade and more with only partial success. On the occasion of the company's residency at the Brooklyn Academy of Music in 1997, Alan Riding in the *New York Times* summarized for readers how issues of expense, size, touring mandate, popularization, and ensemble are ongoing and unresolved 'questions that involve the R.S.C.'s very identity', explaining that '[i]t is the job of

Mr. Noble ... to find the answers'.[112] A year later Simon Callow argued that 'there is today no ensemble in Britain' partly because of the expense, and partly because of a lack of inspiration: 'Somewhere, [the RSC and the National] lost their power to inspire their members to think of themselves as a team, a family, a regiment – an ensemble. Being a member of the RSC or the National became just another job: a rather less well paid job than the one in the West End or in television or film.'[113] Michael Coveney, alleging 'commercial failure and waning artistic credibility', called in 1998 for 'an entire dismantling of the current RSC and an immediate reconstitution of a slimmed-down operation based entirely in Stratford'.[114] The problems of identity were there before 2001 – the controversy around Project Fleet simply put them very visibly on everyone's agenda. The urgent question as 2003 drew to a close was how the RSC could once again 'inspire' actors, as Callow put it, to commit the time and, in effect, the money to the vision of a repertory ensemble company. What *was* the vision?

This was the context of Dench's return to the company. George Bernard Shaw famously described the role of the Countess as 'the most beautiful old woman's part ever written' (a quotation cited repeatedly in the reviews),[115] and it is the obvious Shakespearean role into which actresses who once played Rosalind and Viola mature. Its stage history is punctuated with performances from such theatrical greats as Edith Evans, Peggy Ashcroft, and Barbara Jefford. That said, it is not always the case that *All's Well* is defined in performance by this relatively small part. Depending on the production, the attention might fall on Helena, as played by Juliet Stevenson at the RSC in 1981, or even on the King of France, as played by Alec Guinness in 1953 in Tyrone Guthrie's inaugural season at Stratford, Ontario. The Dench phenomenon, in which the Countess was seen as not just a major casting decision but as *the* casting decision, was something peculiar to Doran's staging. The point is not that the role of the Countess defines the play, but that Dame Judi Dench defined this production.

The importance of this casting choice rested not just with Dench's international star status, nor even with her immense talent as an actor, but with her high-profile opposition to Project Fleet and choice to communicate that disapproval through a letter expressing solidarity with the local community. A few months after Noble's resignation, and while speculation was rife about who would be appointed the next Artistic Director, Dench was once again in the Stratford area to open a garden in Charlecote for sufferers of Alzheimer's Disease. Asked if she would consider a return to the RSC, she replied, 'I see myself working anywhere if they ask me. I think it would depend on finding a role for me.'[116] The RSC finds a role for Dench, and she returns to the RSC not simply to give her Countess, but as a gesture of support for a beleaguered company, post-Project Fleet.

Dench's presence gave to this production, and by extension to the company, the perception of a commitment to the values and ethos of the Hall legacy.[117] It is useful in this specific context to look again at the production publicity. Deirdre Clancy's elegant and rich costume design, in muted shades of silver, dove-brown, russet, and black, was early seventeenth century; the Countess, in an unfitted floor-length gown and ruff, wore her hair swept away from her face. The advertisement for the show, by contrast, while consistent with the production's wintry colour palette, was entirely modern. It featured neither an actor in character, nor an abstract conception of theme, but Dench wearing an un-Jacobean fleece sweater and her own familiar short hairstyle. Why then, if not in character as the Countess, does she look so grave? What is she musing over, as she stares away from the viewer into the middle distance? This publicity image projects at once an idea of the Countess as *grande dame* of the play and the modern performer as *grande dame* of the production. It visually conflates the authority of character and actor in complicated and, for the company at this point in its history, politically essential ways. In the same way as the Countess, in J. L. Styan's words, is 'the still centre which gives the audience faith that all will yet be well', this image of Dame Judi likewise inspires faith that somehow all will yet be well with the RSC.[118]

The strange and difficult play that is *All's Well that Ends Well*, summoning up thoughts of legacies and inheritances, and the imminent death of an older generation alongside the uncertain future of the one coming through to take its place, spoke powerfully to the circumstances of the RSC at the end of 2003. The unexpected nostalgia of Doran's production offered a brief respite from the offstage drama from which the RSC was still trying to extricate itself. When Peter, for example, comments that Judi Dench is 'the moral guardian of this dark-silvery fairy-tale world', and that 'her duet with Gary Waldhorn's shrewd, watchful king has the brilliance, humour, poise and authority of a generous generation that cares less for the price of things than for their value', or when Gross notes that 'There's a much deeper sadness than [the play's] reputation would lead you to expect, and much greater tenderness', Doran's autumnal, bittersweet interpretation comes to seem an extended working-through of the company's recent, painful upheavals.[119]

It is perhaps not surprising then that this production, so supportive of Helena, leaves Jamie Glover's Bertram out in the cold. Sides are clearly taken, with the wisdom of the older generation, and therefore so too that of the audience, resting with the virtue of Helena. Helena and Bertram, old values and modern innovation – it is unsurprising that Spencer, following the lead of the publicity and conflating character and actor in his interpretation of the moving final-scene embrace between mother and daughter-in-law, indulges 'the sentimental fantasy' that 'here is a great performer passing the baton on to another actress of glorious promise'.[120] When the King sharply tells Bertram that the time when he could rely on faith in his honour has passed and the King's good thoughts must instead be won through deeds, Waldhorn's sternness likewise seems to extend beyond the fiction of the play to a different forfeiture of trust. Noble and, by extension, his heir, Michael Boyd, no longer had the option of an appeal to the nation's trust. Not even the assurances of Stanley Wells, setting himself in the academic press the immense task of 'Awaking your faith', could be enough.

However, Doran's production of *All's Well*, described by Peter as 'a healing performance', effected its own peculiar and timely form of recuperative magic. Despite Dench's description of the company as a family, this show was a short, straight run, neither in repertory nor cross-cast with any other production. Although she stood for the Hall legacy, and her involvement was perceived to mark a return to the principles of the 1960s, Dench in fact returned to the company – was perhaps only able to return to the company – through the restructuring set in place by Noble in the late 1990s. This particular troubling narrative, like the ending of the love story in *All's Well*, is left hanging. Although the show was hailed by the national press as a return to form, it remains caught, like Bertram, between old world and new world values, offering no answers to the issue of the identity of the RSC for a new century. The magic was simply to create the illusion of a vision, the illusion of authenticity. What does the RSC stand for? When the governors and directors, perceived to be insiders, no longer have a strong position from which to speak, a world-class production seems to speak for itself. *This* is what it stands for, *this* is why Britain still needs the RSC – the 'this' involving a sleight of hand as wondrous and mysterious as Helena's own royal cure. The appearance of continuity with the company's past and its inherited legacy created the circumstances that could enable spectators to reaffirm their belief in the larger project. The force of this production rested in an uneasy hope that all would be well for Helena and Bertram – and perhaps, too, for the RSC.

Audiences therefore left the theatre in 2002 believing that they had seen Shakespeare's *All's Well that Ends Well*, in sharp contrast to the way some spectators, five years earlier, came away with the lingering impression that what they had seen was not, or at least not quite, *Hamlet*. As analysis of these two RSC productions suggests, authenticity is determined less by textual fidelity than by the extent to which an instance conforms to an insubstantial standard – the work – that seems to exist prior to, and untouched by, production. Doran and Warchus each cut lines and even whole scenes and speeches familiar to readers of *All's Well* and *Hamlet*, but whereas Doran was praised for 'bringing out the treasures that were always there, locked up in the text,' Warchus's textual arrangements became a talking point, a sign of potential adaptation.[121] In the former case, spectators claimed to find the work reproduced in life on the Swan stage, while some *Hamlet* spectators experienced an analogous encounter with the work precisely by marking its *absence* from the site of performance. Thus although the work has no material reality in a text (or anywhere else), it functions in practice as *though* it did, serving constantly to manage the categories of genuine production and its necessary supplement, adaptation.

The impression that the work is an objective standard is of course an illusion, since the work is responsive to, and continues to take shape as the consequence of, changing user expectations. To consider again the Warchus *Hamlet*, growing resistance to popularizing (or 'Americanizing') both Shakespeare's plays and traditions of stage performance – call it the 'Luhrmann-effect' – regulated against identifying the work at this particular moment in the RSC's history with a visually heightened, filmically literate staging, even though Warchus's most striking 'innovations' had been anticipated in previously acclaimed productions. In the case of *All's Well*, reservations about the RSC's adaptive relation to its own institutional traditions had the opposite contextual effect of heightening work recognition. The authority of Doran's production grew out of the way it allowed its audiences once again to remember and to recognize in this performance a 'genuine' idea of an authentic Royal Shakespeare Company. The fluid, contingent work is therefore always at least provisionally knowable as what adaptation is not, deep-seated anxieties about the (impossibility of) stable repetition of the work in its performance instances finding expression in the way the potential for adaptation haunts supposedly legitimate production as its troubling, yet indispensable, 'problem'.

3 Entangled in the present
Shakespeare and the politics of production

I've so far suggested that textual-theatrical instances are *productive* of the work, and that the limits of the work are continually redefined by distinguishing what can be recognized as legitimate productions from adaptations or illegitimate productions. This process becomes especially visible when users disagree about what should count as 'genuine'. As explored in the previous chapter with reference to performances at the Royal Shakespeare Company, looking into claims of adaptive production pins down not the work's 'essence', but rather what prompted failures of recognition of the work among specific audiences at certain times. Another important, related function of naming adaptation is to seem to insulate the work from certain productions with which it remains, nonetheless, closely identified. Calling *Return to the Forbidden Planet* an adaptation falls only just short of describing it as its own work, and yet *as* an adaptation it remains locked in an uneasy tension with *The Tempest*. It is because Shakespeare's works can, logically, never be made free of their adaptations that fears about work perpetuation over time persist. As a category negatively defined by what its adaptations are not, the work as process is never complete. It necessarily contains, in the senses of includes and suppresses, the possibility of its own (illegitimate) transformation.

I want to turn now from anxieties about the work's transmission in text and performance to explore cases that openly declare an adaptive distance from Shakespeare's works, and, in doing so, to consider some other implications of a theoretical model that argues that the work is pragmatically known through production. The intertextual tradition of Shakespearean appropriation which found an early expression in Aimé Césaire's *Une tempête* has become an extensively documented form of creative engagement with the canon. Familiar and even now canonical instances such as Edward Bond's *Lear*, Paula Vogel's *Desdemona (A Play about a Handkerchief)*, and Charles Marowitz's *Hamlet* disrupt Shakespearean production by making the works seem at once recognizable and strange, deliberately intervening in reception histories in order to rewrite them. As Marowitz explains the purpose behind his treatment of *Hamlet*, a collage version is concerned

> to foster another concept ... The change of form inescapably affects the nature of content, but that in itself is not enough. The content must not be accidentally 'affected' in the way that a pedestrian might be 'affected' if he were hit by a bus. It must be refashioned as if, to pursue the metaphor, a pedestrian were hit by a bus driven by a clinical psychiatrist whose aim in knocking him down was to investigate his rate of recovery in response to highly specialized therapies of his own making.[1]

Marowitz's production sought to mount an assault on the character of Hamlet, thereby striking a blow at 'the conscience-stricken but paralyzed liberal: one of the most lethal and obnoxious characters in modern times'.[2] However, the language with which he describes his methodology is revealing in terms of the way he seems to describe the collage simultaneously as both adaptation and an instance of the work. Despite earlier drawing a distinction between the collage and 'the original' it manipulates, Marowitz in the quotation above transforms difference into likeness through the metaphor of the road accident, figuring Shakespeare's work and his critique of it as the same pedestrian at two different moments – before and after he (or it) is hit by a bus. The presumed boundary between work and polemical adaptation momentarily blurs, one merging into the other. This sense that the collage represents the work in trauma is further suggested by Marowitz's report that spectators previously unfamiliar with *Hamlet* were able to convey in discussions after the performance 'impressions [of *Hamlet*] ... as valid, and often as knowledgeable, as those of scholars and veteran theatregoers'.[3]

Marowitz, like those involved years later with the production of the Warchus *Hamlet* for the RSC, is making an argument for engaging with his collage version *as Hamlet*. Not only, to his mind, do spectators come away with apt 'impressions' of the work, but, as later theatrical experimentation in Gothenberg and Wiesbaden showed, the ideas embedded in the collage 'could be transferred back to a straightforward production of the play proper'.[4] There is 'the play proper' and there is the adaptation, but so indistinguishable do they begin to look in Marowitz's analysis of the collage, the metaphor of the bus hitting the pedestrian is needed to explain how collage differs at all from more conventional strategies of production. My point is not to take a stand on which side of the line separating work from adaptation this particular theatrical event falls, since my larger argument is that this is impossible to determine apart from the local debates in which production inevitably participates. Rather, my goal for the moment, as we pursue forms of interventionist production that might seem readily cordoned off from the work as straightforward adaptation, is simply to emphasize the potential contingency of such basic categories by noting the way Marowitz himself seems to insist on an underlying 'original' work that he simultaneously identifies as continuous with its collage-adaptation.

Some other productions, however, seem to operate at a somewhat clearer distance from the work, a new title or additional dialogue and characters making the category of adaptation appear relatively clear-cut. There is Shakespeare's work and then there is Bond's socialist, or Vogel's feminist, adaptation of it – or, to return to postcolonial appropriations, David Malouf's *Blood Relations* and Philip Osment's *This Island's Mine* stand alongside Césaire's *Une tempête* as important adaptations of *The Tempest*. In each of these instances, critique depends on the implicit assertion of a distance between work and adaptation sufficient to enable the adaptation to stake out an independent place from which to return the work's look. The rhetorical importance of this gap is suggested by the way it is reproduced as bibliographical coding in Peter Erickson's early study of appropriation, *Rewriting Shakespeare, Rewriting Ourselves*, the section break in the middle of this two-part book neatly dividing 'Shakespeare's Representations of Women' from 'Women Writers' Representations of Shakespeare'.[5]

Such productions, often speaking from, and to some extent for, disadvantaged identity positions, seek to confront and resist an oppressive canon through strategic intervention. As Helen Gilbert and Joanne Tompkins explain this particular relationship between work and adaptation, borrowing from Helen Tiffin the term 'canonical counter-discourse': 'Rewriting the characters, the narrative, the context, and/or the genre of the canonical script provides another means of interrogating the cultural legacy of imperialism ... Counter-discourse seeks to deconstruct significations of authority and power exercised in the canonical text, to release its strangle-hold on representation and, by implication, to intervene in social conditioning.'[6] Making Shakespeare seem merely contemporary to a modern audience is not enough; 'updating' is entirely secondary to, and might even distract from, the project of reworking the drama to 'decentre imperial hegemonies'.[7] Peter Widdowson, offering something of a checklist of the prevailing characteristics of such production, agrees that 'a clear cultural-political thrust' is perhaps the most important defining feature of the genre. Canonical works are 'revised and re-visioned as part of the process of restoring a voice, a history and an identity to those hitherto exploited, marginalized and silenced by dominant interests and ideologies'.[8]

Martin Orkin has cautioned us not to 'bypass the Shakespeare text' altogether in favour of the 'appropriations, rewritings or even cannibalizations ... [that] have provided a much-favoured field of enquiry in writings on "post-colonial" Shakespeare, particularly in North America'.[9] His concern, writing specifically from a South African perspective, is that the immense critical labour expended on adaptation leaves unexplored the usefulness in the classroom of the 'text itself' in terms of providing one possible set of 'historical perspectives and frames for our own contemporaneity'.[10] But in face of a contingent work, appeals to the text as it supposedly stands apart from production and its necessary supplement, adaptation, are problematic, potentially always returning us to a supposed origin we have ourselves invented. To put this another way, what is recognized (or else will come to be recognized) as the 'text itself' depends on how the work is currently constructed in relation to adaptation, the politics of the work being fully implicated in ongoing processes of production.

My argument that the work is susceptible to change through production might seem only further to reinforce the importance of, and need for, strongly motivated interventions in the politics of the canon and its histories of reception. And yet this instability poses a difficulty for acts of intervention in terms of gaining a purchase in the first place on the changing and permeable boundaries between work and adaptation. Forms of oppositional politics require something relatively fixed to push against – grammatically speaking, there has to be something, inferred or actual, to write back *to*. Writing 'back' to a master narrative would thus seem to depend, at least implicitly, on conceiving the work less as a process than as an already known quantity located somewhere else – so returning us to a familiar model of identity already explored at some length in the opening chapters. As Widdowson explains this tactic of strategically 'reading against the grain', the 'contemporary version attempts, as it were, to replace the pre-text with itself, at once to negate the pre-text's cultural power and to "correct" the way we read it in the present'.[11] Productions that write back, although perhaps less often than Widdowson suggests straightforwardly a matter of replacement, frequently show a tendency to isolate the work rhetorically in the past. As Orkin's discussion of history, Shakespeare, and the South African classroom perhaps suggests, Shakespeare's works seem to speak for a former age (or else, notoriously, for the reactionary values of a present one) to the extent that they can be sealed off from a current moment of revisionist production concerned to adapt the works-as-past in terms of its own priorities. This is thus a politics that works itself out in terms of a binary of 'then and/vs. now'. Cultural, geographical, or ideological differences between work and adaptation are rooted in a perceived temporal gap between work and adaptation enabled by an idea of the work not as process, but as something readily identifiable instead as an *object*.

This tactic is not so different from the way change to the work is informally generated and controlled over time by communities of users who either accept or contest as genuine a newly published edition or the next theatrical enactment. It is only through the pragmatic or actual belief that the work, a process without an origin, exists apart from and untouched by production that one can assert a place from which to categorize and evaluate subsequent productions as potential instances *of* a particular work. Whereas the concern explored in the earlier chapters was a perceived need to authenticate change, here the issue is to mark explicitly certain *types* of departures from the 'source text' as politically desirable. However, to seek to dislodge Shakespeare's works from their place at the heart of the canon through adaptation is often to promote what John Thieme has called a 'characteristically … ambivalent relationship' between work and adaptation since it is to 'combin[e] oppositional writing back with elements that intentionally or otherwise prove to be complicitous, at least to the extent that they leave the Bard's iconic status intact by virtue of using his work as a departure point'.[12] An additional danger in the context of 'motivated' intervention, precisely because to write back is always to write back with the purpose of interrupting the past, is a willingness to suppose that there is an actual rather than merely expedient gap that marks an adaptation as separate in some clearly knowable way from the work. Gilbert and Tompkins argue that: 'Canonical counter-discourse is one method by which colonised cultures can refuse the seamless contiguity between a classical past and a post-colonial present that the empire strives to preserve.'[13] In terms specifically of what one can say about the work and efforts to write back to it, the difficulty here is the inverse predicament to the problems of identity explored in the first two chapters: it is as hard to sustain a category of adaptation that is entirely independent of a fluid work as it is to make the boundaries of that work impervious to production. Somewhat paradoxically, revision being one goal of appropriation, the work that modifies over time is difficult to counter in any predictable manner since it will not remain sealed off in/as the past. The site of adaptation keeps getting entangled, as Marowitz and Thieme in their different ways indicate, and as this chapter's discussion of Djanet Sears' *Harlem Duet* and Robert Lepage's *Elsinore* will show, in the work's ongoing development.

This chapter pursues some of these issues through analysis of two adaptations that insist on, and simultaneously undermine, an ability to sustain an objective distance from the Shakespearean work. My argument is that by intensifying rather than resolving category confusions these adaptations exploit to their own ends the work's inherently adaptive condition. Djanet Sears' *Harlem Duet* is a prequel to *Othello* that narrates the story of Othello's first wife, Billie, abandoned in favour of a white woman. *Othello* is cited rarely by the characters, and only once at any length. Robert Lepage's *Elsinore*, by contrast, a one-man show Lepage describes as 'variations' on *Hamlet*,[14] only uses Shakespeare's words, but scenes are heavily condensed, occasionally spliced together, and overlaid with sometimes spectacular visual and theatrical effects. Each of these productions, with its alternative title, announces an independence from Shakespeare's work, and each of their devisers can be situated culturally, nationally, and even linguistically outside of the Shakespearean theatrical mainstream: Sears is African-Canadian, Lepage French-Canadian (*Elsinore* had a parallel touring life in French as *Elseneur*). At the same time these shows enter into a sustained interaction with the dominant theatrical-critical legacies of *Othello* and *Hamlet*. Through the use of self-conscious theatrical devices, *Harlem Duet* and *Elsinore* produce *Othello* and *Hamlet* by enacting the work's histories of production. In so doing, they suggest how the pasts we construct are shot through with the present, and, perhaps more counter-intuitively, how fragments from those pasts can seem to intrude anachronistically into a later moment. The disruptive potential of *Harlem Duet* and *Elsinore* lies in the way they assert yet at the same time display as flexible and porous the boundaries separating a work from its adaptation. By complicating and drawing into question the work's position 'somewhere else', both of these shows implicate the work in a modern production moment.

Writing the present, exorcizing the past: Djanet Sears' *Harlem Duet*

> I want my students to see Shakespeare's Othello as he is; and to do that, sometimes it might be valuable to see him as someone other than Shakespeare's
>
> Joyce Green MacDonald[15]

> … it is never possible to know who is "possessed" and by whom …
>
> Michel de Certeau[16]

In the essay that prefaces the earliest printed edition of *Harlem Duet*, 'nOTES oF a cOLOURED gIRL: 32 sHORT rEASONS wHY I wRITE fOR tHE tHEATRE', Sears explains that she is troubled by the absence on stage of 'a choir of African voices, chanting a multiplicity of African experiences', and that she dreams that 'one day in the city where I live, at any given time of the year, I will be able to find at least one play that is filled with people who look like me, telling stories about me, my family, my friends, my community'.[17]

Harlem Duet contributes to making that dream a reality by narrating the story of Othello's first marriage and the wife he left for Desdemona. As a pre-history to *Othello*, it gives voice to otherwise occluded voices and writes back to a professional stage history (closely associated with forms of Shakespearean production) that tells of African exclusion from Western theatre:

> As a veteran theatre practitioner of African Descent, Shakespeare's *Othello* had haunted me since I first was introduced to him. Sir Laurence Olivier in black-face. Othello is the the [*sic*] first African portrayed in the annals of western dramatic literature. In an effort to exorcise this ghost, I have written *Harlem Duet* ... [T]his is Billie's story. The exorcism begins.[18]

In writing a story that belongs not to Shakespeare's tragic hero but to his 'forgotten' first wife, a figure of Sears' own creation, Sears breaks with a particular cycle of racial and sexual prejudice, destabilizing the action of Shakespeare's work – literally undermining it – by excavating its narrative foundations. Characterized as an 'exorcism', *Harlem Duet* marks an oblique intervention that seeks to drive out – or ritually write over – a theatrical 'ghost', simultaneously identified with both a canonical work and its (blackface) legacy of performance.

The professional implications of this particular Shakespearean intervention were heightened in the summer of 2006 when Sears entered Canadian theatre history as the first black playwright to have her work performed at the prestigious Stratford Festival of Canada, and the first black director in the festival's fifty-three-year history to lead the first all-black cast of actors. The play was *Harlem Duet*, in repertory at the Studio Theatre from 20 June to 22 September. Although the Stratford Festival is eclectic in its scheduling choices, its reputation largely rests on productions of the works of Shakespeare. Founded in 1953 as a repertory company that renews itself annually, it was directed in its early years by Tyrone Guthrie and showcased an innovative and internationally acclaimed new stage space designed by Tanya Moiseiwitsch. This close association with establishment British culture, once a distinct marketing advantage, has more recently led to complaints that the stagings, casting, and audiences remain trapped in the aspirational values of another generation, perpetuating a conservative and limiting image of a middle-class, white Canada with which younger, modern audiences are increasingly failing to identify.[19]

Stratford is thus widely regarded as the public Canadian face of the sort of exclusionist profession Sears protests against in her preface, and that she seeks to redress through her playwriting. By the time of its Stratford staging, *Harlem Duet* was a play with which critics and many spectators were already familiar. It premiered to acclaim in Toronto at the Tarragon Extra Space in the spring of 1997, and was remounted later in the autumn in a joint Nightwood-CanStage production. The script was published the same year, picking up in 1998 multiple awards including the Dora Mavor Moore Award, the Chalmers Award, and the Governor General's Literary Award. It was then performed at the Neptune Theatre in Halifax, Nova Scotia, in 2000, directed by Alison Sealy-Smith, and two years later off-off-Broadway at the Blue Heron Theatre in New York, again directed by Sears.

Even though the drama was nearly a decade old, its situation within the context of the Stratford Festival – its sudden institutional association with a powerful, mainstream, well-subsidized, and previously almost exclusively white tradition of Shakespeare in performance – gave it a new celebrity. The decision to play *Harlem Duet* at Stratford constituted in itself a theatrical and cultural event that drew to the theatres new audiences.[20] Martin Morrow, writing for the *Canadian Review of Books*, suggests that its revival 'at that bastion of dead white European drama, the Stratford Festival', might offer hope of 'a Black renaissance' in Canadian theatre, while Gary Smith in the *Hamilton Spectator* describes the event as 'iconoclastic': 'Canada's major whitebread playhouse is finally making the effort to be more inclusive and to reflect through this mandate the stories of a country that is no longer a replica of white Europe. It's been a long time coming.'[21] The media sensation prompted by the Festival's decision to include this show on its 2006 playbill resulted from excitement about the event marking a lasting turn in Canadian theatre, and scepticism that it would in time come to seem just another instance of tokenism. As Sears herself explained in a television interview with Clifton Joseph, 'the success of this production can only be told years from now in that if it was the only one, it really wasn't that important. I hope it means the beginning of something. I hope that what "Harlem Duet" leaves another generation is the idea that you can tell your own story from your own perspective anywhere'.[22]

Harlem Duet opens with a Prologue in which an unnamed woman learns that her lover desires another woman. The first clue that this drama might speak in some way to Shakespeare's work comes at the end of the scene when the woman addresses her unresponsive partner by name:

SHE: You love her.
HE: Yes. Yes. Yes.
(He wipes his face with a towel. She stares at the handkerchief laying in her bare hand.)
SHE: Is she White?
   (Silence.)
   Othello?
   (Silence.)

She's White.
(Silence.)
Othello …
(She holds the handkerchief out to him. He does not take it. She lets it fall at his feet. After a few moments, he picks it up.)[23]

The play's Harlem setting 'at the corner of Malcolm X and Martin Luther King Boulevards'[24] shifts across three distinct historical moments: the years leading up to Emancipation (1860–62), the Harlem Renaissance (1928), and the present day. The two central characters, designated in the modern period by the speech prefixes Billie and Othello, feature in all three strands, and the crisis in each period is recognizably the same: again and again Othello abandons Billie for a white woman called Mona or Miss Dessy – versions, one presumes, of Shakespeare's Desdemona. The actor playing this part of the White woman is twice heard offstage in the present-day action but, apart from a brief glimpse of her arm, never bodily enters the performance space (the part of Mona in the Stratford production was doubled by Sophia Walker, the actor who played Amah). Sears thus returns to the issues raised by interracial marriage explored by Shakespeare but sets that debate in revised national and historical contexts, and in exclusively black communities. In keeping with Sears' description of *Harlem Duet* as a 'rhapsodic blues tragedy',[25] the race and gender relations repeatedly played out in all three threads end in violence.

The seemingly irreconcilable positions held by these two (or six) characters on the question of interracial marriage are most fully developed in the present-day thread. Othello, committed to a politics of integration, self-identifies with the teachings of Martin Luther King, Jr., but in some ways his views on assimilation shade into an outright rejection of categories of race. 'Some of us', he tells Billie, 'are beyond that now. Spiritually beyond this race shit bullshit now. I am an American.'[26] With such comments, Othello refuses as inadequate an identity that tries to define him as a member of a disadvantaged racial minority. In *Against Race: Imagining Political Culture beyond the Color Line*, Paul Gilroy sets out the controversial argument that race is an artificial and peculiarly modernist construction that is no longer relevant to a world dominated by a global market. According to Gilroy's analysis, once-clear assumptions about the 'line between white and colored' have been confused by 'the leveling forces of placeless development and commercial planetarization'.[27] In such circumstances, the only appropriate response 'is to demand liberation … from all racializing and raciological thought, from racialized seeing, racialized thinking, and racializing thinking about thinking'.[28] Othello in a similar manner positions himself 'against race'. Arguing that African history and black personhood have been disentangled through education and marketing, and that both are less personally defining than a cultural 'American-ness', Othello rejects what feels to him an imposed role to identify instead with what Gilroy describes as a colour-neutral 'common humanity':

> I am not minor. I am not a minority. I used to be a minority when I was a kid. I mean my culture is not my mother's culture – the culture of my ancestors. My culture is Wordsworth, Shaw, *Leave it to Beaver*, *Dirty Harry*. I drink the same water, read the same books. You're the problem if you don't see beyond my skin. If you don't hear my educated English, if you don't understand that I am a middle class educated man. I mean, what does Africa have to do with me. We struttin' around professing some imaginary connection for a land we don't know. Never seen. Never gonna see. We lie to ourselves saying, ah yeh, mother Africa, middle passage, suffering, the Whites did it to me, it's the White's [*sic*] fault. Strut around in African cloth pretending we human now. We human now.[29]

Unencumbered by what Othello describes as black feminist prejudices projecting images of black men as 'poor fathers, poor partners, or both',[30] Mona comes to embody for Othello the promise of what he might achieve as something precisely *other* than a black man.

This idea that skin colour is not defining of identity prompts from Billie a literally visceral response: 'The skin holds everything in. It's the largest organ in the human body. Slash the skin by my belly and my intestines fall out.'[31] As Peter Dickinson has shown, her attack on Othello's politics as a form of debilitating racial mimicry has strong points of contact with Fanon's study of colonial psychology in *Black Skin, White Masks*: 'at issue [for both Fanon and Billie] is not so much the correct diagnosis of which group suffers from which complex and why but rather that the system that supports such psychological and cultural distinctions – colonialism – is itself constitutively dysfunctional'.[32] Homi K. Bhabha has argued that such mimicry, occupying a troubling and ironic liminal space – '*almost the same but not quite*' / '*[a]lmost the same but not white*' – contains the potential for radical subversion.[33] As Jyotsna Singh explains the position, mimicry exposes the 'ambivalences of colonial authority as it constructs the "other," whereby the colonial subject both resembles and differs from the master'.[34] Billie, however, interprets the situation more straightforwardly in terms of Othello's misguided search for white respect made visible in Othello's desire for – his desire to 'master', as Fanon has it – a white woman.[35] She diagnoses him as suffering a form of 'corporeal malediction' (the phrase, applauded by their landlady, Maji, is Fanon's), reading him as yet another instance of the educated Black man who tries to 'White wash' his life: 'Booker T. Uppermiddleclass III. He can be found in predominantly White neighborhoods. He refers to other Blacks as "them". His greatest accomplishment was being invited to the White House by George Bush to discuss the "Negro problem".'[36] Billie's separationist position, however, shades into an obsession with skin colour that is in turn rejected as racist by her family and closest friends.[37]

This dilemma between the two of them, only further heightened by Othello's impending marriage to Mona and turning on the question of how to live with or against race, never reaches resolution. If one accepts even provisionally Gilroy's claims for a political culture that has superseded modernist constructions of race, this conflict might be seen as actually *beyond* resolution. Billie and Othello, not just exploring competing views within a shared conceptual framework, but trying to speak across incompatible paradigms of race relations, lack a shared 'idiom' by which to arbitrate this conflict. Trapped in what Lyotard calls an instance of the differend, in which to apply 'a single rule of judgment' to simultaneously legitimate yet irreconcilable sides 'would wrong (at least) one of them (and both of them if neither side admits this rule)',[38] Billie and Othello are left not merely with insufficient but even unjust means to negotiate their dispute.

This impasse finds expression in Sears' disorienting dramaturgy. In an interview published after the premiere of *Harlem Duet* at the Tarragon Theatre in Toronto in 1997, Sears explains that a smooth handling of the historical shifts in performance is essential to the development of the play's engagement with race: 'There [had to] be a way not only to have three time periods but to go back and forth through them, not have a moving set, and not have huge changes in the cyc[lorama] … [U]sing three time periods was very important. It gave depth that I wanted. It supported many layers of the play, of the language, and of the contradictions around race.'[39] In the 2006 Stratford production, temporal shifts were suggested by lighting effects, rapid (sometimes onstage) costume changes, and the use of distinctive, easily portable properties such as a hammer and anvil or dressing room table that came to encode each of the different periods. Where the action set in the modern period tended to occupy the whole performance space, the Harlem Renaissance came to be associated with a small area downstage right while the nineteenth-century plot line occupied a similarly localized space downstage left. Movements between periods were reinforced by slight alterations to the way Karen Robinson (Billie) and Nigel Shawn Williams (Othello) spoke and held their bodies as they moved in and out of different historical moments. The importance of this scenic fluidity lies in the way it supports a perception that each of these narrative strands flows into and overlaps with the others. They all share, for example, certain common features: a strawberry-spotted handkerchief, a marriage vow, interracial desire, and violent marital breakdown. The recognition of the actors' bodies in performance – the realization that the same two actors portray Billie and Othello in all three settings – reinforces for spectators as theatrical effect the sensation of a single story repeating itself across time.

The shaping of recurrent moments between the independent strands further contributes to this impression of narrative unity. Act 1.2, the first scene set in the nineteenth century, stages a moment of betrothal between the two slaves, as yet unnamed in the dialogue. Kissing her fingers, he places in her hand a white silk handkerchief spotted with '[l]ittle strawberries', telling her that it is a family heirloom given to him by his mother, and from him to her as 'an antique token of our ancient love'.[40] 'There's magic in the web of it', he responds when she sighs, 'It is so beautiful'. The young lovers then plan their escape to freedom in Canada, where they will live together forever in '[a] big house on an emerald hill'. The scene concludes with a playful and erotic exchange, in which 'Him', kissing 'Her' as he offers a metaphorical topography of her body, figures himself as a claim-staker exploring America.

Moments and phrases of this scene resonate elsewhere in the play. The Prologue, set in a Harlem dressing room in 1928, opens with another unnamed female character (played by Robinson, but not dressed as a slave) holding the handkerchief and asking Othello: 'Remember … Remember when you gave this to me? Your mother's handkerchief. There's magic in the web of it. Little strawberries. It's so beautiful – delicate. You kissed my fingers … and with each kiss a new promise you made … swore yourself to me … for all eternity … remember?'[41] Her repeated injunction to 'remember' in the strand set in 1928 thus anticipates the betrothal dramatized two scenes later in a different, chronologically earlier, strand. Further resonances of Act 1.2 are heard in Act 1.4, a scene set in a late twentieth-century Harlem apartment that closes with a slightly adapted version of the lovers' 'prospecting' ritual (the modern Othello calls himself 'an equal opportunity employer').[42] Not only, therefore, is the linear progression of the opening scenes disrupted, with the betrothal situated *after* Othello's betrayal of his promise to Billie, but what progression one is able to reconstruct from these episodes depends on reading *across* the three historical strands, on interpreting them as repetitions of the 'same' event.

But at the same time that these three stories are drawn together through the recognition of personal names, actors' bodies, or similarities in the dramatic action, jarring differences systematically undermine the possibility of organizing the fragments into a coherent whole. The characters embraced by the name 'Othello', for example, are variously a slave, a black minstrel performer, and a university lecturer. They are all identifiably 'Othello', and yet they are also independent characters who respond to issues of race and gender relations within very specific historical and social conditions. In the earliest historical strand, Miss Dessy needs his protection when her father goes to war; during the Harlem Renaissance, Mona offers him the leading role in a production of Shakespeare's *Pericles*; and in the present day, as a colleague at Columbia, Mona represents opportunity and the allure of the unknown: 'Her mouth to my ear. Knowledge. A desire for that distant thing I know nothing of, but yearn to hold for my very own.'[43] This perception that the three versions are not self-identical is further developed by the way Billie's and Othello's marital breakdown is played out to different conclusions in each of the play's separate, but related, timelines. In the 1860–62 strand Othello is hanged, probably lynched; just over half a century later 'She' sinks a straight-edged razor into his throat; and in the present day Billie is admitted to a psychiatric ward while Othello exits their former apartment to place a call on his cell phone to another member of faculty, Chris Yago.

The conviction that these stories can be resolved into a single narrative is troubled by other slight, but insistent, inconsistencies in the narrative action. Act 2.7 dramatizes in the present day the vow of eternal love first witnessed at Act 1.2. Viewing the Harlem apartment that will become their home and dreaming of the time when they will be able to afford 'A big house […] On a rolling emerald hill', Othello spontaneously asks Billie to jump the broom with him:

> Think them old slaves had rings? Slave marriages were illegal, remember. This broom is more than rings. More than any gold. *(He whispers.)* My ancient love.[44]

Verbal echoes between Act 1.2 and Act 2.7 – 'My ancient love', 'A big house […] On a rolling emerald hill' – suggest that these two betrothal scenes, albeit widely separated in Sears' play and taking place in different historical moments, are versions of the same key event which ultimately leads to the lovers' tragedy. Again, as in the previous examples of resonances of Act 1.2 elsewhere in the play, the spectator is implicitly encouraged to formulate correspondences between the scenes in an effort to draw the fragments together into a single story. But this later version of the betrothal scene, crucially, does not include Othello's gift of the handkerchief.

We know as early as Act 1.10 that Billie received this gift at some point during the strand set in the present because the stage directions indicate that she '*picks up a large white handkerchief with pretty red strawberries embroidered on it*'.[45] Holding the handkerchief, in the Nightwood and Stratford Festival productions the same theatrical property that drifts down from the flies in a pre-show tableau and reappears two scenes later in the 1860 betrothal scene, she prepares to work magic on it that will cause all who touch it to come to harm: 'Othello? [...] Once you gave me a handkerchief. An heirloom. This handkerchief, your mother's ... given by your father. From his mother before that. So far back ... And now ... then ... to me.'[46] This speech echoes Othello's words from the betrothal scene set in 1860:

> It was my mother's. Given her by my father ... from his mother before that. When she died she gave it me, insisting that when I found ... chose ... chose a wife ... that I give it to her ... to you heart.[47]

The language of Billie's soliloquy in Act 1.10 suggests that she was not only given the handkerchief by Othello, but given it in a manner similar, if not identical, to the manner in which 'Him' gives 'Her' the gift in Act 1.2. And yet the betrothal/marriage scene between Billie and Othello as actually played out in modern Harlem at Act 2.7 omits any mention of the handkerchief. The gift of the heirloom remains an aporia in the present-day action that cannot be supplemented through recourse to the other two strands, the 1928 version failing to dramatize the scene, the 1860 version presenting the progression of events in a manner that just fails to fit.

This peculiar structure prompts in the spectator an active engagement with the problems of writing history. Sears fosters the unshakeable belief that these episodes in different temporal moments are repetitions. But it is never clear precisely what they might be repetitions *of*. This perception that one might be able to recover the events that constitute the supplementary, perhaps even explanatory, pre-history to *Othello* is in part generated by the way the action encourages the spectator/reader to formulate connections among the pieces to locate what seems the 'same' about them, coincidences which can then be emplotted as evidence. However, any answer at which one seems to arrive about what happened in the past is destabilized by small details that (just) fail to fit. One is therefore left shoring up versions of what *might* have happened by picking among the fragments, discounting as inauthentic certain clues that might in other circumstances count as evidence. An alternative response to the problem of historical emplotment would be to consider that the strands somehow represent – simultaneously – a single story narrated in pieces in three times, and three independent sequences of events. This methodological acceptance of contradiction, specifically in the context of the conflict at the

heart of *Harlem Duet*, makes available the pre-cognitive *feeling* of the differend, an aesthetic experience of the confrontation of irreconcilable differences typical of what Lyotard terms sublime art. As James Williams
explains it, this affect 'halts our drives to understand, to judge and to
overcome. It does not so much cancel them as leave them in suspense by
welding to them feelings that indicate that a difference is impassable.'[48] It
would be to reproduce as theatrical effect the lack of shared ground
between Billie and Othello, unsettling efforts to ignore or falsely patch
over it. However one chooses to account for these fragments, the activity
of arranging or trying to make sense of them as parts of a (perhaps logically impossible) whole produces a self-conscious awareness of the writing
of history as another form of story-telling.

Afrika Solo, Sears' first play for the stage, offers a fictionalized account of
the playwright's year-long journey through Africa in search of an answer
to the question, 'Where the hell am I from?'.[49] This early drama, conceived in large part as a solo performance and first performed in 1987
with Sears herself playing the central character, is an extended investigation of identity politics. Written in the autobiographical mode, it explores
the complexities of African-Canadian personhood in the context of Sears'
own multicultural background, born to a Jamaican mother and Guyanese
father, and raised in both Britain and Canada. *Harlem Duet*, as comparison
of the titles would imply, marks a shift from one to two voices. The focus
no longer rests on identity as role play, but on forms of interaction
between one and another. In the case of Billie and Othello, this relationship is repeatedly portrayed as one of victimization as each seeks to impose
on the other a particular version of their shared history. Othello's tactic in
the present day, for example, is one of verbal domination. He advocates a
colour-free society – so by extension defending his approaching marriage
to Mona – in a long monologue that attacks Billie's position on feminism
and race. This monologue, that starts towards the end of Act 1.7 and
carries over to comprise the whole of Act 1.9, is listened to by Billie in
silence. In an instance of the differend, silence suggests a 'negative phrase'
signalling that something remains to be said but lacks as yet means of
expression.[50] The awareness that Billie has a response, but not one that
can find voice in Othello's idiom, is brought home in performance. The
action of Act 1.8, set in 1928, temporally and scenically interrupts Othello's long monologue to portray Billie, holding a bloodied razor, respond-
ing to her former lover's arguments in a non-linear, counter-rational
stream of free associations as he lies motionless at her feet:

> Deadly deadly straw little strawberries it's so beautiful you kissed my
> fingers you pressed this cloth into my palm buried it there an antique

token our ancient all these tiny red dots on a sheet of white my finger-
nails are white three hairs on my head are white the whites of my eyes
are white too the palms of my hands and my feet are white you're all
I'd ever and you my my I hate Sssshh.[51]

This short scene can be read back onto the action in the present day as the
reply Billie is unable to phrase, or else interpreted as a working through of
the same conflict in a parallel thread, this time in an idiom that dis-
advantages Othello. Either way, the abrupt and disturbing shifts in context
and tone across these three scenes throw into relief, rather than resolve,
the injustices done by both characters in face of their irresolvable difference. Each victimizes the other through either verbal or physical violence.

This interest in subjectivity and (the failure of) ethical interactions with
the other is reinforced in other ways. Each scene opens with brief audio
recordings of landmark moments in African-American history accompanied by live blues music performed by cello and bass. In the 2006 production, the musicians (Robert Bardston and Bryant Didier) were situated
behind a scrim on a platform above and behind the main playing space so
they could be revealed and hidden by means of simple lighting changes.
Over the music the spectator variously hears, amongst other clips, passages
from the speech Martin Luther King gave at the March on Washington,
phrases from the Emancipation Proclamation, Christopher Darden's
request to O. J. Simpson to try on the bloodied glove, Paul Robeson welcoming the opportunity to play Othello in England, and Malcolm X on
the need to build strong Black communities. This complex audio patterning provides a historically resonant counterpoint to the dramatic action,
implicitly extending the scope of Billie's and Othello's argument from a
private to a public forum, weaving into their 'duet' other voices, other
histories.[52] In combination with the play's multiple timelines, the effect of
this soundscape is of an overwhelming entanglement in a past that is
simultaneously a present – or as Billie puts it towards the end of the play,
either poisoned by her own magic or nearing a complete nervous breakdown: 'Trapped in history. A history trapped in me.'[53]

This sense of a history that is never quite synonymous with a dead or
lost past is picked up by Billie, who tries to explain her sense of time to
Othello through allusion to African ancestor worship:

> Sometimes every moment lines up into one moment. And I'm holding
> you. And I can't tell where I end, or you begin. I see everything. All
> my ancestors lined up below me ...... like a Makonde statue, or
> something. It's like ... I know. I know I'm supposed to be here.
> Everything is here.[54]

Othello jokes that it '[s]ounds crowded', but this conception of history as composed of pasts and presents contained in a single space-time continuum is given visual shape by Sears' dramaturgy. Scene changes, for example, were effected in both the Nightwood and Stratford Festival productions by having the actors in the present-day action who never feature in the other two strands bring on and remove the few necessary properties. These actors would remain in character throughout the change, so creating the effect of historical overlap, an anachronistic intrusion that seemed especially deliberate at those instances when characters from different strands would meet eyes, quizzically, reproachfully, or uneasily. In the 2006 production, Canada, Billie's father (played by Walter Borden), brings on the woolsack for the first change from the present day to 1860 (Act 1, scenes 1–2), then remains on stage for a few moments, hovering on the edge of this other fictional space. Magi and Amah, Billie's landlady and sister-in-law (Barbara Barnes-Hopkins and Sophia Walker), sit comfortably chatting at Othello's portable dressing table in the 1928 strand before the start of Act 1.8, looking hard at Othello when he enters before getting up to leave. The temporal divisions perhaps most noticeably flex, however, during the later scene changes. At Act 2.7, Billie wears into the present day the 1920s flapper dress she wore in the previous scene when she murdered Othello, while three scenes later the 1928 Othello, alive again and about to exit in full minstrel costume, locks eyes with Billie who enters, as though in a modern hospital ward, singing (although not cued in the published script, this final encounter across historical strands is likewise marked in the Nightwood promptbook).

The past in *Harlem Duet* never seems 'over'. This is different from the suggestion that history always repeats itself, or the essentialist position that experiences of love and race are always the same through time. Instead, the recurrences and inexact, troubling repetitions that haunt Sears' dramaturgy and seem to turn history back on itself inhibit the objectification and production of the past as knowledge that de Certeau has argued is typical of the West's 'pathological' obsession with death.[55] Things come back or, more accurately, they were never really gone, a conception of the past as effectual present symbolized by the handkerchief that carries the experiences and emotions of Othello's ancestors, including

> [t]he one who laid the foundation for the road in Herndon, Virginia, and was lashed for laziness as he stopped to wipe the sweat from his brow with this kerchief. Or, your great great grandmother, who covered her face with it, and then covered it with her hands as she rocked and silently wailed, when told that her girl child, barely thirteen, would be sent 'cross the state for breeding purposes. Or the one who

leapt for joy on hearing of the Emancipation Proclamation, fifteen years late mind you, only to watch it fall in slow motion from his hand and onto the ground when told that the only job he could now get, was the same one he'd done for free all those years, and now he's forced to take it, for not enough money to buy the food to fill even one man's belly. And more … so much more.[56]

In a context in which past and present coincide, the problem of history is not just a matter of trying to piece together 'what happened' in order to decide what's true or who's right, but the difficulty of subjecting to analysis something that cannot be distanced from one's own moment. How does one speak of, or for, the past? How does the past continue to speak (in) the present?

Harlem Duet repeatedly turns to the ethical problem of how to voice the other, embedding an instance of the differend (the lack of shared idiom between Billie and Othello that results in violent assertions of power) within a tragedy, or tragedies, of love and race played out across, or in, three separate historical moments. Sears responds to the issues of just representation posed by this complex action by means of story-telling devices that remain unburdened by a search for common ground. Instead of arbitrating the conflict between Billie and Othello, deciding which of them has the best claim to the 'truth' about race relations, or seeking to make logical sense of the discontinuous events she describes in her preface as constituting the black female story occluded by Shakespeare, Sears' flexible dramaturgy accommodates contradiction, indeterminacy, and recurrence. As a slave, Othello is hanged; as a minstrel, he has his throat slit (twice), and yet eventually makes a final exit that is an entrance onto a stage somewhere else; as a professor, he walks out of *Harlem Duet*, into Shakespeare's work. These endings came to seem even more provisional in the Stratford production, as Othello would 'wake' each time from death, suddenly pulling himself to his knees with a gasp to stare at Billie before exiting the stage. Sears' historiography, as distinct from 'Billie's story', engages with the ethics of speaking for the other and the past by positing a form of historical writing in which apparently inconsistent things can *all* happen, and different times can be brought into forms of *reciprocal* exchange and production.

Sears intertwines *Harlem Duet* and *Othello*, adapting the latter by adding to it another voice, and a previously unheard history. What is perhaps more unexpected, however, is the way Shakespeare's work likewise seems to intrude on *Harlem Duet*, altering, in particular, Sears' treatment of the character of Othello. Othello's last line in the present-day strand – 'Chris Yago, please' – delivered from the hallway outside of the apartment he once shared with Billie, is the only line of a cellphone conversation over-heard by the audience.[57] This link to the events of Shakespeare's work, like the one provided by the character of Mona who is likewise contained in the offstage space of *Harlem Duet*, is tentative: fictionally and meta-phorically, Othello's call may not be picked up, and so 'what happened next' remains an open question. And yet the invocation of (Y/I)ago intrudes into the present-day strand from a Shakespearean history that is also this character's potential future to trouble the explanation of race and gender relations provided by Sears' Othello in Act One. Sears has been clear in interview that '[t]he error that people often make is to think [the argument is] one-sided … I'm Billie and I'm Othello. That's the conflict. This is the effect of 400 years of white supremacy [and] what that has done to the psyche of black people.'[58] However, as I will suggest, to the extent that Sears' audience registers the phone call to (Y/I)ago as omi-nous, anticipating that this particular thread will play out according to the tragic events of *Othello*, Shakespeare's work rewrites the even-handed bal-ance with which Sears tries to present as mutually legitimate Billie's and Othello's views on race.

What is it that with the line 'Chris Yago, please' is imported into *Harlem Duet* as though from somewhere else, or another place? It is not, or not just, Shakespeare's text, but rather the history of a work made familiar to successive generations of audiences and critics through production, as Sears' own remarks about Olivier in blackface make clear.[59] This is a history, moreover, that is contested, and far from univocal. Margo Hen-dricks, drawing on Michael Banton's *Idea of Race*, has argued that to trace a genealogy of 'race' is to reveal that 'the concept has never had a fixed meaning':

> In its conceptual shifts, 'race' often leaves residues of previous sig-nifications to inflect current usage … Conceptually and politically, 'race' permitted the [seventeenth-century] English to explain hier-archies of lineage, status, or typology without changing the language. In other words, a writer could describe the inferiority of the Irish 'race' and the superiority of the aristocratic 'race' in the same text with little concern for conflicting meanings, since the text's audience would be expected to supply the requisite definition of the word 'race'.[60]

It would be anachronistic, a potential category error even, to assume that Shakespeare's earliest audiences readily interpreted the colour of Othello's skin as peculiarly defining of 'race'. This is a position Emily C. Bartels has chased down, insisting that Othello is not a racial outsider to Venice – as

Shakespeare's ambivalent subtitle instead suggests, he is 'the Moor *of* Venice', a doubled rather than divided figure, 'defined by two worlds, a figure (like Marlowe's Jew of Malta) whose ethnicity occupies one slot, professional interests another, compatibly'.[61] And yet, as Michael Neill has argued in response to Bartels' essay, there is also something recognizably modern about the way difference – not reduced to, but made visible through, skin colour – provides Iago with the ideological leverage to separate, over time, the tragedy's central lovers.[62] Neill's conclusion elsewhere is that the continuing power of *Othello* lies in how it offers an anatomy of a particular construction of race, laying open to view a discourse it is itself instrumental in making available:

> It doesn't 'oppose racism', but (much more disturbingly) illuminates the process by which such visceral superstitions were implanted in the very body of the culture that formed us. The object that 'poisons sight' is nothing less than a mirror for the obscene desires and fears that *Othello* arouses in its audiences – monsters that the play at once invents and naturalizes, declaring them unproper, even as it implies that they were always 'naturally' there.[63]

At the end of the council scene, seeking to smooth over Brabanzio's perceived loss, the Duke tropes Othello's honour and virtue in terms of a commonplace opposition between 'fair' and 'black' that, especially with Iago's vivid description of an 'old black ram … tupping [Brabanzio's] white ewe' still hanging over the scene, is difficult not to read as an at least glancing allusion to Othello's hybrid status as 'not quite/white': 'Good night to everyone. (*To Brabanzio*) And, noble signor,/If virtue no delighted beauty lack,/Your son-in-law is far more fair than black.'[64] Othello's metaphorically 'fair' colouring – his status as (just as good as) a white Venetian – seems contingent, lasting only as long as his virtue. As others have elsewhere noted, this is a discourse in which Othello himself participates, his own perception of difference making credible the ease with which Iago makes him believe Desdemona has been unfaithful to him with another foreigner to Venice, the Florentine Michael Cassio.[65] A troubled but unfinished thought, 'And yet how nature, erring from itself –', is given words and shape by Iago: 'Ay, there's the point; as, to be bold with you,/Not to affect many proposèd matches/Of her own clime, complexion, and degree,/Whereto we see in all things nature tends./Foh! one may smell in such a will most rank,/Foul disproportions, thoughts unnatural!'[66] Desdemona's 'unnatural' decision to marry Othello renders suspect her honesty, seeming to confirm adultery as an act in keeping with her predilection for 'disproportion[ate]' matches. It is only because Othello is already as immersed as the other Venetians in certain ways of thinking about identity that Desdemona's choice of husband becomes, even for him, a sign of moral corruption.

The phone call to (Y/I)ago invites, even encourages, the spectator/reader to bring this modern-day narrative thread to a provisional resolution by reading into *Harlem Duet* the tragic course of *Othello*. However, to anticipate that *this* Othello falls prey to (Y/I)ago's manipulations is to activate in the intertextual space between work and adaptation a peculiarly modern notion of American race relations and psychological trauma – it is, in effect, to be firmly positioned with Billie against Othello in a debate about identity. The supplemental effect of Shakespeare's work is thus to intervene to rewrite Othello's claim that he's 'beyond this race shit bullshit now', implicitly insisting that he is still defined by his colleagues – and by himself – in terms of his skin. What is perhaps most unsettling about this moment is the realization that Sears is not 'writing back' to Shakespeare so much as she is *being written back to by* Shakespeare. One turns to a Shakespearean future to satisfy questions about 'what happens next' in Sears, but once arriving at a conclusion, or premise, about that as yet unwritten history, one then *returns* to a Shakespearean past constructions of race as they are defined in *Harlem Duet*. *Othello* no longer seems situated apart from, or even prior to, *Harlem Duet*. A relationship of exchange is instead triggered, a dynamic process of production in which one marks Shakespeare's work continuing to take shape in response to, at the same time as it seems to ground, adaptation.

A growing sense of unease about the identity politics espoused by the modern-day Othello is further sharpened in the scene immediately following in which the actor playing the part(s) of Othello returns a final time, now as an entertainer in the 1928 strand. In the 2006 production, Williams sat alone at his dressing table, dressed in a tuxedo, applying to his face the minstrel's mask. As he worked with the black and white greasepaints, he rehearsed a line from Shakespeare's council scene as though testing the words in his mouth: 'It is most true; true, I have married her./It is most … /It is most true; true, I have married her.' As he completes his minstrel's costume, and gaining confidence with Shakespeare's language, he stands and directly addresses to the theatre audience a monologue that, given this character's complex metatheatrical situation (an onstage Othello rehearsing in a supposed offstage space the part of Othello that he will never play in performance), functions simultaneously in the manner of a soliloquy. This private rehearsal that doubles as a public performance is a condensed and adapted, yet recognizably Shakespearean, version of the speeches in which Othello explains to the Duke the 'witchcraft' he used to win Desdemona in marriage:

It is most true; true, I have married her.
For know, but that I love the gentle Desdemona
(She) questioned me the story of my life
From year to year – the battles, sieges, fortunes,
That I have passed. These things to hear
Would Desdemona seriously incline;
But still the house affairs would draw her thence,
Which ever as she could with haste dispatch
she'd come again, and with a greedy ear
Devour up my discourse. Which I, observing,
Took once a pliant hour ...
And often did beguile her of her tears,
When I did speak of some distressful stroke
That my youth suffered ...
  ... My story being done,
She gave me for my pains a world of sighs.
She wished she had not heard it, yet she wished
That heaven had made her such a man. She thanked me,
She thanked me ...
She thanked me ...
She thanked me ... . [67]

The delivery of this soliloquy in which Othello describes what he believes
Desdemona first saw in him to love is powerful and unsettling, precisely
because of the complexity of the stage image presented to the theatre
audience. Instead of actor, role, and embedded role coalescing in a single
coherent stage identity, the character of 'Othello' flickers as different layers
of the work's production history become simultaneously visible. What the
theatre audience hears is Othello's testament to Desdemona's unpreju-
diced sight, a version of the claim he makes to Billie in the various strands
of *Harlem Duet* that 'Mona sees my gift', and that the 'White women I
loved saw me – could see me'.[68] But what the audience *sees* is a composite
figure whose body is physically overwritten with the racist codes of
'blacked-up' performance – minstrelsy, of course, but implicitly also the
conventions of black-face production that dominated classical Shakespearean theatre until as late as the last quarter of the twentieth century. Both
of these actors, Williams and Sears' 1928 Othello – as Olivier did – 'play
at' the stage Black man. Cast in the position of the absent white lover who
gazes at the black man's performance of 'Othello', the audience becomes
suddenly caught in what Singh has described as Desdemona's 'complicity
in the production of the "exotic" Moor'.[69] The metatheatrical layers written on the body visually collide to trouble an 'authentic' speaking position,

evoking instead white theatrical constructions of black identity. Hugh Quarshie has commented that, '[o]f all the parts in the canon, perhaps Othello is the one which should most definitely not be played by a black actor', since this casting choice might seem to naturalize assumptions about race in a way that is avoided by a white actor who takes on (and at the end of the show sets aside) both Shakespeare's part and the theatrical signs able to code difference.[70] What is so disturbing about this scene in *Harlem Duet* is the way it exposes 'race' as performative at the very moment it allows Shakespeare's/Sears' 'Othello' to seem to persuade himself that his white lover has access to his 'true' self. For the audiences watching the history-making Stratford production in 2006, the challenges of sight, race, and the continuing production of *Othello* within the Canadian theatrical establishment were perhaps not resolved, so much as further deepened. Mimicry is transformed into a spectacle of political disempowerment which undermines Othello's faith in Desdemona's ability to see him for who he 'really' is, further troubling a willingness to share a belief that on any level he is – or we are – beyond race.

Despite its simultaneous setting in 1860, 1928 and modern-day Harlem, the unscripted 'future' of *Harlem Duet* as Othello leaves the stage to marry Desdemona remains implicitly located in the tragic 'past' of Shakespeare's early modern English work. Sears constructs a history for Billie and a pre-history to *Othello* by relating three intersecting narratives of the past, each of which stands in an adaptive relation to the others. This methodology offers a non-chronological model of production that speaks in useful ways to the politics of adapting Shakespeare. The work, as I have already argued, is never cut off from its production in the present, although one invokes a belief in the work's fixed existence in order subjectively to regulate change. This means that even motivated interventions – productions that seek to alter reception of the work in some specific way – are not apart from the work, but rather constitute the next layer in a continuum. In this rich palimpsest of production (one might alternatively draw on Billie's image of the Makonde statue), past moments are never fully gone or lost. Instead, not unlike the way the temporal threads of *Harlem Duet* can flex to enable contact or exchange across time, present formations of the work remain open to intermittent or unexpected intrusions from past layers of production. In such a model of recurrence, writing back to Shakespeare is always writing *with* Shakespeare, and *Othello* is less countered than *en*countered. The duet highlighted by the play's title thus extends beyond the fictional action – the play of voices between Billie and Othello – to reference as well Sears' artistic entanglement with Shakespeare. Or as 'She' comments to 'He' as the action begins (the abstract speech prefixes here seem especially apt), 'We keep doing this don't we?'.[71]

By inviting recurrence Sears opens up possible alternative relations of production, rather than, as Widdowson would have it, setting out to 'negate', 'correct', or 'replace' a supposed original work, a model of confrontation that seems potentially to result in versions of the impasse staged between Billie and Othello.

Othello, however, is not the only Shakespearean ghost to haunt Sears' play. In the 1928 strand, Othello is given the opportunity to perform not the great tragic roles to which he aspires – Hamlet, Othello, Macbeth – but Pericles, 'the prince of Tyre'.[72] *Pericles*, a late play that dramatizes broken families and travels far from home, offers another intertext, particularly in terms of the portrayal of domestic relationships between parents and children. Billie's mother died unexpectedly, leaving behind a grieving husband, Canada, and a daughter who was too young at the time even to have memories of her mother in adulthood. Although Canada's dead wife never returns from the grave, and the reversal of family misfortunes as dramatized in Sears' play is only tentative, what *Harlem Duet* takes from Shakespeare's play is the bitter-sweet tone of tragi-comedy. In the eighteenth and nineteenth centuries, the idea of Canada for refugee Black Americans represented full citizenship, land, and the promise of a new life, an idealism given voice in *Harlem Duet* by the slaves' dream of 'a white house, on an emerald hill, in Canada'.[73] But in the strand set in modern-day Harlem, in the aftermath of centuries of disappointments and frustrated ambitions, Sears shifts African hopes of freedom from an actual destination – 'Canada freedom come' – to the challenges embedded in a home symbolically located 'at the corner of Martin Luther King and Malcolm X boulevards'.[74] This reorientation is embodied in the character of Billie's father, a character who was a late, but to Sears' mind essential, addition to the play: 'I paid for this man to read the part of Canada, the father. But I don't know why the character came, I just knew he had to be there and I don't know now how the play could have done without him.'[75] Billie, tellingly, never does make it back to Canada, the place of her birth – Canada comes to her. The promise of new beginnings, key to the regenerative power of Shakespeare's late plays, is evoked in the final scene of *Harlem Duet* when Canada tells his daughter-in-law that he plans to stay in Harlem indefinitely: 'Oh, I don't think I'm going anywhere just yet – least if I can help it', he says. 'Way too much leaving gone on for more than one lifetime already.'[76]

Othello, as noted previously, seems trapped by the narrative shape of Shakespearean tragedy. Billie's future, by contrast, seems haunted by *Pericles*, a late play ambiguously positioned between comedy and tragedy. In her preface, Sears proposes to counter an imaginatively and professionally restrictive theatrical canon in order to 'dream [her]self into existence'.[77]

However, in working through this legacy, she enacts a more complex historiography in which it is not always clear who is writing, or being written by, whom. Joanne Tompkins, writing about *Afrika Solo*, has characterized Sears' conception of personal and national identity as rehearsal for an endlessly deferred performance, as a process of preparation that fits her 'to continue rather than complete'.[78] *Harlem Duet*, I want to argue, models a relationship between adaptation and work by extending to the identity of the Shakespearean work this engagement with 'provisionality and change' in place of an impractical 'desire for "getting it right"'.[79] As my citation from de Certeau at the head of this section suggests, the writing of possession, like the writing of history, is an uncertain practice. Sears in the end seems to write back to *Othello* – or, to return to the language of her preface, she 'exorcizes' the past – precisely by making space in a present moment of production for those ghosts to return.

Dancing with art: Robert Lepage's *Elsinore*

The example of *Harlem Duet* suggests that to appropriate Shakespeare's works is to enter into a complicated process of reciprocal exchange, one not fully in the control of the modern deviser. Instead of being the passive object of revisionist adaptation, the continually evolving work 'escapes' a past to which it has been at least rhetorically consigned to intrude on and potentially redirect current production. With the work in a state of perpetually coming into being, the boundaries separating it from adaptation are never sure – in effect, the work seems to recur in adaptation because the work is always itself undergoing something like an adaptive process.

Elsinore, in this context, marks a useful point of comparison with *Harlem Duet* even though, despite Lepage's French-Canadian base, 'no reviewer has noticed … *any* immediate social or cultural signification' to his treatment of *Hamlet*.[80] A one-man show, enacted in its earliest touring life by Lepage himself – a white French-Canadian man speaking the lines, when performed in English, with an assumed British accent – *Elsinore* weaves into its fabric and so raises for examination the cultural legacies and performance histories of *Hamlet*, another of Shakespeare's most canonical works. *Elseneur*, the French language version, premiered in Montréal in November 1995 before transferring to Québec City, and then to Sherbrooke in December; the English language version, *Elsinore*, was the one most often staged over the next two years at theatres in Toronto and Ottawa, the United States, Britain, and continental Europe. Despite an extensive foreign tour, the financial circumstances imposed by Ex Machina's touring mandate mean that the company's audiences are mostly 'Western, Northern, and metropolitan'. As Jennifer Harvie and Erin Hurley comment: 'Ex

Machina's shows may travel extensively ... but the destinations of their pilgrimages are remarkably homogeneous: major metropolitan international festivals, mainly in Europe.'[81] Devised specifically for an international touring circuit that constitutes something of a privileged, even élite, community, *Elsinore* plays with this audience's expectations of the canon and their ability to recognize in Lepage's production this most canonical of works.

Lepage's exploratory methods of making theatre, where a production evolves out of rehearsals and continues to change over the course of its run, speak in provocative ways to a conception of the work as continuous process.[82] His devised shows are always and continually 'unfinished'. Lepage expects *Lipsynch*, for example, a collaboration between Ex Machina and Northern Stage that opened in February 2007 in Newcastle, England, to evolve from four and a half hours to about nine hours in length by the time it premieres at the London Barbican in September 2008, in part as the result of spectator input. 'I don't think about rehearsing a show', Lepage explained to Lyn Gardner at the time of the Newcastle residency. 'We just play. People bring in objects and ideas and we play around with them and improvise, and we wait and see what happens. Over a period of time, the show gradually reveals itself to us ... Often, particularly towards the end of the process, I think of myself less as a theatre director and more as someone who just directs the traffic.'[83] In the case of *Elsinore*, a version or adaptation of an already known work, this dynamic is further situated within a long history of *Hamlet* production. I want to argue that by overtly playing, and playing with, the stage traditions (and occasionally even the textual traditions) associated with *Hamlet*, Lepage presents the audience with the doubled spectacle of an evolving production *and* evolving work. Rather than locating the site of production *beyond* the supposedly fixed margins of the work, *Elsinore* self-consciously situates itself *within* this palimpsest – or, as suggested by Lepage's choice of title, within the work's architectural walls – so continuing to 'write' what *Hamlet* might yet become.

Lepage has long seemed fascinated more by the activity, than product, of theatre. In a scene from *Da Vinci* (1986), his earliest solo devised piece, a blind Italian narrator recites 'A Brief Anthology of Artistic Creations Which Have Defied the Rigid Rules of the Tape Measure'.[84] Standing alone on stage, Lepage manipulates a retractable measure to summon up in quick series the pyramids, the Statue of Liberty, the Great Wall of China, Big Ben, the Mona Lisa, jazz, *Jaws*, Michael Jackson's moonwalk. As the fictional narrator illustrates the point that iconic art is 'impossible', or at least beyond rational explanation, the onstage actor delivers a virtuoso performance of canonical and popular art that itself seems comically and impossibly to exceed rules (and rulers). The audience is engaged by theatrical method – not just what Lepage plays (the Mona Lisa, the Statue of Liberty), but how he plays it. *Elsinore*, another solo show performed a decade later, likewise plays with iconic art but on a far larger, and more sustained, scale. Instead of a short scene, audiences were presented (depending on when they saw the show) with a set of variations lasting up to three and a half hours;[85] instead of enacting multiple works of popular and high culture, Lepage offered 'sketches' of *Hamlet*; instead of a tape measure, the technology with which Lepage played and on which his theatrical effects depended was a huge onstage monolith that could be raised, lowered, and revolved.

This engagement with theatre as play extends beyond *Elsinore* to Lepage's subsequent one-man show, *Far Side of the Moon* (2001). Here the opening sequence presents the audience, lit by house lights, with a huge reflective surface spanning the width of the stage. Lepage stands in front of the polished metal, facing it. Looking at the reflections of himself and the spectators, and with the spectators watching the reflections of themselves and the solo performer, Lepage talks to us about growing up in Québec during the decades when the Americans and Soviets were racing to put a man on the moon. Near the end of this monologue, the wall begins to rotate to become a low ceiling, and as the house lights dim and the audience is blinded by strong white footlights, Lepage steps underneath and behind the wall, and the show begins.

Far Side of the Moon opens with a personal narrative that seems to offer an explanation, as it were, of the autobiographical origins of the performance and the terms in which one might begin to understand what is about to unfold. However, this sense of a privileged insight into the performer/author's perspective is overlaid with an awareness of the theatricality of the form that communication takes. This account of childhood memories is presented as a self-consciously crafted stage moment. Spectators are encouraged simultaneously to attend to the actor who is in an uncertain fictional space, both in and out of character, themselves who, pictured in the reflective surface, seem no less part of the autobiographical performance, and the technology by which the doubling effect is created. We have Lepage, physically and emotionally, and we don't.

This effect of placing barriers or mediating devices between himself and his audience has become something of a hallmark of Lepage's theatre. The polished metal surface featured in *Far Side of the Moon* was previously used in *Coriolan* (1993) to dramatize an impressionistic homoerotic encounter between Coriolanus and Aufidius on the battlefield, a naked fight that was also a dance that showed the warriors spinning around each other as though moving independently of gravity. The use of a letterbox set elsewhere in that production likewise served a distancing effect. The window or slit through which the audience watched the performance was a narrow rectangular shape about half the height of the actors, and there was a flat platform that could be positioned behind and at the bottom edge of the aperture. In those scenes that did not make use of the platform, spectators watched the actors from the waist up; where the table was used, the spectators saw the actors from the hips down, unless the actors knelt or sat. This choice of set made for some provocative stagings of key moments. Most controversially, in the scene in which Volumnia pleads with her son not to sack Rome, spectators saw Volumnia crouched on the platform in front of Coriolanus who, standing on the platform, was visible only from the waist down. Coriolanus's face was out of view – in effect, offstage – until he cried (in French), 'O mother, mother! What have you done?', and collapsed onto the table. The British press, on the whole critical of the production, repeatedly turned to this moment to indicate the limitations of the letterbox set. Paul Taylor of the *Independent* suggested that 'it's unclear quite what you gain from concentrating on Coriolanus's khaki knees and awkward hands rather than on his facial reactions during the climactic scene of maternal entreaty'.[86] Charles Spencer, likewise objecting to the set in the *Weekend Telegraph*, claimed that: 'This fatuousness even extends to the magnificent climactic moment in which Coriolanus finally learns pity. We are unable to see his facial reactions as his mother urges clemency, and one of the most moving scenes in Shakespeare becomes a ludicrous farce.'[87]

What is so striking about these responses is their frustrated, even irritated, tone. These spectators want the freedom to look: they want to see the actors' bodies; they want to see facial reactions; they want to partake vicariously in the characters' anguish. Denied visual access to the actor's whole body in the scene outside the walls of Rome, and so kept at a distance from the character's pain, they withdraw their voices – much in the manner of the Roman plebeians from whom the hero's scarred body is likewise withheld in the gown of humility scene. In effect, the theatrical spectacle replicates the *experience* of disappointment and eventually rage that characterizes the citizens' (lack of) interaction with the tragic hero. The critics' assumption seems to be that spectators should be moved by Shakespeare's works in performance. However, to varying degrees, the *Far Side of the Moon* and *Coriolan* fail, or are not concerned, to deliver that theatrical effect. Our attention, instead, is insistently drawn to the theatricality of the performance event.

Elsinore, if anything, exaggerates this effect of emotional distance. Spectators who caught the show in London, England, when it toured for one week to the Royal National Theatre (4–11 January 1997), entered the

Lyttleton Theatre to see three contiguous floor-to-ceiling screens, onto which was projected an image of the night sky. The show opened with the faint sound of howling wind. An impassive male voice, accompanied in the darkened theatre by a vibrating blue sound wave projected onto the screens on either side of the central screen, began speaking:

> *The castle at Elsinore. A platform before the battlements.*
> *Enter Hamlet.*
> HAMLET: The air bites shrewdly. It is very cold. It is a nipping and an eager air. What hour now?
> HORATIO: I think it lacks of twelve. No, 'tis struck. It then draws near the season wherein the spirit held his walk. Look, my Lord, it comes!
> *Enter Ghost.*
> GHOST: I am thy father's spirit … [88]

As the disembodied voice – speaking the dialogue complete with speech prefixes and stage directions – began to deliver the Ghost's message of murder and revenge, a white spot picked out a golden breastplate of armour fixed to the middle of a wall, now positioned in place of the central screen. With the final lines of the scene ('Exit Ghost. Exit Hamlet'), the wall was lowered backwards to the floor. When it slowly returned to the vertical, one discerned a central aperture resembling a doorway in which was suspended a figure seated in a throne. Chic in a pair of sunglasses, and framed in a projected playing-card border that alternated between the King of Spades and Queen of Hearts, Lepage played Claudius and Gertrude welcoming Rosencrantz and Guildenstern. His voice was electronically modified as he shifted between the two roles, an effect further underscored by body movement and gesture. When the courtiers (inferred, not seen) were sent to seek out Hamlet, the wall fell back again, descending around the still seated Lepage, to form a level platform. As Robert Caux's music swelled, the wall, now detached from the throne and with the doorway closed off, rose to meet the two side screens. Onto this flat expanse were projected production credits on the left and right screens, the impassive bricks of the castle's exterior, and the title 'ELSINORE'.

Projected images, electronically rendered voice and sound effects, doubling techniques, and an ever-transforming machine at the centre of the stage foregrounded, metatheatrically, the play's non-representational staging. One's absorption in plot and character was at best intermittent, checked by a constant awareness of technological process as the wall/floor/ceiling on and around which Lepage moved was raised, lowered, and revolved. British audiences had been primed for a hi-tech *Hamlet* not just through familiarity with Lepage and his oeuvre (this was his fourth production in seven years staged at the National), but also by the huge advance publicity generated by the non-appearance of *Elsinore* at the Edinburgh Festival the previous August due to a faulty rivet.[89] If London theatregoers knew nothing else about the show, they knew about its set: the machine at the heart of the performance that had failed, spectacularly, five months earlier at an estimated cost of £100,000 in lost revenue.[90] A rhetorical opposition between spectacle and work evident in media coverage at that time – that a definition of theatre as 'two planks and a passion' is betrayed when 'computerised sets and electronic wonders' take over from 'living actors delivering the words, sometimes the music, of human writers' – became even more entrenched after the London press night.[91] Reviewers complained that *Elsinore*'s treatment of *Hamlet* foregrounded Lepage's spectacle at the expense of Shakespeare's words. Michael Billington, who saw the production in Oslo before it arrived in Britain, argued in the *Guardian* that this 'hi-tech version of Hamlet reduces the play to a box of tricks in which the human dilemma is upstaged by LePage's [*sic*] visual ingenuity ... Text is subordinated to image, idea to effect and the chemistry of interplay between actors to the faint narcissism of solo display.'[92] Alastair Macaulay for the *Financial Times* lamented that 'the poor old Danish play has been skewered, laid out on the slab, cut up, reordered, and turned into a flashy one-man show, a cold array of theatrical effects'.[93]

These reviews criticize Lepage's visual display as self-indulgent showmanship; spectacle has its place in Shakespearean theatre, but only when it is in the service of the words, and not the other way around. Ironically, a tension between words and visuals was likewise a concern for Lepage. In conversation with Andy Lavender, he comments that:

> I'm a bit burdened by people coming to see Lepage play Hamlet – and of course there's absolutely no interest in seeing me perform Hamlet. What's interesting is to see how I cut up the story and devised theatrics out of that [...] how does it change the story, how does it bring insight to some parts of the story? So it's ... an experiment.[94]

An experiment in story-telling, then, in two distinct parts: script and theatrics. The controversy and media attention in Britain surrounding Lepage's technological 'boldness' obscured a significant part of what he himself considers interesting about the play, 'how [he] cut up the story'.[95] Studying Lepage's devised pieces raises the sort of issues of textual indeterminacy explored in the opening chapter in relation to Shakespeare's works: one is confronted with many non-identical versions of the 'same' thing. In its earliest form, the performance had a running time of three and a half hours; by the time it reached London, England, it was half the length; when it toured to the Brooklyn Academy of Art in New York a year later with Peter Darling, rather than Lepage, at its centre, the sequence of the scenes (and some of the stage business) had been rearranged yet again. The script of *Elsinore* published in *Canadian Theatre Review* as the 'revised' Darling version is the script as performed in Ottawa in September 1997, but as scripts and recordings archived at Ex Machina indicate, the opening scenes had been rearranged yet again by the time *Elsinore* arrived in New York the following month, the show no longer opening with the 'To be or not to be' soliloquy.[96] Lepage's insistence that his theatre is a process of play – always evolving in response to the reactions of collaborators and spectators – means that *Elsinore*, like *Hamlet*, exists as a series of versions. Since textual instability comes as standard with Lepage's theatrical creations (even when talking about pieces such as *Elsinore* based on literary drama), to analyse the production is necessarily to focus on one or more synchronic moments, or to talk about an abstraction – the work of *Elsinore*, or perhaps *Hamlet* – constructed from non-identical production instances.

Christopher Innes, in a thoughtful discussion of Lepage's complex links to mainstream and alternative theatre, argues that *Elsinore* is '[d]irectly comparable' to Charles Marowitz's 'Collage Hamlet'.[97] While comparisons are available in terms of running time, or the challenge to expectations these two performances of *Hamlet* presented to their respective spectators, *Elsinore* is not precisely a collage. It cuts lines, and sometimes whole scenes, but the overall shape of the story played in London was surprisingly *undisruptive* of work expectations.[98] Indeed, what was perhaps most startling about the way Lepage shaped the script was not its radicalism, but its utter familiarity. Whether one considered it a production or adaptation of the work, *Elsinore* remained easily recognizable as a 'Hamlet' show through its manipulation of the stage and editorial traditions that have grown up around *Hamlet* as text and performance.

Polonius's famous precepts to his son were gone, as were his instructions to Reynaldo about how to take a 'carp of truth' with a 'bait of falsehood', yet Lepage's interplay of words and images preserved a view of this senior counsellor as a meddling fool. We first encounter him when he informs the King and Queen that their son is mad for love of Ophelia. Costumed in a heavy robe, wearing glasses and an obviously fake beard attached with a band around the back of the actor's head, Polonius delivers his circumlocutory speech all the time trying to keep his balance and position steady while the platform on which he is standing, with an open rectangular trap in the centre, spins beneath him. The image – his character note – is that Polonius endeavours busily to get nowhere. Hamlet's letter, projected in oversized colour behind him, and to which he directs our attention with the aid of a wooden pointer, completes the image of a bustling, pedantic schoolteacher lecturing his silent listeners. The flat platform rises, lifting Polonius with it, to create a wall, leaving the counsellor standing in the open central aperture. As the doorway, previously the trap around which he was stepping, turns counter-clockwise one final time, Polonius 'falls' out of one scene and into the next, where he finds himself looking up at Hamlet's legs (an effect made possible through the collaboration of Pierre Bernier as a body double for Lepage), as the prince reads on a ladder in the library.

The production's treatment of Claudius likewise combined an unexceptional interpretation with extraordinary theatrics. The vision of Claudius as a powerful gamesman/politician, suggested by an early visual identification with the King of Spades, was enhanced in his scene with Hamlet after the murder of Polonius. This meeting between prince and king was staged as a confrontation at opposite ends of a table. The effect of dialogue was created by Lepage, seated facing the audience, spinning the table hard through 180 degrees while simultaneously transforming his body language and voice to paint in turn a stern Claudius and an ironically bitter Hamlet. The revolving table punctuated the cut and thrust of their exchange, while the playfulness of Lepage's solution to the problem of dialogue in a one-man show intensified a reading of their struggle for power as a tense and deadly game. Spectators were left with this image of male competition as they went into intermission, but they returned at the top of the second half to a composite vision of female frailty: Lepage as the Queen incorporating into his/her narration of Ophelia's 'muddy death' fragments of the young woman's songs. As Gertrude finishes her monologue and sings the first stanza of 'Saint Valentine's day', Lepage removes the Queen's heavy dress to reveal Ophelia's white shift below. Ophelia moves centre stage to lie on a large sheet, bathed in blue light. As the machine, its aperture open (in which empty space she is lying), slowly rises around her, she struggles with the billowing sheet but is finally engulfed by it as the set completes its transformation from floor to wall.

In her four short scenes in *Elsinore*, Ophelia is portrayed as emotionally confused and physically abused. Scene nine spliced together Ophelia's account to her father of Hamlet's erratic behaviour with Hamlet's verbal attack on her in the 'nunnery' scene, as Lepage shifted fluidly between Ophelia's vulnerability and Hamlet's brutality with the aid of lighting and voice effects. This stunning counterpoint concluded with Ophelia's 'O, what a noble mind' lament, after which she collapsed to the floor. As Robert Caux's swelling, heavily modified, and repetitive electronic treatment of

Hamlet's misogynist 'you jig, you amble' speech filled the theatre as a coda to the scene, Lepage slowly stepped away from the female 'dress' (the effect of a dress was created with a dappled screen) to pull on a male shirt in full view of the audience, only then exiting the stage to re-enter as Hamlet. *Elsinore* offered provocative gender shifts within and between scenes, as Ric Knowles has noted.[99] And yet Lepage's shape-shifting presentation of Ophelia, like his portrayal of Polonius and Claudius, combined innovative staging with a conventional interpretation of character, reinforcing a metaphorical reading of Ophelia-the-character, and a literal reading of Ophelia-the-role, as consumed by Hamlet. Her mimed drowning, by contrast, drew on the work's parallel life in the visual arts. Lepage has noted *Elsinore*'s indebtedness to painting, explaining that he became 'interested in this play [*Hamlet*] mainly through people who painted. It's a play that has been painted a lot.'[100] Her haunting and solitary death scene brought to life in performance a familiar, even iconographic, offstage moment of female fragility, madness, and beauty already known to spectators through, in particular, the Pre-Raphaelite paintings of Arthur Hughes, John Waterhouse, and, most famously, John Everett Millais.

An attention to the palimpsest-like quality of *Hamlet* – one's experience of Ophelia's death as layers of theatrical, textual, and cultural production traced one on top of the other – ran throughout *Elsinore*. The narrative introduction, locating the action at '*The castle at Elsinore. A platform before the battlements*', rephrases a description of place for Act 1.1 first introduced by Capell, elaborated on by Malone, and conventional well into the twentieth century, thus overtly situating *Elsinore* in relation to the sort of mediated and modernized editions through which readers typically come to *Hamlet*.[101] Lepage's treatment of Rosencrantz and Guildenstern was likewise wittily attentive to the stage history of these two bit parts. Simultaneously alluding to their lack of individuating features, and citing a piece of traditional comic business that transfers that inability to distinguish them to Claudius and Gertrude, Lepage's Queen in her first scene pointed the line 'Thanks, *Guildenstern* and gentle *Rosencrantz*' to seem to correct her husband's previous misidentification of the courtiers. Playful echoes of a Stoppard-like identity crisis with respect to Hamlet's schoolfriends might be discerned elsewhere in *Elsinore*. Unlike Fortinbras who – in another example of traditional stage practice – was cut entirely from the play, Rosencrantz and Guildenstern were part of the action, but they always 'appeared' offstage. In the second scene, welcomed to Elsinore by the King and Queen, their silent presence was implicitly located downstage, among the spectators. In the next scene, when they encountered Gertrude's 'too much changèd son', Lepage as Hamlet stood in the doorway in the centre of the wall while live video projections of his head and shoulders captured on fixed cameras stage left and right were fed to the screens on either side of him. The audience had access, in other words, not to the two courtiers, but to how they, separately, saw Hamlet, two slightly different perspectives to which Lepage comically called attention as he turned his head quickly from one friend to the other, seeking, but failing to get, an explanation for their visit.

The way Lepage 'cut up the story' and developed theatrics out of what remained thus shaped a performance of *Hamlet* as seen through its history of production; by necessity, this created a conventionalized, even clichéd, interpretation of character and narrative. Reviewers who saw *Elsinore* at different stages of its development in the theatre note the familiarity of its perspective on *Hamlet*. Ian Shuttleworth, after the Nottingham press night, described the piece as having 'surprisingly little to say about Hamlet', while Tom McSorley, reviewing it on CBC Radio 1 as presented in Ottawa the following year with Peter Darling, considers describing this approach 'the Coles Notes of *Hamlet* for the technological age'.[102] Lavender, who saw the show in London and then documented in Québec City the process of rehearsing Darling in the role, comments that 'Hamlet is pictured, still, as the brooding malcontent, Ophelia as the fragile victim of male fantasy. The staging erodes some boundary lines, but still depends upon stereotypical images ... which it sustains almost as archetypes.'[103] Ric Knowles, quipping in his introduction to the published script of *Elsinore* that 'to read the play is to be reminded of the old joke about a student's dismissal of Shakespeare's *Hamlet* itself as nothing but a pastiche of familiar quotations', glances at my argument by tentatively suggesting that 'Lepage in *Elsinore* is less concerned with adapting, interpreting or producing *Hamlet*' than 'in the ways that the play's words and iconography have entered contemporary discourse'.[104]

Elsinore tells a tale of true and betrayed friendships; of troubled relationships to women and sex; of suicide and mortality; of power struggles between men. The direction in which the production developed over the course of its two-year tour, foregrounding Hamlet's trauma and his efforts to trap his uncle, only strengthened further a dominant narrative of filial loss. The version performed by Darling at the Brooklyn Academy of Music opened with an anguished Hamlet sitting in a chair listening to (or reliving?) the Ghost's tale of murder, an encounter that seemed to prompt the 'To be or not to be' soliloquy, while the idea for 'The Mousetrap' was shifted from its placement in the London staging after Polonius's encounter with Hamlet in the library to follow hard after the King welcoming his spies, Rosencrantz and Guildenstern, to Elsinore. The effect of such alterations was to focus attention on Claudius, the murder, and Hamlet's revenge. Significantly, the final image before Hamlet's death in the New

York staging was of the prince erasing his uncle's presence by seeming to wipe clean a floor-to-ceiling screen on which appeared a frozen still of the dead King's face.

Elsinore, then, is an experiment in deploying innovative theatrical form to convey an idea not of the text, but of the *work* as it has taken imaginative shape through textual-theatrical production. To assume that Lepage is playing Hamlet is to misidentify the project; Lepage is playing *Hamlet*. It is not the character but the iconic work that is filtered through his solo performance, accompanied by the machine he called the play's other 'dancer'.[105] The piece missing from *Elsinore*, however, the gap in Lepage's performance that left spectators unable to find Hamlet in the *Hamlet*, was the effect of interiority. Lepage's voice, filtered through microphones and fed through computers, and delivered in a flat, understated tone with something approaching a Royal Shakespeare Company, rather than his own, Québécois-inflected English, accent, was criticized as disengaged, drained of energy. Commenting on a moment where the live actor faces, in profile, a reversed and enlarged projected image of himself to create the multi-media effect of Hamlet in dialogue with Hamlet/Horatio (see Figure 2), Nick Curtis of the *Evening Standard* writes that it is 'as if the multiplied image were giving a deeper insight into Hamlet's psyche. Well, it doesn't.'[106] Jane Edwardes admits that there is 'technical wizardry galore … But if there is a heart to this piece, it is not one that beats with any vigour.'[107] Billington likewise argued that the show's form made for a cold performance: '[Lepage's] work on Shakespeare … always seems emotionally underpowered. In Elsinore, for all the breathtaking skill of Carl Fillion's design, he seems to be holding the mirror up to art rather than to Nature.'[108]

The London reviewers insisted that a performance of *Hamlet* had to get beyond surface effects. They wanted 'deeper insight', to feel the production's beating 'heart', to see, as Michael Coveney put it after watching the show in November at the Nottingham Playhouse, 'the soul beneath the skin'.[109] It is Lepage's emotional detachment, his failure to get into the head and psyche of Hamlet the character, that was criticized as bad acting, weak interpretation. Although the 'two planks' missing from Spencer's theatrical formula were not mentioned explicitly, the production's lack of passion was. *Hamlet* in the late-twentieth century, it would seem, necessarily requires Hamlet's passion. Not encouraged to identify with the suffering of the central character – not given, as it were, a piece of Hamlet – these spectators objected that the show had no heart, no soul, no centre.

But this, one could argue, and to appropriate Benedict Nightingale's review headline, is 'Missing the point'.[110] Lepage did, and did not, deliver

Figure 2 Robert Lepage in rehearsal for *Elsinore* at the Musée d'art contemporain, Montréal, Canada (1995). Photo: Richard-Max Tremblay.

the 'universal' dimension for which this play is typically prized so highly. Lepage's performance furthers an understanding of how Shakespeare signifies within self-referencing traditions of production. *Elsinore*'s ability to speak 'to' and 'for' the world (or at least that small, Northern corner of the world to which the production toured) rested not on a supposed 'humanity' at the heart of the story, but on a self-conscious manipulation of the situation of *Hamlet* at the heart of the Shakespearean canon, and the circulation of the work through production – the skull, the madness, the voice from beyond the grave – *as* art.

Lepage's performance drew attention to his protean changeability from man to woman, from prince to king to counsellor, and back again. Curiously, though, the body beneath the vaguely Elizabethan costuming always displayed the same neat moustache, picke-devant beard, and high forehead accentuated by a wispy, dark, receding hairline. These choices seem especially remarkable given that due to a childhood injury Lepage, himself, has no hair. Playing all of the characters in *Elsinore*, Lepage oddly resembled not himself, or even the usual portrayal of a blond Danish prince, but *Hamlet*'s author, Shakespeare. The effect of the London performance was of watching the likeness of an image, known to us only through engraving and portraiture, perform acrobatics across and within a constantly changing space that represented the castle at Elsinore. *Elsinore*, by this light, is less about releasing or revealing the passion of Hamlet (an emotion, Lepage argues, this character lacks),[111] than it is about watching an actor grapple with a monolithic, yet unstable, cultural icon: Shakespeare's *Hamlet*.

Hamlet consisted in this production of surfaces and images that Lepage explored and displayed by means of what he calls 'theatrics': actorly technique and the visual effects enabled by a custom-built, multi-media set. The performance event thus physicalized the experience in the late-twentieth century of ranging across the many and shifting contours of a canonical work, making it seem both recognizable and unfamiliar. Instead of developing insights into the 'mind' of Shakespeare's protagonist, this production records the traces left by one performer's encounter with *Hamlet*. To splice together Billington's paraphrase and Lepage's metaphor for the machine at the heart of the production, Lepage was not holding the mirror up to art – he was dancing with it.

'*Elsinore* makes a spectacular introduction to state-of-the-art theatre wizardry', writes Robert Butler in the *Independent on Sunday*. 'It just seems odd to involve Shakespeare.'[112] But the 'theatre wizardry' Butler admires is what makes visible a process of production that, in Lepage's words, 'change[s] the story'. Lepage's attention to the formal aspects of *how* the work is perpetuated, and to what effect, allows him to play the work as historical palimpsest, as an ongoing process of textual-theatrical evolution. It is by such means that Shakespeare becomes 'involved' as something other than a detached bystander. Shows such as *Harlem Duet* and *Elsinore*, preoccupied in their different ways by the histories of production out of which *Othello* and *Hamlet* take provisional shape, draw attention to the fluidity of the boundaries separating work and adaptation. The work's identity – insofar as it can be said to have an 'inherent' identity – is shown to consist of an unpredictable and never finally completed interplay between production and reception conducted by, and among, a partici- pating community. Crucially, as both of these shows suggest, the work's identity is responsive to textual and theatrical probing, like the walls of *Elsinore* that become floors and then walls again as Lepage moves around and through the space. To the extent that a methodology of 'writing back' situates Shakespeare's works elsewhere than at the site of revisionist pro- duction, it bolsters precisely where it seeks to counter. Insulated from the critical debate and with the potential for intervention always located somewhere else, Shakespeare's works come to seem impervious to sub- sequent generations of creative and interpretative enquiry. By stressing instead the extent to which these works are entangled in the present – not countered by *some*, but potentially *always* written again through produc- tion – *Harlem Duet* and *Elsinore* stimulate a critical awareness of the work as process. The emphasis shifts from what one knows now to what one might be able to recognize in the future as Shakespeare's works.

4 Adapting media

ShakespeaRe-Told by the BBC

As was seen in the context of stagings of *Hamlet* presented by Lepage and Warchus, means and styles of production that challenge one's assumptions about the medium of transmission can provoke a crisis of work recognition. If one's idea of Shakespearean theatre is technologically minimalist, essentially defined by 'two planks and a passion', then a staging such as Lepage's that relies heavily on 'computerised sets and electronic wonders' will seem, at best, far from the heart of what one considers the authentic work.[1] One might even choose to insist that a category shift has been effected, and that this is not an instance of the work at all, but something new, perhaps an adaptation. Alternatively, and especially as distinctions among performance media continue to blur, such features of production might come to seem, or might already seem to others, unremarkable, this adjustment of expectations permitting innovation to be folded into an evolving consensus about the supposed essence of the work.[2] Parallel technological developments have likewise confronted production of the work in the textual instance, especially with regard to the continued expansion of electronic editing and the internet.[3] Curiously, however, far from generating controversy and anxiety about what should count as a genuine textual instance of the work, humanities computing has more often been embraced as providing *improved* access to the work.[4] While my larger argument is that there is no fixed work to which one can gain access, what seems certain is that as capabilities such as full-text searching and on-screen facsimile reproduction become increasingly ordinary (to note just two of the more common applications of electronic text), the potential for such technology to influence a pragmatic conception of the work is enhanced.

In terms of performance, probably the most significant (because most prevalent) technological development to trouble recognition of the work in the instance is the advent of film and television. It is not unusual to see filmed Shakespeare – even 'full-text' productions – automatically categorized as adaptation; even Branagh's *Hamlet*, advertised as the 'writer's cut', was nominated at the 1997 Academy Awards for 'Best Adapted Script'. The implicit assumption here is that Shakespeare's work is only legitimately produced as literary text (and perhaps also live theatre), while all other forms of production are inherently adaptation. However, as electronic editions become more prevalent, and the boundaries dividing live theatre and film in multi-media stage productions become increasingly porous, this division into 'original' and 'secondary' media comes to seem tenuous, even unsustainable.

This chapter explores how innovations in the medium shape perceptions of the Shakespearean work. My focus will be on *ShakespeaRe-Told*, a four-part television series mounted in 2005 by the British Broadcasting Corporation (BBC). I have taken broadcast television as my example partly because of its ready accessibility to potential consumers: it seems likely that the Reduced Shakespeare Company's ten-second performances of the works on *Jeopardy!* in 2005 were seen by more viewers than any live production of Shakespeare staged in the same year. Television might further seem an apt site for analysis since it represents in Shakespeare studies a relatively neglected medium of production.[5] By looking beyond live theatre and film to focus on television, this chapter seeks to isolate how a recognition of Shakespeare's work – both what one thinks it is and how one comes to know it – is caught up in, and shaped by, technologies of production. I begin by analysing how the works were updated and reinterpreted for a twenty-first century British audience. The next two sections address in turn scriptwriting and camerawork in order to investigate how the BBC uses such elements of production to reinvent for television not Shakespeare's words, but something like a convincing 'Shakespeare effect' that is available to be read by viewers as consistent with the work. Finally, I consider the impact of interactive digital technology specifically in terms of the way this 'add-on' educational component, while ostensibly enabling a recovery of the original words in their historical moment, foregrounds the producerly contributions of an active viewer to the ongoing construction of Shakespeare's works. This last section of the chapter is particularly attentive to broadcast television as a technology that is itself undergoing rapid change.

Strategies of appropriation: Shakespeare's 'divorce comedies'

The BBC launched *ShakespeaRe-Told* as part of a New Shakespeare Season aired in the autumn of 2005.[6] Each Monday at 8:30 p.m. throughout the month of November a ninety-minute production of one of Shakespeare's plays was broadcast on BBC1. This BBC Drama initiative, modelled after the award-winning *Canterbury Tales* series televised two years earlier, included three comedies and a tragedy: the series began with *Much Ado About Nothing*, continued with *Macbeth* and *The Taming of the Shrew*, and concluded with *A Midsummer Night's Dream*.[7] As with the *Canterbury Tales*, the goal was to produce four distinctive retellings of selected works of a classic author for modern television audiences. To this end Executive Producers Laura Mackie (BBC Head of Drama Series and Serials) and Patrick Spence assembled for each drama an almost entirely independent creative team, each with its own writer, director, director of photography, music composer, and cast.[8]

All of the dramas are relocated to modern-day Britain, the scriptwriters finding for Shakespeare's settings local and familiar analogues. *Much Ado* is set in a Wessex television studio, with Benedick and Beatrice portrayed as antagonistic news anchors; *Macbeth* unfolds in the kitchens of a three-star Michelin restaurant in Manchester; *Taming*'s Katherine, who comes from a wealthy London socialite family, is a volatile parliamentary figure seeking election; and the confusions of *Dream* are played out during a two-day engagement party hosted by 'Theo Moon', Hermia's father, at a wooded holiday resort park in northern England. The emphasis is on rendering Shakespeare's plays contemporary in terms of situation and social attitudes by incorporating into the action physical surroundings, material objects, and behaviours that might be presumed to be well known to the BBC's projected audience. Characters send video messages by mobile phone, they get married in churches and pampered in spas, they travel by plane, bicycle, and taxicab, they put out the garbage and they feed the children.

Apart from a scattering of Shakespearean lines, the plays are fully rescripted. Short and easily recognized phrases are fitted into the modern dialogue (Macbeth, his wife tells him, is 'too full of the milk of human kindness'), while a few longer speeches, such as the soliloquy in which Benedick persuades himself that the 'world must be peopled', are loose paraphrases of a well-known passage. In some instances the appropriations are more deliberately underscored. 'I would lead you up and down', Puck explains, grinning at the camera, 'it's my theme tune'. A sense of collusion in Puck's pranks encouraged by his frequent direct address to camera is heightened here for those viewers who recognize his 'theme tune' without prompting. In *Taming*, by contrast, the distance one occasionally registers between the modern script and Shakespeare's language is usually a function of the Petruchio character's eccentric, larger-than-life personality – 'I've come to wive it wealthily in Padua', he declares inexplicably to 'Harry' (Hortensio), as he slumps into a chair in the middle of a comfortable living room in what looks like Battersea, London.

Such practices of modernization are by now not unfamiliar strategies of production, with the works interpreted – some might say 'adapted', a distinction to which I will return later in the chapter – in order to make them feel contemporary. The challenges that attend on efforts to update Shakespeare's action and characterization are perhaps especially visible and acute in the case of *The Taming of the Shrew*, a play that has long been at the heart of ongoing debates about gender politics and the canon. Famously attacked as a brutal and objectionable portrait of male–female relations by commentators as varied as Charles Marowitz, Michael Billington, and Shirley Nelson Garner, this early comedy has come to seem something of a modern 'problem play'.[9] Its very notoriety, however, is probably precisely why the comedy was chosen ahead of popular mainstream works such as *Hamlet* or *Romeo and Juliet* for inclusion in a modernized television drama series. It remains one of the most topical of Shakespeare's plays not despite, but because of, what George Bernard Shaw derided as its 'lord-of-creation moral'.[10]

The show's scriptwriter, Sally Wainwright, had met with success two years earlier on the *Canterbury Tales* project with the proto-feminist classic *The Wife of Bath's Tale*. Perhaps surprisingly, Wainwright chose not to use this next commission to make a similarly strong feminist intervention, but to develop instead strong motivation for Katherine's decision to marry – and stay married – to a feckless Petruchio. This production thus deflects rather than confronts the work's critical legacy by reconfiguring marriage as an issue less of female exploitation than of male vulnerability. Katherine is presented as a physically and verbally abusive Member of Parliament who is prone to making a public spectacle of herself. She follows up an assault on a subordinate whose inadequate briefing made her seem a 'political pigmy' on *Newsnight* by throwing over a table in a high-class restaurant while lunching with her mother and supermodel sister, later storming out of a party after reportedly breaking a guitar over the head of another guest. Albeit not a realistic portrayal of a modern, image-savvy politician, this level of farce quickly establishes Katherine as recognizably Shakespeare's comic heroine. In keeping with a range of critical and theatrical interpretations, this production variously implies as the source of her anger sibling rivalry, parental neglect, personal eccentricity, a lack of sexual interest in men (her mother warily asks if she 'shop[s] around the corner'), and pent-up sexual frustration, with quite a lot made of the fact that she has never had an offer of marriage, has never been in a relationship of any account, and at thirty-eight is still a virgin. By multiplying possible causes for her anti-social behaviour, Wainwright makes Katherine's violent proclivities legible through the ready caricature of the career woman driven by a competitive edge that, in its single-minded ruthlessness, comes to seem grotesque.

It would be reductive, however, to argue that the film in any simple way stigmatizes career women to celebrate an ideology of domesticity. All of the Minola women – mother and daughters – are independently wealthy, and Bianca is no less successful in her career than Katherine in hers. The spectator first sees Bianca surrounded by paparazzi at an Italian airport, the use of a medium-range slow-motion tracking shot reinforcing her status as a supermodel by picking up on the familiar signs of beauty and glamour visually encoded, for instance, in television commercials. She regularly gets, and rejects, offers of marriage, choosing for herself an Italian 'boy' out of a crowd of people checking their bags onto a flight. Lucentio, travelling to England as a tourist, is subsequently invited to her London flat to tutor her in Italian. It is at this moment that she dismisses her besotted personal manager, Harry, announcing that she will get married 'when Katherine does'. Bianca is thus presented as an empowered woman in command of her money and sexuality, while it is the relatively silent Lucentio, without a command of the English language, who is objectified as the subplot's sexually desirable, silent marriage partner.

Marriage comes to seem one option among many, rather than a state to which a woman necessarily or even ideally aspires. Since there is no parent in Wainwright's modernized setting with the absolute authority to negotiate an arranged marriage, motivation has to be found for Katherine to choose a husband for herself, a decision that is ultimately driven by political expediency. Her parliamentary mentor, John, is crucial to this plot development. With Baptista reinvented in the sphere of the family as a mother and former supermodel (the part is played by Twiggy Lawson), John takes on an unofficial function as the primary role model in Katherine's public life, advising her to marry by obliquely referring to her status as a single woman in terms of 'certain [*pause*] lifestyle issues' that might impede election. He later assures her that her hasty choice of partner is a 'stroke of genius'. Leadership of the party and a residence at Downing Street constitute the bait that makes the idea of a husband for Katherine – 'to anyone', as John puts it – seem feasible.

The marriage plot is thus recast in terms of Katherine's explicit consent and approval. Although she first meets her future husband while trapped in a lift, and so has no means of escape from their first encounter, she *chooses* to meet him for lunch the next day, and *agrees* to accompany him over the weekend to see his family estate. His eligibility is settled during that visit when she learns that although he is penniless, he is the 16th Earl of Charlbury. This matter of the title is used by Wainwright to lever an unexpected gap between production and work, this central character gaining a title but losing a name. When first questioned in the elevator, he names himself through a projected relation to Katherine: 'I'm – going to marry you.' The next day, when he calls to confirm a non-existent lunch date, Tim, her assistant, passes on the message that a 'bloke rang to say you're having lunch with him'. When Katherine asks for his name, the answer is simply: 'Didn't say. Said you met him at Bianca's party.' A few scenes later, a reporter tells Bianca that Katherine is marrying the '16th Earl of Charlbury' on Saturday; this is likewise how Tim identifies him to John at Westminster. The name Petruchio is entirely, and it would seem deliberately, erased from the television drama.[11]

And yet clues that link this modern shrew-taming earl to Shakespeare's Petruchio allow the loss of his name to pass almost unnoticed. The first explicit mention of taming occurs after the marriage. Having just been threatened with divorce at the airport by his wife of one hour, the Petruchio character telephones Harry to tell him to join them on honeymoon in Italy. 'She wants a bad marriage, I'll give her one!' he drunkenly threatens, adding ominously: 'And then I'm going to tame the bitch.' The violence of his language later translates into physical abuse when an argument at the villa escalates into what looks set to be a rape, Petruchio throwing a protesting Katherine on the bed and claiming sexual relations with her as a husband's right. When he suddenly steps away from the bed to announce, to Katherine's clear disappointment, that he will have sex with her only if she starts being nice to him, the spectre of a Marowitz-like brutality is replaced with the troubling yet no less familiar spectacle of the unruly woman who secretly desires of a husband social and sexual mastery. Finally, however, almost despite itself, the programme's portrayal of the shrew-tamer is undercut by an utter lack of motivation: Petruchio, seduced from the first by Katherine's outspoken belligerence, is given no reason to wish her 'conformable as other household Kates'. His impulsive decision to leave them stranded at their secluded Italian villa is driven by need not power, as he seeks ways to put off their return to England and so the divorce that seems the inevitable consequence of his decision to turn up late to the church, drunk and dressed like a woman.

A major consequence of the work's reinvention as a twenty-first century television drama is thus the intrusion of divorce as the circumstance able to redirect entirely the portrayal of husband–wife relations. Why, having married a man she now regards as 'a moron', 'a freak', and a political liability, would Katherine choose to *stay* married to him? Somehow Katherine has to have motivation to choose a husband not only before, but after the wedding. Wainwright, in keeping with a familiar strand of theatrical interpretation, develops audience sympathy for Petruchio by presenting him as psychologically fragile.[12] His offer early on to show Katherine the derelict estate he cannot bring himself to sell but equally cannot afford to keep comes to represent more than eccentricity or a misguided sense of aristocratic privilege when he reveals it was there he was raised by his father when his mother 'cleared off' when he was six. Anxiety about a man's ability to be lord and master in his own home is reworked in this film as a male fear of female abandonment, with family and divorce providing the coordinates around which a peculiarly modern idea of marriage is constructed. The turning-point in their relationship occurs through Harry's intervention – not on the road to Padua, but one evening at the honeymoon villa, where he explains to Katherine that: 'Basically, he's just a mixed-up, emotionally needy exhibitionist who needs someone to think the world of him.' In an off-hand comment that in its specificity recalls the divorce of Petruchio's parents, Harry explains that he will never be 'one of the adults … he is no more than about six, probably'. At this, Petruchio walks past them, carrying Katherine's supposedly lost luggage. Threatening to throw her case in the pool unless she promises 'unreservedly and without sarcasm' to be nice to him, Petruchio starts a count-down from ten. The stand-off is resolved without a concession on either side: Petruchio ruins her clothes, and Katherine gives him his kiss.

Male insecurity likewise provides the context and motivation for Katherine's final speech of wifely duty. Asked for her opinion during the family row occasioned by her sister's demand for a pre-nuptial agreement, and noticing her husband flinch when her mother insists that 'We live in an age of divorce', Katherine announces to Bianca that she should be grateful to have a husband to take care of her. Her depiction of a marriage in which the husband works to support a wife who stays at home watching television notably bears little relation to the show's narrative circumstances or conceptual framework, given that Harry is the only man in the room (apart from Lucentio's translator) who works for a living. Both Lucentio and Petruchio are supported financially by their high-flying career wives, with Petruchio, as becomes clearer in the programme's 'after-story', staying at home to raise their children while Katherine goes on to become Prime Minister. This speech on female duty thus seems as meaningless as the pre-nuptial agreement that Katherine moments later tells her husband never holds up in court. But like the legal document, it functions as an important symbolic promise of intent. The fact that Katherine delivers a speech of marital obedience explicitly obviates any need for divorce – and so for even the possible security of a legal safety net – since it offers an unconditional affirmation of the institution of marriage.

The BBC's productions of *Much Ado* and *Dream* likewise struggle with Shakespeare's comic marriages. In *Much Ado*, for example, Hero and Claude (Claudio) are never reconciled after his humiliation of her at the altar, the film playing with viewer expectations of the work to challenge the politics of romantic desire. The action shifts from the abandoned wedding reception to a hospital ward when Hero hits her head and falls into a coma. What follows that night when her friends and family leave the hospital is a version of the display of penance performed by the mourning groom outside of the tomb, here played as a bedside monologue between Claude and the unconscious Hero that is as familiar a trope of television hospital drama as is the nurse who finally enters to usher him firmly into the hall.[13] As the camera tracks Claude leaving the ward, the soundtrack takes an ominous turn, lights start flashing at the nurses' station, and hospital staff rush past him towards the room he has just left; forcing his way back into the room, Claude discovers – at the same time as the viewer – Hero sitting up in bed, the filmic clues at first interpreted as evidence of death in fact marking her unexpected recovery.

Whereas spectators and readers are usually privy to the plot to fake Hero's death, this production situates the spectator with the groom, using the generic conventions of television drama to persuade the viewer that Hero might indeed be dead. This trick ending that is in fact consistent with the shape of the work (the slandered woman must 'die to live') prepares one later on to interpret as yet more false clues Hero's new-found determination to seek a life independent of the jealous control of either husband or father. As this penultimate scene closes with Hero looking silently at Claude as he pleads with her to give him reason to hope they might yet marry 'sometime in the future', the camera cuts to a signboard reading 'sometime in the future', and from there to Benedick dragging a pacing Claude into a registry office where the guests have already gathered. This second wedding seems a lower-key repetition of the first, the implicit answer in the affirmative to Claude's appeal for forgiveness, until Claude suddenly notices that Benedick is standing on the wrong side of his best man. As the two of them switch positions and Beatrice enters with Hero in attendance, the programme concludes with the prospect of a single, rather than double, wedding.

This second trick ending is part of the production's complicated interrogation of Shakespeare's treatment of affective relations, a focus enabled by reconceiving Don John's resentment of the honours heaped in war on Claudio as a melancholic obsession with – or rather, in this character's mind, 'love for' – Hero. The expression of a man's love for a woman through a jealous control of her sexuality, an aspect of the work that is already problematic for many twenty-first century readers and spectators, is made more troubling in this production by finding in 'Don' a near-criminal counterpart to Claude. Reservations about Hero's possible motivations for going ahead with the marriage are overlaid with questions about whether, and how, Don's and Claude's possessive attitudes towards Hero might differ. A peculiarly Shakespearean take on the nature of love is explored at length the night before Hero's and Claude's ill-fated wedding day, Beatrice and Benedick parsing the poem he plans to read the next day in place of the best man's speech – Shakespeare's sonnet 116 ('Let me not to the marriage of true minds'). 'Original', Beatrice dryly comments. This familiar sonnet with its injunction against alteration functions as an affirmation of love and marriage, the poem serving as the seemingly prescient expression of Beatrice's and Benedick's feelings for each other. As they reach the final line, the would-be lovers simultaneously conclude that since the poet *did* write, and men *have* loved, 'therefore Shakespeare must be right'.

Beatrice and Benedick make a claim for Shakespeare's supposed power to speak across the ages to the essential truths that lie at the core of human relations. However, the revised ending which takes a stand on abusive, even potentially murderous, marriages and the problem of loving 'not wisely, but too well', is worked through to a very different conclusion. This production in effect builds into its interpretation of the work a self-aware critical apprehension of *Much Ado*'s gender politics. Why *would* Hero marry Claude? *Should* one 'admit impediments' to forms of jealous love so readily susceptible to corruption? The interpretative attitude embedded in the decision to summon up, only to deny, the possibility of Claude's and Hero's marriage is the prospect that Shakespeare's works are never just 'told' – and that at least in this particular instance, for this particular audience, he did *not* get it right.

Early in *Taming*, Harry describes Katherine to Petruchio as 'a dyke, or mad, or Hitler – or something', telling him that her sister claims she is still a virgin. 'It's not what you want, is it?', he comments, 'Not in this day and age.' In each of these instances, what exactly one wants 'in this day and age' – of marriage, of Shakespearean romantic comedy – presses awkwardly to the fore. Even Helena in this series' production of *A Midsummer Night's Dream* at first rejects 'James' Demetrius after their night in the woods, refusing to be his 'consolation prize'. These uneasy comic resolutions speak to the insistence with which the works are interpreted as domestic tales about marriage and the family, especially as these institutions have been complicated by women's professional careers: Shakespeare's works as (re)told by the BBC become readily legible to modern-day viewers in terms of the challenges posed by a liberal heterosexual feminist politics. While this bias is in part a consequence of the series' orientation towards comedy, the exclusion of cross-dressed comedies such as *Twelfth Night* and *As You Like It* (or even *The Merchant of Venice*) narrows the opportunities to stage sexual diversity that have become commonplace in theatrical production. Same-sex orientation, when it is not ignored altogether, is either demonized or tightly inscribed within male heterosexual fantasy. Thus Petruchio, future father and house-husband, is quick to make clear as he walks up the aisle in make-up and women's clothes that he is a transvestite, not 'a poof', while Bottom's pornographically coded 'dream' includes the promise of lesbian desire staged for male sexual pleasure as two women dressed in classical Greek attire embrace in Titania's bower. Katherine, by contrast, stigmatized as a 'dyke' and portrayed (along with Beatrice) as a woman nearly past her marital prime, is saved in the end through the love of a good man, a clichéd character arc that once again privileges traditional – albeit in this particular programme gender-inverted – family values.

Even *Macbeth*, not self-evidently one of Shakespeare's most domestic of plays, becomes principally a story of complex family relations, the impetus for 'Ella' Macbeth's murderous ambition linked firmly to a mother's emotionally troubled response to the death of a child. The solution to the literary riddle 'How many children had Lady Macbeth?' turns out to be 'one' – a premature child who lived for three days. For Peter Moffat, the show's scriptwriter, the opportunity to cut through speculation about Lady Macbeth's cryptic reference to nursing a baby is one of the pleasures of this sort of project: 'you get to make a choice. I thought it would help our understanding of the character if we just said it – that she had a baby who lived for [a] while and then died'.[14] According to Keeley Hawes (Ella), this information 'gives an insight into why she acts as she does. It doesn't excuse it, or make her a more sympathetic character exactly, but it makes her more accessible to a contemporary audience.' Not prompted by any indication of wavering resolve on the part of her husband, Ella's mention of breast-feeding a baby becomes a narrative end in itself, the couple living the pain of her memory of giving birth to, then grieving after the death of, a child. This disclosure functions to project an image of Shakespeare's Lady Macbeth as both wife and mother *manqué*, a woman suffering the mental after-effects of a very precisely located loss.

Writing Shakespeare's *Macbeth* for television

By reconceiving setting, language, and action, these programmes seek to make Shakespeare more accessible to twenty-first century British television audiences. But can one still claim them as genuine instances of Shakespeare's works? Or have the works been so altered in production that one must regard the programmes as adaptations – as not 'fully' Shakespeare's works – or else as *new* works authored by someone or something else, perhaps modern scriptwriters or the BBC Drama department? In a way, the ambiguous identity of the transvestite, Shakespeare-quoting 16th Earl of Charlbury speaks to the problem of discerning work from adaptation.

He is, and he is not, Petruchio. He is the 16th Earl of Charlbury, but viewers are free to bridge the identity gap potentially occasioned by the BBC's production choices to find in this titled but nameless character, Petruchio. The need to supply the elided name emphasizes the extent to which recognition is always a contested, evaluative process – this character *achieves* the name 'Petruchio' only to the extent that he conforms sufficiently to one's expectations of Shakespeare's shrew-tamer. This pragmatic process of gauging when something is 'like enough' likewise guides work recognition, continually fashioning and redefining its accepted limits. This section will explore further issues of work recognition and the attendant problem of adaptation as they bear on television drama, focusing in particular on Shakespeare's language.

The scriptwriters were acknowledged as important creative contributors to the series, but, importantly, they were not presented as the 'authors' of the shows they scripted. On the contrary, each programme was identified through interviews, publicity, website material, and, eventually, DVD extras with a wide range of artistic personnel. In addition to the four scriptwriters (David Nicholls, Peter Moffat, Sally Wainwright, and Peter Bowker), the series was chiefly aligned with the names of two Executive Producers – one of whom (Laura Mackie) was joint Executive Producer with Franc Roddam on the *Canterbury Tales* project, and so particularly closely associated with the modernized format. There were also four directors (Brian Percival, Mark Brozel, David Richards, and Ed Fraiman), and a team of well-respected and celebrity British actors including Shirley Henderson, James McAvoy, Bill Paterson, Billie Piper, Rufus Sewell, Imelda Staunton, and Johnny Vegas, all of whom were well known to British audiences for their work on television, stage, and film. Curiously, though, instead of marking a dispersal of authority, the perhaps counter-intuitive effect of this proliferation of names is finally to cause one to fall back on 'Shakespeare' (and perhaps by extension 'BBC Shakespeare') as the name able to encompass and give purpose to all the others.

Unlike *10 Things I Hate About You* or *She's the Man*, Hollywood films that elide more or less entirely their respective indebtedness to *Taming of the Shrew* and *Twelfth Night*, this series explicitly defines itself as 'Four modern interpretations of Shakespeare plays'.[15] *ShakespeaRe-Told* thus positions itself within a long and continuing history of Shakespearean performance: this 'new' drama, the marketing implies, is at the same time 'classic' drama. Such genre identification guides producers' scheduling and advertising decisions, while for viewers it firmly situates the series within a certain horizon of expectations (in turn reinforced by scheduling and advertising decisions). The cultural coordinates that perhaps most readily give meaning to the series are educational value (the vague perception that the shows will be somehow improving), the English-language canon, and the BBC's own traditions of production of great classic literature, especially but not exclusively in relation to Shakespeare (one thinks, for instance, of the much earlier BBC–Time/Life Complete Works series, but also of series such as *Pride and Prejudice* and *Bleak House*). Since many viewers will come to the drama with prior knowledge of the plays – if only a hazy classroom memory of plot and character – the way the series simultaneously enacts and disrupts expectations of 'Shakespeare' as a generic category becomes a significant, and not necessarily alienating, part of the viewing experience.

So while the producers are frank about a level of interpretation that might lead some viewers to describe the project as adaptation, *ShakespeaRe-Told* is nonetheless positioned as instances of the works, able to 'bring Shakespeare' (as one publicity blurb puts it) to a twenty-first century audience. To take up again from the first chapter Grigely's insight into the historical situatedness and constant reinvention of text – into the inevitable failure, as it were, of textual reproduction – it seems not inconceivable to identify as Shakespeare's *Macbeth* a BBC production with clear generic links to Shakespeare that is entitled *Macbeth*. But despite the BBC's efforts to shape audience expectations in such a way as to permit an at least provisional identification of the series with Shakespeare, the loss of Shakespeare's language proved for some viewers an unqualified and insurmountable barrier to recognition. Sir Trevor Nunn, former Artistic Director of the Royal Shakespeare Company and Royal National Theatre, was one who spoke out against the decision to rescript the plays, insisting that fidelity to language is the touchstone of the work: 'I'm concerned that none of Shakespeare's language is to be involved in these films. Ultimately for me, it's the language that matters – no language, no Shakespeare ... What we find in his language defines how close we are getting to Shakespeare.'[16]

Nunn is not alone in laying a priority on language, playwright and director Stephen Poliakoff and RSC Voice Director Cicely Berry, for instance, arguing seven years earlier at a roundtable discussion hosted by the RSC that 'the magic of Shakespeare's writing' lies in the language: 'When we start to lose the language, that's the end.'[17] Significantly, however, Poliakoff's and Berry's attacks on efforts to 'simplify Shakespeare or dumb him down', like Nunn's after them, are fuelled by productions that they perceive to have made unacceptable textual alterations. Despite the authoritative positions from which all three speak, they are entering into a public debate, seeking to persuade others of the validity of their opinion about what should count as Shakespeare. The very fact that they feel motivated to stake a claim in this debate at all suggests the extent to which the artistic and political boundaries defining the plays and 'the end' of Shakespeare are drawn precisely in response to such exchanges. The occasion for the RSC roundtable, as discussed in Chapter 2, was Matthew Warchus's *Hamlet* and the director's widely publicized call for a ten-year moratorium on productions of Shakespeare. Arguing that '[p]arts of *Hamlet* are actually rather badly written, and we shouldn't be afraid to say so', Warchus clearly struck a chord with at least some members of the audience at the roundtable discussion who offered a series of comments to the effect that theatre companies should experiment even *more* freely with the plays. Their views understood in context, it becomes plain that Poliakoff and Berry are defending a particular – not necessarily self-evident – position. Revealingly, their uncompromising stance on the need not to be complacent about the importance of language was prompted by the opinion, voiced from the floor, that Shakespeare's works and texts are not self-identical: 'The stories are good, universal themes and that's what we are interested in, so why not tamper with them?'

The issues here concern the point at which interpretation ('tamper[ing]') disables recognition of the work in the instance, and the degree to which Shakespeare's works, as distinct from either text or performance, are indeed defined by language. I want to pursue this particular problem of adaptation specifically in relation to the demands of writing *Macbeth* for television. As already explained, the death of a child provides the primary narrative context for Ella Macbeth's madness and death. After 'Joe' Macbeth plans the attack on Macduff's home, the camera cuts to a close-up of Ella in profile narrating a gruelling labour, a Caesarean birth, and the baby's eventual death. The sound of murmuring voices and cutlery suggests, however improbably, that she is at her usual place, greeting guests at the front of the restaurant. Growing curiosity about her unseen listener(s) is answered at best uncertainly when the camera at length cuts away to reveal the indistinct outline of two customers who are calmly shown to their tables, the camera then quickly cutting again to a slightly elevated distance shot of the restaurant floor in which Ella is captured staring impassively into the middle distance. The poise and clarity with which the history of the baby's life is recounted are thus opposed to an opaque and disorienting visual narration of the actual moment of telling, the camera's disruption of viewer legibility (should the speech be read as a monologue? as an internalized soliloquy?) marking the character's deteriorating mental stability. The action shortly after cuts to the rooftop of the restaurant from which Ella, her washed hands raw and bloody, falls to her death, the camera pausing over the sight of her lifeless body on a garbage skip below.

The report that she is dead is thus heavily augmented for television with the dramatization of what is transparently a suicide. Questions one might have about the circumstances surrounding Lady Macbeth's untimely death are dispelled, and as with other trajectories in the series, whether comic or

tragic, Ella's tale is brought to an unambiguous end. These 'new interpretations' are often directed towards enhanced character motivation and
clarification of Shakespeare's action. *Much Ado* sketches in the history
behind the long-standing animosity between Beatrice and Benedick with
an extended pre-show sequence, and locates the cause for Don (John)'s ill-
defined misanthropy in feelings of emotional abandonment and sexual
obsession; *Taming* not only makes explicit Petruchio's straitened financial
circumstances (he owes £54,000 to the Inland Revenue), but cites identity
politics as the reason behind his unconventional wedding garb, rounding
off the comedy with a series of picture album snapshots that reveal the
birth of triplets and Katherine's rise to parliamentary power. Such
moments explain events that might otherwise seem perplexing (Petruchio's
costume at the church), expand on hints only lightly touched upon (Beatrice's casual reference to a prior emotional attachment to Benedick), or
else provide a firm sense of closure (Katherine and Petruchio went on to
raise a family and run the country, whereas Macbeth's wife killed herself
by jumping from a roof).

Moffat explains this pattern of story-telling in terms of the conventions
of writing for television: 'You have to fill in the gaps for a 21st-century
television audience … Shakespeare very often leaves things unresolved,
whereas the rules of television say you have to finish what you've begun.'[18]
Writers for *ShakespeaRe-Told* thus shape Shakespeare's works for the televi-
sion-literate viewer who has certain narrative expectations of how a story
will be told, but who no longer relies on expository dialogue to grasp even
complex plotting. Telling a story for television is in large part a visual
exercise, and *Macbeth*, like the other programmes in the series, relies at key
moments on contrived filmic techniques to encode villainy, to signal hal-
lucination, and to express the intrusion into everyday life of the surreal
world of the weird sisters (imagined here as three binmen). Given the
dominance of non-verbal narration, it seems especially curious then that
the language of *Macbeth* should be no less stylized than its camerawork, the
show's heightened and even poetic dialogue drawing attention not just to
what characters say, but also to how they say it. The opening dialogue, for
example, is given over to the binmen as they eat lunch in the cab of their
truck, perched in isolation in the middle of an immense wasteland of garbage. The challenge of making sense of their allusive and heavily accented
language as they discuss meat sandwiches, restaurant slop, and Macbeth,
especially as the scene's visuals are already slightly distorted through almost
impossibly tight camera angles, creates the disorienting sensation of not
being able fully to get one's bearings on a nearly but not quite ordinary
scene. The programme then moves into what feels like a second introductory
sequence with a scored filmic montage developing a set of interwoven

storylines that converge on the restaurant. Sustained dialogue resumes when Macbeth, heaving a raw pig's head onto the preparation counter, calls over his apprentices to give them a master class in knife skills.

Like the binmen, Macbeth is immediately set apart from other characters by his distinctive language patterns. As he slices and tears the pig's flesh from its head, he instils in the would-be chefs gathered around him the rules of butchery – 'respect' and 'no waste' – that double as life lessons. In another long monologue, Macbeth remembers the complex sensory experience of eating roast sparrow, describing the sound and feel of crunching down on the bones as a sort of childhood epiphany. The deliberate artistry of this narrated memory implicitly links the sensuality of meat and the sensuality of words, food preparation and poetry emerging as analogous aesthetic forms. The only character to rival Macbeth's wordcraft is Duncan, who recounts as defining the childhood memory of his mother waking him before dawn to watch his father slip into the shed to butcher a sleeping Tamworth pig. When asked if his father killed the animal in its sleep out of kindness, his mother 'gave [him] the truth' rather than the answer she knew he wanted to hear: '"The meat," she said, "tastes better."' Sounding like each other, and nobody else, Duncan and Macbeth are verbally positioned as potential rivals.

This aural patterning, however, shifts with the plan to knife Duncan in his sleep, the crime seeming in this particular setting a monstrous travesty of the art of butchery since it produces meat that can only be wasted, not consumed. The kitchen, a space previously filled with shouting and music, falls increasingly silent. Days and nights within the windowless walls of the restaurant become indistinguishable, the viewer caught up, like the Macbeths, in the disorienting experience of insomnia. The temporal and linguistic strangeness of this new world is captured in a short scene that takes place shortly after the murder of Duncan is discovered. Summoned by an out-of-hours knocking at the door – whether it is late afternoon or the early hours of the morning is impossible to tell from lighting and costuming cues – Macbeth admits into the kitchen a well-dressed stranger who starts rummaging through cupboards and pulling knives from the wall, demanding to be told the secret he knows 'Michelin man' wants to confess, promising leniency if he is not made to work for his 'pound of flesh'. This tense episode is played as one long monologue, Macbeth, as uncertain as the viewer about the visitor's identity, standing to the side, silent. Concluding that the problem is always vermin in the sewer, this garrulous porter-cum-health-inspector offers an uncanny inversion of the life, meat, and art speeches previously heard from Macbeth and Duncan, describing as 'tragic' the remorseless certainty with which the exterminator is able to kill fecund, but behaviourally predictable, rats. Telling Macbeth that he sees what he is, 'a man who is committed to running a clean kitchen', this comically disturbing figure disappears as suddenly and inexplicably as he arrived.

This new image of a wordless Macbeth increasingly dominates the film as his distinctive, heightened register is taken up by other characters. A version of the 'signifying nothing' monologue, for example, is here delivered by the binmen. Warning Macbeth to beware Macduff as they throw bags of waste into the back of their truck in the alley by the restaurant, the enigmatic binmen explain that they have access to the 'whole story':

MACBETH: How – how do you know these things?

BINMAN 1: The whole story is here. From flaunted sperm in banana-flavoured rubber, right through to the yellow hacked-out gob of ancient drunks. All of life.

BINMAN 2: And the Special Brew.

BINMAN 3: Dipping needles.

BINMAN 1: All the great excitements that get us from cradle to the grave. The sound and the fury.

BINMAN 2: It all ends with us.

BINMAN 3: Incinerated.

BINMAN 2: Obliterated.

BINMAN 1: No more.

BINMAN 2: Yesterday's breakfast, yesterday's meat, yesterday's men.

BINMAN 3: All our yesterdays.

BINMAN 2: All our tomorrows.

ALL: [*driving away*] Bye bye, bye bye, bye bye … [19]

This rich passage of dialogue, with its repetitions, oppositional phrases, and stichomythic rhythm, reduces to detritus 'all of life', with the bleak expanse between birth and old age, yesterday and tomorrow collapsed into a vision of bodily emissions – the 'flaunted' sperm and the 'hacked-out' expectorate – as discarded urban waste. Everything ends with the collection and disposal of meat and men, the repeated shot of the garbage truck at the dump coming to seem in this light an emblem of despair. In terms of the production's manipulation of linguistic registers as the sign of power, the reassignment of this monologue further marks the alienation of Macbeth from himself, his once accustomed creativity and authority appropriated after the murder of Duncan by characters as various as the binmen, the porter-cum-health-inspector, and Billie, his second-in-command in the kitchen, all of whom come to seem threats to his authority.

This treatment of a script for television is conspicuously wrought, the characters' verbal artistry drawing attention to the scriptwriter's craft as art. This encourages in turn a curious bifold perspective on the category of authorship (a faultline already implicit in a series that is simultaneously 'new' and 'classic' drama), with the modern author 'writing' the canonical author. Moffat, accommodating what he calls the rules of television, modernizes Shakespeare's words, introduces visual sequences in place of expository dialogue, develops psychological motivation, and brings narrative trajectories to firm closure. However, he also *disrupts* viewer expectations of television dialogue to make the language sound in places self-consciously elevated. In a film preoccupied with the production and corruption of art, the craft of the scriptwriter lies in the way that his (re)telling for television reproduces not Shakespeare's poetry, nor even a modernized paraphrase designed to approximate for a later age what might be supposed to be the effect of the language of *Macbeth* in the period of its earliest theatrical production, but a treatment of language that in its patterning and stylization seems overtly literary – or, more specifically, 'Shakespearean'.

Moffat writes what at times registers as strange television dialogue. This is different, however, from Shakespeare's language sounding strange on television, which was often the effect generated by the BBC–Time/Life films. It is precisely because Moffat's language can be accepted first as authentic television that there emerges the potential for it to be recognized subsequently as authentic Shakespeare. Moffat, in short, authors Shakespeare for a new medium and a new millennium by projecting a distinctive authorial *effect* that is consistent with modern perceptions of the canon as high art.[20] Paradoxically, it is this slanting proximity to the work, one's ability to hear the 'Shakespeare' in Moffat's *Macbeth*, that makes an interpretation 'based on the play by William Shakespeare', as the title credits put it, less self-evidently adaptation. The more closely *Macbeth* approaches a poetic style that might be (mis)recognized as Shakespeare – or rather, as it approaches what sounds within the specific context of the broadcast medium 'Shakespearean' – the more the art of the television scriptwriter challenges implicitly the boundaries of what can be recognized as an instance of the authentic work. They are not Shakespeare's words, but this programme might yet be Shakespeare's *Macbeth*.

Mediated proximities, or much ado about 'noting'

The previous section questioned how conventions of television might contribute to evolving conceptions of Shakespeare's works, particularly in relation to the intersection in production of language and medium. Of course, when the BBC last attempted to mount full-scale productions of the works, critics tended to stress the impossibility of playing Shakespeare on television. A recurrent observation at the time of the monumental

BBC–Time/Life series which began in 1978 its marathon broadcast of thirty-seven productions was that although television with its small screen and poor quality image is necessarily a dialogue-intensive medium, Shakespeare's convention-heavy stage language is ill suited to the typical three-camera studio format.[21] Arrangements of actors within the small frame became a predictable range of head-and-shoulders shots, and the complaint was that experimentations with language and mise-en-scène were frequently insufficient to prevent distractions in the home intruding on the viewing experience. As Michèle Willems concludes her analysis of the distinct styles that characterized directors' work for the series: 'Producing Shakespeare with the resources normally expected on the small screen has too often resulted in attracting attention to the fact that Shakespeare did *not* write for television.'[22]

Since the conclusion of the Complete Works series in 1985, the BBC has explored ways of broadcasting Shakespeare on television as varied as the documentary format of BBC2's Bard on the Box series in 1994, the Animated Tales on BBC2 (1992–4), and productions of live theatre transmitted on BBC4 (Peter Brook's *Hamlet* in 2002, and *Richard II* and *Measure for Measure* from Shakespeare's Globe in 2003 and 2005, respectively). Each of these types of production presents distinctive answers to the problems and opportunities posed by the medium, with 'Shakespeare on television' emerging over the past thirty years as a catholic house embracing a wide and overlapping range of possible formats. In yet another configuration of 'Shakespeare' and 'television', *ShakespeaRe-Told* elides through wholesale updating of language and situation the lack of fit between theatrical and televisual media so apparent, in different ways, in the BBC–Time/Life series or the broadcasts from Shakespeare's Globe, in effect producing these works as drama made for, not translated to, television. This section shifts from a focus on the interplay between language and work production to consider how strategies of visual narration peculiar to the televisual medium might further contribute to an effect of work recognition.

ShakespeaRe-Told draws for the most part on a familiar range of filming techniques that through repeated use have become naturalized as television's supposedly transparent window onto a fictional world. Scenes are usually filmed from possible, but not actual, human perspectives, the shot-reverse-shot sequence is commonly used to listen in on a conversation between two characters, and editing practices create what seems an 'invisible' cut from one frame to another by showing first a character's glance and then the object of the glance, the sequence of shots seeming 'naturally' to follow the look. These sorts of shooting and editing practices construct what Tony Wilson calls television's 'regime of vision', a highly conventionalized, and yet precisely because of that believably realist, visual narration.[23]

Registering such filming techniques – when they are working most effectively, subliminally – as everyday and unexceptional allows one to accept the viewing experience as uncontrived.

However, and fittingly for a series that flirts with issues of production and adaptation, *ShakespeaRe-Told* also marks the extent to which assumptions about 'everyday' television are themselves being reconceived. Low lighting, tracking shots, extreme close ups, camera positions strikingly above or below eye height, digitally enhanced images, and point of view shots – devices which at one time seemed more cinematic than televisual – create idiosyncratic effects that overtly require decoding and interpretation. One is sometimes aware, in other words, not just of the story unfolding, but of how it is being told visually, the aesthetics of the programme foregrounding as artfully constructed (and so as less unproblematically 'real') both the image and one's perspective on it. Such compositional complexity is consistent with what John T. Caldwell identified in 1995 as a shift towards 'televisuality'. Technological improvements such as new film stocks and more mobile cameras in the production industry, and a prevalence of bigger screens, sharper digital images, and surround sound systems in consumers' homes, have led to greater experimentation since the late 1980s in mainstream television. As television has increasingly invested in 'visual style' (to use Caldwell's phrase) in terms of its manipulation of image and sound, and become proportionately less dependent on wordy expository dialogue, traditional conceptions and expectations of the medium as being 'more like' radio or 'more like' film have been challenged.[24]

Viewers, according to Caldwell, are not only gaining greater sophistication in terms of their ability to decipher increasingly complex mises-en-scène, but have become fluent readers of presentational style. Television programmes can juxtapose competing generic styles reminiscent, for instance, of newscasts, soap opera, commercials, or documentary, they can borrow visual effects suggestive of film, and they can even cultivate a deliberately 'retro' look from earlier generations of television programming without being in danger of alienating their projected audiences. This is not to imply that every programme will draw on such 'semiotic abundance', or that viewers necessarily seek or accept this kind of display as typical of the medium, but simply to highlight the availability of an emergent, peculiarly televisual, aesthetic.[25] The at times self-conscious camerawork and editing of a series such as *ShakespeaRe-Told* implicitly construct the viewer as a media-literate 'reader', one who is engaged with the BBC's handling of the conventions of mainstream television as another property of the work in this particular production instance.

In *Macbeth*, for example, the attack on Billie (Banquo) is filmed in a wooded park, Billie and his son 'Freddie' biking quickly along the trails. A juddery hand-held camera takes either Freddie's view on his father ahead in the distance or assumes an undetermined but clearly motivated perspective, racing at the cyclists and (impossibly) cutting without collision across their paths into the bushes. This artful and fragmented filming style raises as an unanswered question the identity of the third presence in the park, implying solely through camerawork the presence of supernatural forces. *Much Ado*, however, is perhaps the film which integrates this self-conscious visual play most fully into its methods of story-telling: *Much Ado* is not only on television, but *about* television and its production in, and for, an increasingly mediatized culture. The programme's self-reflexive attitude is captured in the many scenes set in an imagined Wessex television studio. The action of the drama takes the viewer behind the camera, as it were, to watch the roles played by producer, director, editors, make-up artists, and newscasters in the production and broadcast of local regional news. Cameras and teleprompters, frequently featured in the television frame, become ordinary parts of the programme's mise-en-scène, technical jargon used in the production gallery while the show is live on air cues opening credits, commercial breaks, and movement between cameras, and one watches the constant interaction between gallery and studio floor that happens by means of headset, earphone, and two-way intercom. Occasionally human error intrudes to disrupt the show's smooth broadcast: Don, the newscast's first director, is late on his cues, there is momentary confusion about which camera the meteorological reporter, Hero, is supposed to address, the live broadcast suddenly cuts to an embarrassed Benedick caught checking for food between his teeth.

The overall effect of these meta-televisual scenes is complicated. In part they reinforce as an important aspect of the aesthetics of broadcast television the effect of 'liveness', the sense that this action is transmitted (as though) live directly into one's living room.[26] At the same time, however, a constant engagement with the production of television images disturbs an illusion of camera transparency, serving instead as a constant reminder that this 'liveness' effect is itself fabricated. The exchange of wit on set between Beatrice and Benedick as they prepare for their first co-hosted show is watched through a studio camera that happens to zoom in and out on their exchange, a device used again after Benedick has fallen in love, the repetition visibly marking the transition in their relationship. At other times one watches nested images – a television visible in the frame relaying the action on set (either on or off air) – or else the screen image as a whole is deliberately degraded, in effect transforming one's television at home into a studio monitor. This insistent use of technology exposes, rather than reinforces, the reality effect typically associated with television, with the camera lens, the screened image, and the embedded monitors working in different ways to impose a distance from the action, making of the passive viewer a self-aware watcher.

This attention to the production of images trains viewers in a knowledge of their situated vantage point, encouraging one to be suspicious of even seemingly unmediated narration. The ability of the camera to mislead or even to trick the unwary viewer into making false assumptions that must be subsequently corrected is flaunted in the show's opening moments as one watches characters who will eventually be identified as Beatrice and Benedick separately getting ready to leave their respective flats. Watching the cuts between the two spaces, the viewer infers they are preparing for a date with each other, a reading that is finally contradicted only when Benedick directs his taxi to the airport. As Benedick sends a text on his mobile phone, the storyline darkens: the upbeat, slightly tongue-in-cheek soundtrack (Tom Jones's 'Help Yourself') dies away, and Beatrice, already seated at an expensive restaurant, picks up the text message. One's revised understanding of this mostly dialogue-free sequence is confirmed when a waiter appears at the table with a bottle of champagne to tell her that 'The gentleman said to say, "No hard feelings"'. The camera quickly cuts to a storyboard that reads 'Three years later', and from there to Beatrice in the news studio, startled out of her reverie by an insistent voice calling her name on the intercom. Beatrice's gesture as she is brought back to the present-day world of the studio recontextualizes this moment of rejection as her (impossibly omniscient) *memory* of it, throwing into question the assumption that one watched the action unfold, as it were, 'live'. This pre-show sequence explains the animosity between Beatrice and Benedick, and provides for Beatrice, in particular, strong character motivation; beyond this, the way it wrong-foots viewers' expectations and so draws attention to one's lack of direct access to events raises as an interpretative issue the formal story-telling conventions of television.

Viewers are caught out again while watching a private conversation between Beatrice and Leonard (Hero's father and the show's producer) that takes place after hours on the newsroom set. After he persuades a reluctant Beatrice to work again with Benedick, Leonard reveals that he has also decided to fire the director, confiding to Beatrice (and so to the viewer) that Don is alcoholic, incompetent, and not well liked by his co-workers. The intimacy of their exchange coincides with the intimacy of the televisual medium to situate the viewer within the scene as an unacknowledged and privileged auditor to a confidential exchange. Suddenly, however, one's viewing position shifts to the darkened gallery overlooking the set where the scene one had been watching from the studio floor continues, now captured on a small monitor. Only when Don leans into the television frame to ask Leonard through a microphone if he would like to speak with him does one realize that this character, like us, has been silently listening in on their dialogue. His unexpected interjection exposes the viewer no less than Leonard and abruptly reconstructs as eavesdropping what had previously seemed a conventionalized, and so unproblematic, spectatorial presence.

The camera's visual preoccupation with what and how one sees further triggers an awareness of how often one watches and is watched in the course of everyday life. Characters are constantly being televised, whether as part of the mass circulation of news and entertainment, or just as a result of the commonplace surveillance of public spaces by means of closed circuit television (CCTV). *Much Ado*, of course, is a play alert to encounters either accidentally overheard or else purposely staged for the benefit of a hidden listener/auditor. Borachio overhears the plan for Don Pedro to woo Hero on Claudio's behalf, and is in turn overhead by the Watch explaining how Claudio was gulled to believe as true the counterfeit spectacle of Hero courted by a lover at her bedroom window; Benedick and Beatrice, like Claudio, but to less potentially tragic ends, are separately tricked when they are framed as supposedly unseen witnesses to false and deliberately planted information. Hearing is figured as eavesdropping; watching as spying – with both activities demanding careful interpretation in order to discern false performance from true intelligence.[27] *ShakespeaRe-Told* takes this 'noting' motif and extends it to the now familiar conditions of a mediatized information culture dominated by mobile phones, text messaging, and television cameras.

This is particularly evident in the way Benedick is tricked into believing Beatrice loves him through the simple device of making him believe that audio technology affords him a neutrally positioned peripheral stance on a scene taking place in the gallery. A conversation involving Leonard, Hero, Claude, and 'Peter' (Don Pedro), the director who returned with Benedick to work on the show after Don's demotion, first comes to his attention when it is piped, seemingly in error, into his dressing-room; when the sound suddenly cuts out, he sneaks into the studio to continue listening furtively through a headset. By such means, the eavesdropping Benedick is himself transformed into a spectacle surreptitiously watched from above by the conspirators. Much like those viewers previously 'caught' watching Leonard and Beatrice, Benedick wrongly assumes that his adoption of a fly-on-the-wall stance guarantees him a privileged and unproblematically mediated perspective on the scene being relayed to him through audio. The comedy, both for the characters-turned-actors in the gallery and the viewer at home, rests in their perception of a larger contextual frame and of Benedick's manipulated and unwitting position within it.

This training in the potential duplicity of media technology – a suspicion of television, and of telecommunications more generally – is reinforced by the way Claude is persuaded of Hero's infidelity. Working on his jealous and violent temperament the night before his wedding, Don 'confesses' to Claude in the hotel library that he and Hero are lovers, producing as confirmation of their affair signed photographs and text messages sent from her mobile phone. The scene, played as a two-hander in which one character, Iago-like, plants doubts in another's mind which lead him to mistrust the woman he loves, causes this plot line to shade into the much later *Othello* in terms of its treatment of marriage, male friendship, and betrayed faith. These resonances between the plays are further heightened when Don, without recourse to accessories, gives Claude the 'ocular' proof he demands. Watching Hero from his hidden vantage point out of earshot down the hall talk to Don at the door of her room, then using his mobile phone to hear Hero, now inside her room, deny Don's presence with the words he cannot see him suggest to her, Claude misinterprets this fragmented evidence, believing he sees and hears what Don directs him to see and hear.

Don's deceptions are only unravelled after the wedding, when the security guard, 'Mr Berry' (Dogberry), and his assistant, 'Vincent' (Verges), piece together for Benedick the evidence gleaned from what had previously seemed their comically vigilant security checks. Mr Berry saw Don steal the photographs during the fancy dress party, and Don was caught on CCTV taking Hero's phone from her bag at the office; at the end of the library scene, the camera cuts to a vantage point in the hall where one becomes suddenly aware of Vincent watching unseen, with us, the conversation between Don and Claude. Benedick's 'challenge' back at the hotel after Claude humiliates Hero at the altar consists in showing him how he has been tricked, making explicit precisely the same lessons in uncertain perspective and biased information transmission the viewer has been implicitly trained by the camera to attend to over the course of the programme. What follows is a public confrontation in which Hero demands a reason for Don's malice, a motive for his actions. This scene, without an equivalent in the work familiar to spectators and readers, blurs once again the boundaries separating *Much Ado* from *Othello* as the bewildered victims of slander try to understand not 'what' but 'why'. Unlike Don John, who runs away, or Iago, whose refusal to speak makes him seem a cipher of evil, this Don cites as his inspiration unrequited love.

The directness of this face-to-face exchange and its ability finally to expose Don's deceit and obsession might seem to confirm a profound suspicion of telecommunication, especially the way confusions can proliferate as one consequence of an increasingly mediatized and mediated world.[28] But the ease with which Claude(/io) is persuaded of Hero's dishonesty is not peculiar to *ShakespeaRe-Told*. On the contrary, a recurrent motif of this work in its various instances is the manipulation of evidence enabled by a jealous mistrust of female sexuality; all that changes in this instance of production are the resources available to the slanderer. Television cameras and mobile phones are thus not in themselves the problem – indeed, if one considers Mr Berry's timely intervention, they could just as easily be understood as contributing to the solution. However, the ability accurately to interpret the evidence presented to one's eyes is shown to depend on an increasingly sophisticated knowledge of the potential of electronic media and the conventions within which they operate.

This programme meta-televisually foregrounds the realization that personal communications devices and technologies of remote observation and surveillance (either selectively mediated by a camera operator or, as in the case of CCTV, impassively and endlessly recording information) have become a condition of modern existence, altering assumptions of what constitutes the 'normal' operation of perception in twenty-first century Britain. This in turn has consequences for one's assumptions about, and so knowledge of, Shakespeare's works, especially a work such as *Much Ado* that is preoccupied above all with the manipulation of perception. The work cannot remain exactly what it was four hundred years ago, or even twenty years ago, in part because the audiences who must discursively apprehend it by means of its instances have been conditioned to 'see' differently. For this reason, it is not self-evidently the case that *ShakespeaRe-Told* 'translates' the works to television (a choice of words that presupposes an innately adaptive and alien medium). On the contrary, the series integrates into its formal strategies of story-telling modern communication technologies that – to the extent one has come to take them for granted as ordinary parts of daily existence – *already* inform in fundamental ways one's perception of the legitimate boundaries of Shakespeare's works.

(Re)Telling *Dream,* building digital Britain

Where *Much Ado* plays with and critiques perception, particularly in relation to the way evidence can be mediated and potentially compromised by modern communications technologies, the final programme in the series, *A Midsummer Night's Dream*, addresses the manipulation of sight itself. *Dream* exhibits many of the same formal and thematic characteristics of the earlier films, particularly in terms of its narrative interventions, stylized camerawork, and preoccupation with marriage and female agency. Theseus and Egeus are conflated in the figure of Theo Moon, Hermia's irascible father, with the Duke's marriage to Hippolyta reconceived in the film's closing scenes as a renewal of vows between Theo and 'Polly', his wife of twenty-four years. Theo and his guests think they are at the holiday park to celebrate the engagement of Hermia to James Demetrius, but Puck informs the viewer that they have been brought there by the fairies in order to give supernatural forces the opportunity to help Theo and Polly resolve an impending separation. Thus the crisis at the outset of the programme from a fairy perspective involves not unmarried, but married, lovers, the conflict between Oberon and Titania doubling the escalating tensions between Theo and Polly.

A metaphorical connection between sight and (sometimes false) understanding is made readily legible through stylized camerawork signalling the transformative effect of the 'love juice' dropped into the eyes of Lysander, Demetrius, and Titania. Extreme close-up shots of a sleeper's eye held open and a drop of liquid falling in slow motion through the air are followed by a low rumbling sound and a high-contrast, rapidly accelerated pastiche of associatively linked faces and situations. Such effects suggest the television viewer is given privileged access to dreams, specifically to the sleeper's mind's eye at the moment his or her mental visions are redirected by the power of the drug. The suggestion that the viewer's own sense of sight is no less vulnerable to manipulation is introduced in the opening scene. The programme begins in an empty forest clearing: one hears the sound of a man and a woman arguing but can see nothing other than little sunbeams flitting through the air. The shot then cuts to Puck sitting up in the trees who, in a direct address to camera, offers to better our eyesight through the application of an eyewash. As with the drugged lovers later, one watches the drop fall in slow motion, the picture swims as the liquid hits the camera lens with a low rumble, one glimpses flashes of what can be identified on a second viewing as moments in the film yet to ensue, and then, as the camera turns back to the forest ground, one suddenly sees what had previously been imperceptible: Oberon and Titania standing in the clearing, playing out again the scene of their argument. As Puck notes, 'Things aren't always what they appear to be'. This idea that there exist alternative realities if only one could see them thus extends beyond the fictional world of the film to include the viewers watching the programme. Within the narrative space of *Dream*, love juice functions to distort visual and mental sight; when considered from the point of view of the television audience, Puck's eyewash provides viewers with a fuller and more accurate perspective on the unfolding action.

The difference between the visually innovative *Much Ado* and *Dream* in terms of their treatment of perception and sight rests in the disparity between electronic devices such as newsroom cameras and mobile phones, and fairy magic. This distinction, however, is ultimately not as important as it might at first seem since the effect of a self-consciously privileged access to a supernatural world can only be created in *Dream* by means of the technological resources of television, thus generating for the viewer, as with *Much Ado*, an acute attention to medium. When the series was first broadcast in Britain, this effect was further reinforced by a continuity announcement at the end of each of the four shows which instructed viewers to 'press red now' to go interactive with the programme they had just watched.[29] For those with analogue television, the invitation to press a non-existent red button on their remote controls seemed to summon up the promise of another world as inaccessible to their eyes as the fairy world of *Dream* is to the eyes of the young lovers. But for those others – the Bottoms of Britain? – who found themselves in November 2005 in a position to abandon a technologically imposed and culturally learned relationship of passive consumption to enter an interactive 'red button' environment, *ShakespeaRe-Told* provided an encounter with a largely novel and still evolving conception of television as transformed and redefined through digital transmission. In this section I will investigate the way *ShakespeaRe-Told* invests in contradictory discourses of authoritative production depending on whether one considers the programmes, or the programmes in relation to their interactive supplements. This uneasy tension is a feature of the series' political and ideological implication in issues relating especially to digital literacy and the BBC's unique mandate among British broadcasters as a 'trusted guide' to change.

The interactive component received no mention in reviews of the series, which were on the whole mixed, many reviewers clearly bemused by these so-called interpretations. Robert McCrum, for example, unable to locate in the changed storylines and modernized language the 'literary inheritance we call "William Shakespeare"', recommends sending the BBC drama department 'back to the Arden and the Oxford texts to discover that you don't need to "reinterpret" Shakespeare', claiming the season 'is inventive, often wildly so, brave, and occasionally interesting. It is also a tragic failure and a dreadful waste of money.'[30] Thomas Sutcliffe acknowledges midway through the month-long season that the series should be commended for offering modern writers a commission for a one-off television play and the opportunity to stretch beyond the limits typical of more conventional television programming. 'On the other hand,' he continues, citing the previous night's airing of *Taming* as a good case in point, 'we are entitled to consider these plays as if they were just one-offs, and when you do that, it can be quite hard to credit that anyone would broadcast something so silly and implausible if Shakespeare weren't standing surety for the whole affair.'[31]

Sutcliffe's assumption is that the BBC was persuaded to undertake the series not because it necessarily makes for outstanding television drama, but because the BBC (or its anticipated audience) considers Shakespeare's plays worth broadcasting in any format. The political and educational agendas underpinning this series, however, are perhaps more complicated than Sutcliffe's analysis suggests. The idea for the *Canterbury Tales* series, the model for *ShakespeaRe-Told*, grew out of a desire back in 2001 for 'a piece that reflected life in the new century'. The stories were pitched as 'enduring' tales that 'embody the timeless themes of love, lust, greed, power, anger and bigotry – human emotions that are as relevant today as they were six hundred years ago'.[32] Similarly universalizing assertions about Shakespeare's drama have long been commonplace, so it seems not entirely surprising that the BBC might follow up its success with a sequel based on a few of the plays. The format, however, is not exactly reproduced. Specifically, the *Canterbury Tales* series lacked the interactive supplement accessed through one's television immediately following the broadcast of *ShakespeaRe-Told* by means of 'red button' technology. Pressing the red button took one to the actor David Oyelowo, who, pictured outside of a weathered stage door, introduces the viewer to the interactive format. A short clip is then shown of actors dressed in black and playing in a white box who perform a scene or speech from the work just broadcast. In each case the actors work from an unmodernized script. When the clip ends, Oyelowo invites each viewer to use his or her remote control to choose among four options (see Figure 3). The selections include interviews with actors, writers, and directors on the making of the series ('Performers'), and listening to Oyelowo offer a voiced-over commentary on the structure of the language and choice of vocabulary while watching the actors repeat their performance ('Glossary'). Another set of interviews with British scholars and media figures such as Sir Peter Hall, Kathleen McLuskie, and Michael Wood provides biographical details about the author and information about the earliest socio-historical conditions of theatrical production ('Context'), while the fourth option offers a thematic approach to the works, relating them to modern points of reference as varied as music festivals and drug culture, *EastEnders*, and protests against the war in Iraq ('Theme'). Viewer interaction is limited to arranging and choosing among these four pre-filmed, programme-specific clips, a level of involvement presented by Oyelowo as an opportunity to 'follow your own path to create your own story'.

Digital interactivity thus links education, Shakespeare, and the BBC in what has become a familiar nexus of authority, and one notes without surprise that the New Shakespeare Season was timed to coincide with the release of the BBC–Time/Life Complete Works as an anniversary box-set DVD collection. It seems doubtful, however, that *ShakespeaRe-Told* will enjoy the same shelf-life as the earlier series, which, despite widespread

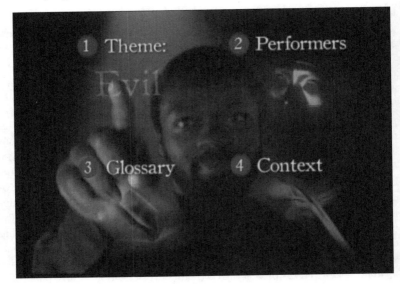

Figure 3 Interactive menu, *ShakespeaRe-Told*, British Broadcasting Corporation. *Source*: http://www.bbc.co.uk/drama/shakespeare/interactive.shtml; site accessed 12 August 2008.

reservations about the critical merits of many of its productions, has served as a pedagogical tool in classrooms around the world for the better part of three decades. The decision, in particular, to rescript the language undoubtedly compromises the usefulness of the programmes as a certain type of illustrative performance resource for teachers of English literature. Moreover, topical jokes such as Snug's tentative guess that Bottom with his ass's head is trying to impersonate the footballer Ruud van Nistelrooy, or Malcolm's blundering reference to Gordon Ramsay ('we don't use that name in this kitchen,' Billie tells him, 'it's bad luck – we just call him the Scottish chef'), will not only inevitably and quickly date but are so culturally specific as to have currency only with an audience keenly attuned to trends in British popular culture.

However *ShakespeaRe-Told*, unlike the earlier series, is not dependent on selling itself as providing either enduring or universal readings of Shakespeare's works.[33] Its educational impact rests instead in an irreproducible broadcast moment when viewers were invited to press the red button, and what was 'performed' in homes across Britain was television itself, as reinvented through digital technology. When one looks beyond the Shakespeare content to examine the medium of performance, the purpose of commissioning, filming, and broadcasting modern versions of the works comes better into focus. To return to Sutcliffe's observation, Shakespeare does indeed stand 'surety' for the series, but not quite in the manner he suggests; rather than serving as a specious guarantor of quality, Shakespeare's works provide a familiar entertainment vehicle for a certain form of mass education in new technologies. The BBC is reaching out by means of an already tested narrative formula to a self-selecting audience base whose interest in Shakespeare might well predispose them to take advantage of, or *wish* to take advantage of, the opportunity to go interactive. Although the interactive component of the programme was made simultaneously available on the BBC-hosted *ShakespeaRe-Told* website, the point, at least at the moment of broadcast, was not to redirect viewers from television to the internet but to get them to use their television in an unaccustomed way, gaining a greater comprehension of what digital offers and how to use it, and so prompting among analogue and digital viewers alike a reconception of the medium of television.

The motivation for this initiative reflects the complex relationship to market forces and centralized government that has characterized the BBC since its inception in its current form in 1927. While it is in the Corporation's own commercial interests to train up users in new technologies, the government equally demands of the BBC this critical educational role, an expectation enshrined in the White Paper that was prepared throughout 2005 and released in the spring of 2006, which sets for the BBC in its next charter period the responsibility of 'Building Digital Britain'. In the government's eyes, technological developments are proceeding 'at an unprecedented, often bewildering, rate', and the BBC, perceived by the public as 'a "trusted guide" to new technology and the new experiences that come with it', is ideally positioned to draw British viewers into this new world.[34] The branding of the series as 'BBC' and 'Shakespeare' discussed above thus speaks to the BBC's unique mandate among broadcasters to provide the 'practical help and advice' to make possible a nationwide switch to digital by 2012.[35]

The decision to transmit the series on BBC1, a channel that can be received by both analogue and digital televisions, is therefore a significant broadcasting choice. Instead of catering to an audience that has already converted to digital with a distinctive genre of 'Shakespeare' programming – as with the decision to broadcast on a digital channel (BBC4) Peter Brook's *Hamlet* and live productions of *Richard II* and *Measure for Measure* from Shakespeare's Globe – the BBC made the changing shape of television felt by every viewer who tuned into *ShakespeaRe-Told*. Analogue viewers, denied access to the interactive site, were enticed to make the switch to digital, while recently converted digital viewers were introduced to the

benefits and capabilities of digital technology and to a greater understanding of how to use it. The educational impact of *ShakespeaRe-Told* is
precisely *not* tied to series longevity, and not just because this particular
technology will probably be obsolete within five years. The potential of
the series as a learning tool for new technologies was almost entirely fulfilled at the moment of transmission because of the irreproducible nature
of the red button experience: there is no way to access the interactive
environment when watching the films by means of recorded playback
devices. Even as broadcast four months later on BBC Canada, the programmes, stripped of their interactive technology, assumed a very different –
more backward-looking – cultural and educational significance.[36] As audiences become more sophisticated digital users, their relationship to the
red button, an object which functions at the moment as a metonym of
television as a transforming and so newly unfamiliar medium, will itself
inevitably alter. *ShakespeaRe-Told*, a broadcast event directed at a local
audience at a particular moment in the continuing evolution of British
communications technology, thus intervenes simultaneously in popular
conceptions of the works of Shakespeare and the media by which they are
currently told.

With the conclusion of the British broadcasts at the end of November,
the educational potential of *ShakespeaRe-Told* shifted from television to the
internet, with ancillary material facilitating a 'do it yourself' attitude to
production in terms both of Shakespearean interpretation and film. The
adjustment of priorities in the two years between 2003 and 2005 can be
gauged through a comparison of the BBC-hosted websites for the *Canterbury Tales* and *ShakespeaRe-Told* projects. The Chaucer site, illustrated with
stills from the six programmes, has clickables leading to a photo gallery,
video clips, a prize quiz, a downloadable screensaver, supporting material
about the programmes in the forms of a 'Producer's Intro' and 'Episode
Guides', and educational information about how to write for television
('Get Writing'). The *ShakespeaRe-Told* site supplements these pages with an
online murder mystery game ('The Seven Noble Kinsmen'), an invitation
to 'Explore Shakespeare Interactive' which streams to one's computer via
broadband the material that was first made accessible through digital television,
and '60 Second Shakespeare'. This last option, aimed explicitly at schools,
opens into nested information pages and video tutorials designed to communicate and inspire, training students in the digital media skills they require
to create their own one-minute film or audio interpretation of Shakespeare
in performance. Schools were invited to submit their productions to the
BBC through the six months to May 2006 for posting on the *ShakespeaRe-Told*
site and review by their peers. By constructing them as producers, the
BBC makes of students knowledgeable consumers of digital media.

The BBC thus foregrounds in a variety of ways an awareness of television as a medium itself undergoing major changes. Television no longer looks or performs entirely according to conventional expectations, and the shift for viewers from an attitude of mass passive consumption to one of personalized interactivity enabled by digital technology radically blurs the boundaries separating television from, say, the internet or even computer games. Functionality is expanding to the point where existing conceptions of television no longer seem adequate or appropriate.[37] This is a lesson that the BBC embeds in *ShakespeaRe-Told* precisely by making the medium visible *as* medium through devices such as stylized camerawork and language, situated perspectives, and the development of interactive environments.

Given what might be perceived by some viewers as unwelcome change to a medium long taken for granted, it is then perhaps no surprise that the BBC returns to the works of Shakespeare, grounding technological innovation in stories likely to register with a British audience as both comfortably familiar and, especially as televised by the BBC, quintessentially British. The potential for viewer alienation was likewise assuaged by building into the series allusions to popular British television culture. To return briefly to *Dream*, Bill Paterson and Imelda Staunton, much-loved stalwarts of British television, are cast in the roles of Theo and Polly, while in Titania's bower the offer made to Johnny Vegas (Bottom) of a familiar pyramid of wrapped chocolates provides a camp visual citation of the long-running Ferrero Rocher television advertisements ('You are spoiling us, monsieur'). Vegas himself, a household name in British television comedy, famously starred three years earlier with a knitted monkey – in what seems an apt intertextual link – in advertisements launching the erstwhile ITV Digital channel. These sorts of common points of reference (among them the works of Shakespeare) help to ease the transition from analogue to digital transmission, encouraging viewers to continue to recognize in this transformed medium, television.

The BBC promises its viewers 'television Shakespeare', but *ShakespeaRe-Told* makes apparent how both of those terms – along with viewer expectations of them – have undergone revision in the twenty years since the completion of the BBC–Time/Life Complete Works broadcasts. The differences between the two series are more deep-seated than the matter of modernized language and settings, choices McCrum attacks as a failure to safeguard Britain's 'literary inheritance'. Television is not what it was. As a broadcast event *ShakespeaRe-Told* spoke to a moment when innovations in technology made expectations of television briefly visible as conventionalized, rather than as innate to the medium, before a new model of television–viewer interaction could itself be learned and in turn taken for granted. Viewer familiarity with Shakespeare was used to introduce 'television' as an altered discursive structure, so driving up, in the words of the 2006 White Paper, 'media literacy amongst all social and age groups'.[38] But alterations to the means of production cannot be introduced without implications for the work; such innovation sets in motion a feedback loop which influences conceptions of Shakespeare's work and so in turn assumptions about its legitimate reproduction.

Whether *ShakespeaRe-Told* should be categorized as 'interpretation' or 'adaptation' is a question that cannot finally be resolved since the authority of the work, itself under constant negotiation, is conferred on, rather than found in, the production instance. To put this another way, to seek to determine in any absolute sense the series' status as either interpretation or adaptation is to ask the wrong question of production since there is no fixed original the essence of which can be repeated or captured through performance. The point is rather to look *beyond* the instance at hand to the surrounding contextual circumstances to determine how, at this moment and for a particular community of users, the work is being defined (and redefined) as a conceptual tool. On this basis one can then determine whether a particular instance of production is likely to count – and for whom – as a 'genuine' repetition of the work.

ShakespeaRe-Told offers a fascinating example of this authorizing process in action since the series constructs for different communities of users contradictory notions of the work, the divide, tellingly, falling along the line that separates analogue from digital viewers. On the cover of Bowker's script of *A Midsummer Night's Dream*, pictured on the website as one of two quiz prizes, one can read that it is subtitled 'An Adaptation'. However, with just one notable exception that I will return to consider below, the only other place this term appears either on the website or in advertising and other BBC-supported material is behind a clickable offering a brief description of historical stage traditions found deep within the 'Seven Noble Kinsmen' computer game. The terms preferred by the BBC are 'updating' or 'interpretation', both of which foreground continuities with, over departures from, the works. There is no suggestion that these films are not adaptations, but one notes that the BBC itself seems satisfied to perpetuate fuzzy boundaries. These programmes based on television scripts that carry the same titles as plays written by Shakespeare are – as the graphically hybrid title of the series implies – simultaneously Shakespeare 'Told' and Shakespeare '*Re*-Told'. This slippage around a (possible) prefix speaks both to the complexities of 'Shakespeare' as origin and a reluctance to declare whether these are genuine or adapted instances of the works, the producers leaving it finally to the consumers to recognize in the programmes both/either television and/or Shakespeare.

These boundaries shift, however, as soon as one goes 'interactive' to explore the material broadcast as an exclusively digital supplement to the series. It is as though *ShakespeaRe-Told* itself exists in two versions. The first version, directed at users without digital capability, strongly implies that these broadcasts, like any instance of production, are 'interpretations'. The other version of the series – the one that comes with an interactive supplement – freely situates the four broadcasts as 'adaptations' of original works. The interactive environments share a common introductory sequence in which Oyelowo, about to enter a theatre by its stage door, pauses to invite the viewer to join him in what amounts to a special 'behind-the-scenes' tour of Shakespeare's works:

> You are about to embark on a fascinating interactive journey that will take you right to the heart of Shakespeare's plays, and I will be your guide along the way. You've just seen the BBC's modern adaptation of [*fill in title*]. Now we're going to use modern technology to explore a scene from this play in its original language. For each week that BBC1 brings you a contemporary reworking of one of Shakespeare's stories we will allow you to explore that particular play in greater depth. We're going to show you a defining moment from the play. We've staged the scene in a simple theatrical space to allow you to concentrate on Shakespeare's words, as the drama of Shakespeare's stories was created by words alone. With the scene as your starting point you'll have the chance to discover more about Shakespeare's players, history, themes, and language. You'll be the one to follow your own path to create your own story. Come with me and let's see if we can find a new way to interact with Shakespeare.[39]

These prefatory remarks present what follows as a return to an authorial original. To take up Oyelowo's invitation is to make the 'journey' from the margins of the work 'right to the heart of Shakespeare's plays'. The viewer's remote starting point (figuratively outside of the stage door which comes to stand as the material sign of privileged access) is defined by the programme one has just watched on television – now no longer figured as an interpretation but as a 'contemporary reworking' and 'modern adaptation'.

Although one is eventually asked to select among four options ('Performers', 'Glossary', 'Context', and 'Theme'), one can only reach those options by first passing through a staged episode that has been identified by the producers as 'defining'. The way these embedded performances are situated in relation to the full-length television productions is instrumental to a perception that one is now gaining privileged access to the real thing. Oyelowo introduces the excerpt shown to *Much Ado* viewers, for example, by explaining that the interactive site's performance of the Watch over-hearing Borachio bragging to Conrad follows 'the original play' in show-ing the deception of Claudio 'carried out with the aid of Don John's vile henchman Borachio'. Once past this scene, Oyelowo summarizes what viewers will encounter if they choose the 'Performers' option by explaining that: 'Our modern adaptation of *Much Ado About Nothing* is set in a world renowned for its shallowness and deceit – TV. To hear how and why this world was picked, select our second option and listen to the insight of our writer, David Nicholls, talk about bringing the play to the small screen.' The implicit suggestion is that, unlike an adaptation for television set in a newsroom, the BBC's unelaborated and unmodernized staging of Act 3.3 for the interactive environment offers a suitable launching-off point for an in-depth exploration of the 'drama of Shakespeare's stories', created in his own time 'by words alone'. This returns the viewer to the belief, explored earlier in relation to objections to some modern productions set out by Berry, Poliakoff, and Nunn, that Shakespeare's works survive in the words. These short excerpts – the others include Katherine's final-scene mono-logue (delivered by a male actor), Macbeth's dagger soliloquy, and Titania awakening to Bottom's song – are presented as the 'unadapted' instances of production by means of which one gains greater insight into Shakespeare's works, a process which in turn allows one to formulate an informed assessment of the 'adaptations' one has already watched on television.

The sleight of hand achieved by this interplay between original broad-cast and red-button supplement is to persuade the viewer that the perfor-mances encountered in the interactive environment are 'neutral' instances of the works. And of course they are not. To continue for the moment with the *Much Ado* example, even this 'simple theatrical space' assumes a modern period setting when the actors playing Borachio and Conrad, looking somewhat like film mobsters, enter the white box set wearing black suits, ties, and hats, with Borachio sporting a heavy gold necklace; the Watch is likewise dressed in a black shirt and trousers, but his lower status is signalled through the lack of a tie, jacket, and hat, and his regional dif-ference is marked with a Welsh accent. Playing the Watch not as a group but as a single actor perched above the other two on top of an up-ended white block is a good example of theatrical economy, but it has important interpretative consequences: the Watch's end-of-scene dialogue is trans-formed into a short monologue, the pronouns used by this character are altered from 'we' to 'I', and his interjections, scattered throughout Bor-achio's tale, are delivered as asides to the audience. Curiously, this latter production choice (presumably introduced because there is nobody onstage to whom this character might direct his lines) is subsequently pre-sented as an essential part of the work. Viewers who select the 'Glossary' option learn from Oyelowo that 'Shakespeare puts the audience in a privileged position – possessors of knowledge of which the characters in the play remain unaware – and he reinforces the importance of this position by having the watchmen *talk directly to the audience* in asides' (my emphasis). A few other lines and words are likewise reassigned or in some cases cut, and this stand-alone scene is given a firm sense of comic closure when Borachio's and Conrad's willingness to obey is punctuated by the Watch collapsing in surprise in a faint.

This example in fact nicely demonstrates the extent to which 'the drama of Shakespeare's stories' is *never* created in performance 'by words alone'. It also points up the complexity of the process by which one recognizes the work in production once interpretation is admitted as a component part of what constitutes a 'genuine' instance. Without the benefit of fixed criteria (such as Goodman, for example, devises), an assessment of the in/authentic repetition can only rely on judgement and context. One is perhaps disposed to regard this staging of a scene from *Much Ado* as a genuine repetition of the work, despite its modernizations, interpretations, and language adjustments, precisely to the extent that one is directed to find and evaluate interpretative distance between two production instances, one categorized as staged performance, the other as televisual adaptation. My point here is not to argue that textual revisions somehow invalidate production, but to foreground the way this production – inset within and contextualized by an interactive educational site, which is in turn inset within and contextualized by the *ShakespeaRe-Told* series – generates, rather than discovers, an authentic Shakespearean work to which it then claims fidelity.

What seems most surprising, even paradoxical, about the BBC's treatment of the scenes embedded in the interactive site is precisely that they are 'staged' in a 'simple theatrical space'. Another part of what evidently makes these performances recognizable as authentic instances of the works is the way they are coded as specifically *theatrical* instances of production. This effect extends well beyond Oyelowo's verbal introduction to the interactive environment: the viewer is invited to walk through a stage door rather than into a television studio, the white box set and black costuming reproduces a familiar and peculiarly theatrical minimalist aesthetic, the sound of the light breaker being thrown at the beginning and end of each of the sequences creates the effect of live, instead of filmed, performance. Even the direction to camera of the Watch's asides in a stage whisper is a device borrowed from theatre that draws the television audience into the enactment by seeming to break the fictional illusion. The implicit suggestion is that genuine as opposed to adapted production of Shakespeare's works is theatrical rather than televisual – even when transmitted on digital television. Technology is ostensibly set aside as a hindrance rather than an aid to production, with performance seeming more closely to approach the work the more completely it is stripped bare to reveal in a 'pure' form Shakespeare's words. In effect the BBC marks these productions as authentic by seeming to embrace the 'two planks and a passion' school of thought mentioned at the beginning of this chapter.

Particularly interesting then is to mark the way advanced communications technology contributes to this illusion of 'liveness'. In the enactment from *Dream*, for example, the aesthetic of the spare theatrical set and minimalist casting is maintained by means of computer graphics, animation bringing to life a vibrant fantasy world in which Bottom is transformed and Titania attended in her bower by an entourage of fairies. An ass's head which seems to move with Bottom is sketched as a black and white line drawing over the actor's head, and the same technique is used quickly and lightly to introduce and erase flora and fauna from the frame; the three fairies, by contrast, are represented as small animated splodges in primary colours that when summoned fly out of Titania's mouth to float in the air, attending on Bottom. Computer animation is thus superimposed on the BBC's 'simple theatrical space' in order to invent the fairy world as a dynamic space that is perceptibly distinct from the mortal world, and digital technology is folded into the 'theatrical' production with minimal disruption since it specifically functions to reinforce a sense of the fairies' otherness.

These embedded performances of scenes from the works are thus presented as though they were live theatre, but without the 'once-removed' effect of an actual live performance filmed for television broadcast. By such means, the viewer seems to gain privileged access not just to an interpretation but also to the real thing, Shakespeare's work itself. Crucially, the most important factor contributing to this effect of authenticity is not Oyelowo's commentary, nor even the carefully managed illusion of a neutral and theatrical staging, but the way the viewer is situated within this interactive environment as a producer – less a passive consumer than a participant integral to the decision-making activities on which production depends. Those who follow Oyelowo through the stage door implicitly agree to collaborate with him on a pioneering, technology-aided encounter with Shakespeare's words to 'see if we can find a new way to interact with Shakespeare'. The effect of choosing among the options thereafter is to generate the sense that one is actually making real-time decisions that shape real-time interactions with the works in production. Theatrical 'liveness' is reinvented as an effect of digital interactivity, the viewer's own 'performance' seeming to discover, while actually participating in the ongoing construction of, Shakespeare's work. As with the films from which this supplement takes meaning and purpose, the works of Shakespeare are generated in the space *between* production and reception. This realization of the work as an event, as a process of dynamic interplay between an instance of production and its user, is captured in the medium of digital television by an invitation to play and to learn, or, as the BBC puts it, to 'press the red button now'.

5 Textual origins

An unusual performance of Shakespeare took place in North American homes on 26 April 2005. As part of the '2005 Ultimate Tournament of Champions', a week-long contest of skill and knowledge televised on NBC's *Jeopardy!*, Alex Trebek asked three contestants – David Triani, a high school administrator from Moorestown, New Jersey, Chris Miller, a retail specialist from Louisville, Kentucky, and Ryan Holznagel, a writer originally from Forest Grove, Oregon – to name 'each Shakespeare play that will be performed from start to finish by the Reduced Shakespeare Company'. Miller's request near the end of the round, 'Shakespeare $400, please', cued an audio-visual clue in which three actors wearing vaguely period costumes and carrying toy swords and a wine goblet performed, in about eleven seconds, a play in which all the protagonists died. The full-text script and pre-filmed performance is stored on-line in the 'J! Archive':

> 'Boo-oo!'
> 'Bl-bl-bl-bl! Mad! Ow!'
> 'Poison!'
> 'Mother! Treachery!'
> 'Agh-hh-hh-hh!!'
> 'Ugh!'[1]

The correct answer, of course, phrased to accord with the gameshow's conventions of response, is 'What is *Hamlet?*'.

Jeopardy! rewards with cash the speed with which contestants are able to respond to clues on the board. Part cryptic crossword, part *Trivial Pursuit*, the show's format is typically characterized by abbreviation and wordplay. As performed by the Reduced Shakespeare Company, *Hamlet* is abridged to a web of interlocking verbal and visual citations. There are four words (mad, poison, mother, treachery), five characters (the Ghost, Hamlet, Laertes, Gertrude, Claudius), and a set of sound effects and theatrical gestures that suggests other-worldly behaviour ('Boo-oo!'), semblance of madness ('Bl-bl-bl-bl!'), stabbing ('Ow!'), consumption of wine at sword point ('Agh-hh-hh-hh!!'), and falling down dead ('Ugh!'). In order for this embedded citation to work as a successful *Jeopardy!* clue, a significant proportion of the television audience must be able 'correctly' to recognize in this performance *Hamlet*, and only *Hamlet*.

Probably few people would answer the question 'What is *Hamlet*?' in quite the same way as the Reduced Shakespeare Company. However, Holznagel's answer and the studio audience's ready laughter attest to this group's shared ability to recognize the work in this short passage of sound effects, dialogue, and stage business. Such recognition is in turn productive of the work in terms of reinforcing the dominance of these particular properties, characters, and events as defining. Parodic and farcical though condensed Shakespeare may seem, the conclusion one is forced to draw from the points scored by Holznagel for his correct response is that, at least in this context and for these spectators, '*This* is *Hamlet*'.

The Reduced Shakespeare Company, inspired by Tom Stoppard's *Fifteen Minute Hamlet*,[2] first gained attention touring a show that sets out to perform the entire canon of thirty-seven plays in under two hours. The comedy of *The Complete Works of William Shakespeare (abridged)* rests in the effect of wrenching Shakespeare's works from their usual high culture context to set them within a vaudeville performance. All the parts are played by just three actors, and their fast-paced, high-energy delivery style relies heavily on audience interaction and farcical slapstick. Tone of voice, histrionic posturing, and fluid shifts in and out of character create the effect in performance of invisible quotation marks around the Shakespearean language (the published play text uses actual quotation marks to create the effect of two registers, the words marked as 'Shakespearean' visually embedded as citation within a larger drama).[3] The actors also provide frequent, supposed impromptu commentary on their live performance, providing onstage the parodic annotative paratext that will help audiences interpret what they are watching as they watch it. Thus an explanation of Shakespeare's comic conventions as formulaic and self-plagiarizing prompts the company to perform all of the comedies simultaneously as a single conflated work; a free interpretation of *Titus Andronicus* as a cooking show is contextualized as concept theatre; and an actor's collapse during Hamlet's 'To be or not to be' soliloquy is excused through an analysis of the speech as emotionally taxing. The company's long-lived popularity thus at least partly rests in the way the actors editorialize Shakespeare's works and the details of their own theatrical production of those works, so making the joke available to non-specialists who have read or seen on stage relatively little of the canon.[4] In effect, they teach audiences what they need to know about the works in order to enjoy how this production sends up both the works and the conventions associated with their modern production.

Perhaps especially curious for live performance, the company plays to comic effect with the conventions of not only theatrical but also textual production. The show opens with Daniel Singer introducing Jess Borgeson – 'a member of the Company who is one of California's pre-eminent Shakespearean scholars' – who enters dressed after the manner of a stuffy professor (tweed jacket, spectacles) to deliver 'a brief preface' to the complete works.[5] Borgeson's preface, attacking the way popular culture has 'systematically compromised' an ability to comprehend Shakespeare's genius,[6] begins as a university lecture that slowly and ironically transforms into its performative near-relation, the evangelical television sermon. This introduction is followed by a biography of William Shakespeare delivered by Adam Long, the third member of the company, who nervously enters with cue cards as though making a school presentation. His account of Shakespeare's life opens with the year of his birth, continues with his marriage to Anne Hathaway and the apocryphal account of the bard as a young man caught poaching a deer, his arrival in London, and retirement to Stratford. In retirement, Long continues, 'he dictated to his secretary, Rudolf Hess, the work "Mein Kampf," in which he set forth his program for the restoration of Germany to a dominant position in Europe'. Shakespeare, of course, then went on to annex Austria and invade Poland, committing suicide at the end of the Second World War with his mistress, Eva Braun. Long's biography concludes with Shakespeare's burial in Holy Trinity.[7]

This extended introduction highlights the educational regimes through which Anglo-North American students are typically brought to a knowledge of Shakespeare's works, with the comedy depending on the audience being readily able to mark the company's ludic interventions in everyday performative events such as the university lecture and school presentation. What further distinguishes and complicates this critique of Shakespeare's cultural situation, however, is the way these actors, seeking to perform the complete works of William Shakespeare, in fact perform on stage *The Complete Works of William Shakespeare*. Opening with a scholarly preface and continuing with a biography, the Reduced Shakespeare Company is not just playing the works but the one-volume *book* in which those works are now commonly circulated, with performance explicitly constructed as actors' theatrical replication of editorial print production. As Singer explains while providing continuity between Borgeson's and Long's introductory portions: 'Those of you who own a copy of this book know that no collection is complete without a brief biography.'[8] So pervasive is this sort of appended scholarly apparatus, it has become a defining part of what the company recognizes as constituting the 'complete' works. This parody of the modern conventions of print production is likewise evident in the published edition of *The Complete Works*, which displays the text literally and figuratively resting on a foundation of pseudo-scholarly annotation, so broadly replicating the hierarchical division of the editorial page into text and commentary which is now taken for granted.[9] This editorial annotation, with its authoritative tone, is in some ways typical of the genre. Besides glossing difficult words and providing contextualizing historical detail, it notes variant readings found in the early editions, considers emendations suggested by previous editors, and comments on performance options. However, as with the preface and biography, this scholarship is consistently wrong ('"*tyrannous*"; dinosaur-like'), banal ('"*Italy*"; a small country just north of Africa and left of China. Shaped like a boot'), and/or misleading ('"*O, happy dagger! This is thy sheath*"; this line again plays on the penis-as-a-sword metaphor … the sight of the young actor portraying Juliet "unsheathing" Romeo's would have provoked much general mirth among the groundlings').[10]

This edition thus adapts to the print medium the slapstick clowning that characterizes the troupe's live performances. The careful account of the stage tradition of 'Booga, booga, booga' as a comic sound effect in an 'unbroken line' from 'Samuel Pepys' diary in 1598' [*sic*] through the bowdlerizations of the Victorian period to cheek-flapping variants found on the modern stage is the editorial counterpart to Adam's pratfall as he trips and lands on his face just as another actor mocks the taboo against saying 'Macbeth' in a theatre.[11] However, the joke also partly depends on the experienced reader's ability to recognize how this absurdly copious commentary (with jumps in the numbering, the footnotes run to 11,188 entries) satirizes the quirks and shortcomings to which the modern mediation of the works in print is vulnerable. That the RSC's text and editorial apparatus may seem to some readers partial, unreliable, or discriminating in peculiar ways is part of the point: Shakespeare's works are shaped by those who produce them – perhaps most powerfully by means of the print editions in which form they are studied in classrooms. The interpretative effect of this comedy is uncertain. Taken as satire, it might seem to imply that *all* editions are potentially 'misproductions' – or adaptations – of the works. Alternatively, taken as farce, it might imply instead that the sorts of problems of scholarly mediation found in this comically abridged spoof are avoided by competent editors. Everyone knows, after all, that the man who authored 'Mein Kampf' and invaded Poland was Hitler, not Shakespeare. These are historical facts that Adam, ridiculously, gets wrong. What then would seem to separate a textual instance of the work from its adaptation, the Oxford *Complete Works* from the RSC *Complete Works*, is a commitment to getting the history right.

Shakespeare and the Problem of Adaptation has so far largely drawn its case studies from performance, even though the theoretical approach developed in the opening chapter to the distinction between work and adaptation has clear applications to print production. My purpose has been to challenge the perception that performance is an extension of text in order to make the point that text is not an ontological origin. Through experiences of performance *and/or* text one comes to learn and form opinions about the dramatic work; it is this acquired and evolving set of assumptions which then functions as the seemingly objective, fixed origin against which instances of production can be measured. However, because the dramatic work is by definition impossible to fix, yet functions so powerfully and persuasively to regulate perceptions of authenticity, its force is often identified with text, the form of production still most closely associated with the hand of the author. One implication of my argument is that this always doubled production is what distinguishes drama from, say, literature, while linking it as an art form in certain key respects to music. Another implication is that other forms of production – short stories, graphic novels, ballets, operas, coffee mugs – while not insignificant in terms of reinforcing Shakespeare's cultural influence, are generically adaptive forms. The question then is not how performance departs from or otherwise 'adapts' text, but the shifting criteria by which *both* texts and performances are recognized – or not – as instances of a certain work. The evolving identity of the work is shaped over time in response to debates that occur specifically in relation to text and performance, drama's two forms of production, about what should count as 'genuine' repetition and, especially where consensus fails in the course of those discussions, allegations of adaptive practice.

This final chapter will therefore address in a more sustained way issues of adaptation as they bear on the production of Shakespeare's works as reading texts. Specifically, I want to consider some continuing efforts on the parts of theatre historians and textual scholars to recover the works' earliest moments of textual-theatrical production. My larger goal is to reflect on some of the current intersections between historical research and editorial rationales, and so to consider how, when it comes to textual production (as opposed to theatrical production), appeals to the past continue to shape attitudes towards what can be recognized as 'genuine' textual instances of Shakespeare's works. To start, one should note that to undertake an act of textual production is always to risk adaptation since any reader, or group of readers, might fail to recognize the work in the instance. This is precisely the force of criticisms of modern editorial practice mounted by performance and theatre history scholars such as Alan C. Dessen and Don Weingust. Dessen has long advocated non-interventionist editorial policies, arguing that the way editors mediate text for readers erases or misrepresents potential evidence of early modern staging practices.[12] In 'The Editor as Rescripter', for example, the final chapter of *Rescripting Shakespeare*, he provides numerous examples where editorial directions in print editions offer not the only, nor even arguably the best, staging option available. Drawing on his own and others' research into early modern theatre conditions, he shows how stage directions and their placement in Shakespeare's early quartos and Folio are more workable than editors have imagined, and Dessen provides a keen sense of the interpretative possibilities closed down by editorial intervention. The burden of Dessen's chapter is that: 'Choices must be made. But on what basis and by whom?'[13] And while accepting that errors and inconsistencies in the earliest texts should be cleared up by the editor for the reader, he concludes this chapter by advising caution: '"If it ain't broke, don't fix it."'[14]

The problem, of course, is knowing when, and how, a text is broken. The upshot of Dessen's analysis is not that the earliest texts of Shakespeare's works are 'unbroken' and therefore should be left untouched by editors, but that editors tend to botch their repair jobs, effacing the evidence on which theatre historians depend and to which any reader should attend. This issue of history and evidence takes a slightly different cast in Weingust's book-length defence of acting techniques advocated by Patrick Tucker and Neil Freeman which are grounded in study of the orthography of the Shakespeare First Folio. Weingust's point is that by 'cutting through the layers of editorial "improvement"', actors can develop 'performance choices that some would claim are more faithful to a sense of either authorial intention or at least the rhetorical milieu from which the works originate'. Whether or not a capital letter or line break can be securely attributed to Shakespeare is not relevant: 'The Folio orthography becomes a simple alternative means of textual study, one well suited to the temporal demands of theatrical production. Folio-based techniques provide actors with not only technical assistance, but also a less tangible, though no less important, moral authority bound up with the supposed intentionality of the playwright'.[15] Particular arrangements of words and punctuation may not be authorial, but if modern actors can find new interpretations as a consequence of a belief that such arrangements originate with Shakespeare, or are at least 'Shakespearean', then preserving them offers an aid to rehearsal. Examples of such opportunities include cues embedded in dialogue pauses, page layouts, and irregular verse lines that variously signal gestural emphasis, simultaneous speech, and character development.

Weingust is therefore critical of interventionist editorial procedures, especially those associated with the Greg-Bowers school, since they neglect to preserve the textual cues such acting methods find theatrically useful, and he implicitly promotes instead the 'variety of alternatives [that] have begun to appear, including editions by Freeman and Tucker themselves'.[16] *Acting from Shakespeare's First Folio* offers a clear example of my argument that groups of users *confer* authority on textual, no less than theatrical, instances, having already devised for themselves pragmatic notions of the work and its essential properties – if capital letters and line breaks printed in a specific edition (i.e., the Folio) are ranged among the essential properties of the work, then any edition that fails to include them will be open to the charge of editorial revision (or 'rescripting') and adaptation. The point that Freeman's Applause editions have achieved a significant market presence even though advocates of Folio acting have not persuaded many textual scholars of the bibliographical merits of their hermeneutic strategies simply reinforces the point that the defining limits of the work are provisional and contested.

Not surprisingly, however, Weingust runs into trouble when he tries to do more than make an argument from utility, when, for example, he tries to show that the Folio has (along with Freeman's and Tucker's edited texts of it) better relative authority as an instance of the work than the 'plethora of Shakespearean editions' currently 'rushed to market' that sustain, in his view, 'the goals of the New Bibliographers'.[17] It remains unclear in what objective ways Freeman's and Tucker's editions could be regarded as especially reliable. Setting aside an inability to know whose – if anyone's – intentions are encoded in the Folio printing and whether one finds anything more than one's own desire for meaning through a close analysis of orthography, there remains the difficult issue of the editorial correction of textual error and the rationales editors devise to support such intervention. Freeman, in the course of preparing his Applause editions, corrects what he considers Folio misprints through consultation of the early quartos and the three later seventeenth-century folios. But where all orthographic peculiarities are potentially significant, what constitutes a category of obvious error? Perhaps even more urgently, on what methodological grounds can Freeman introduce emendations into what Weingust calls a process of 'uneditioning' without ultimately producing a text which seems in practice suspiciously like an ill-theorized return to the 'editioned' editions to which it is ostensibly an answer?[18]

Setting out to critique the received text and the editorial rationales that underpinned its production throughout the better part of the twentieth century in order to advocate Folio acting techniques, Weingust overlooks the point that *every* modern edition, 'copies' of the Folio included – like every modern theatrical performance – is potentially vulnerable to failures of recognition, and so to rejection as adaptation. Even facsimiles, as we are now well aware from the debates generated, for example, by Randall McLeod's brilliant and polemical contributions to the 'unediting' debate, are mediated documents, and so open to accusations of editorial mis-representation.[19] As Laurie E. Osborne explains: 'The Folio facsimile is a picture of the Folio, created by editors who have decided how much to reduce the page size, who give their introductions, and who choose which particular Folio or Folios they will photograph and present. The medium which *we* have decided can offer an uncorrupted view of Shakespeare's text is ... a historically grounded intervention in the text.'[20] More provoca-tively, even an actual copy of the Folio is not self-identical with itself over time:

> We may 'return' to the material text [of *Twelfth Night*] dated 1623, but what we find there, what exists there, cannot be confidently ascribed to be what was there for the 1623 reader, or for the 1790 reader who knew Malone's [1614] dating or the reader from 1830 who knew Collier's revised date of composition [of 1601]. Like those past read-ers, we cannot erase our historical moment, but 'going back to the Folio' can create a dangerous illusion of getting back to origins.[21]

As discussed in the opening chapter, unmediated production of the work is not an option unless one carefully and arbitrarily limits what constitutes the work by returning to something like Goodman's criteria of 'accurate spelling'. But even in that extreme case there is still the potential need for editorial labour whenever one considers that the earliest agents of pro-duction – an author, a reviser, a compositor – didn't really 'mean' that turned letter, misaligned speech prefix, or duplicated word. Again, this is the persistent problem of the editorial identification and emendation of error. The question is not *whether* one will mediate through production, but how. At the heart of the editorial project is the issue Goodman takes for granted – how one knows when a work is 'accurately spelled' in its instance, including a first instance.

Few people these days set out to prepare definitive editions. Scholars seem more readily willing to accept the position, articulated half a century ago by Fredson Bowers, that editorial method relies fundamentally on 'critical judgement', and to endorse Gary Taylor's comment that emen-dation, far from being a science, is 'all too obviously an art'.[22] These now commonly repeated assertions are worth pausing over. No single editorial production is likely to be taken, on purely objective grounds, as *the* textual instance of the work, and potentially quite different editions, prepared on the basis of opposed rationales, can equally claim to be 'genuine' productions. In some ways this only makes more pressing the need to insist, as Weingust does, that some editions are better than others: as with theatrical production, the 'genuine' textual production depends on users recognizing the work in the instance. The difference, perhaps, is that while many users feel competent to judge theatrical production (as with some other forms of art, there operates the criteria that 'I know what I like'), textual production, when it is noticed at all, seems an arcane, specialized discipline beyond the ken of ordinary users. When it is asked outside of a theatre, the question 'What did you think of it?' tends to refer to the specific production instance; when asked in a classroom, the question usually refers instead to the abstract work, the editor's interpretative choices implicitly accepted as providing transparent access to that work. The effect of this is to push debates about vandals and adapters, so familiar in relation to theatrical production, out of the public, and more squarely into the scholarly, domain. As a result, Bowers' guess that those scholars 'whose opinion is powerful enough eventually to shape the form of the edited texts that penetrate to the schools' might number fifty – 'They might well be fewer, perhaps considerably fewer' – probably still holds.[23] Publishers and general editors, influenced by the cutting edge textual scholarship of their day, devise the series others accept and read as (instances of) the works. This institutional condition of limited access to the power to make the decisions that will influence what will count as a textual instance of the works in part explains why professional arguments among textual scholars are so vigorously, even ferociously, pursued. The need to persuade and sway those fifty scholars – possibly even eventually to be numbered *among* the fifty – is the only way one can secure the means to shape perceptions of the work in its textual instances.

John Jowett's and Gary Taylor's claim that the Folio text of *Measure for Measure* is an adaptation offers an important and influential case of textual scholarship that seeks to revise substantially the distinction between work and adaptation with regard to past and future textual productions of *Measure for Measure*. Their argument is particularly timely to revisit in light of the long-awaited publication by Oxford University Press of *Thomas Middleton: The Collected Works*.[24] In *Shakespeare Reshaped*, Jowett and Taylor argue that this earliest printing derives from a theatrical playbook, no longer extant, that presented a text of Shakespeare's work as it had been cut, rearranged, and supplemented by Middleton with new dialogue and a song for a late revival in 1621. Elsewhere I have described adaptation as the work's necessary supplement, the inevitable consequence of consumers comparing a particular theatrical or textual instance against their actual or pragmatically held beliefs about what constitutes, for example, *Measure for*

Measure. Since there are no criteria according to which one can ensure the work's stable perpetuation over time and simultaneously in two media, one can only keep relearning (and so potentially renegotiating) what will count for the moment as its essential properties by naming supposed infringements in its production instances. Adaptation is therefore always a 'problem', always implicitly or explicitly fraught with rhetoric of fraudulent or criminal activity, precisely because it is the concept by which one manages anxieties about work preservation.

Jowett's and Taylor's research is thus especially interesting since it is analogous to the conservationists arriving at the National Gallery with new infra-red technology to reveal that their supposed Caravaggio is not quite what it seems – not quite a fake but not quite the real thing, either. They then proceed to recover the Shakespearean work they believe has been obscured in print since the publication of the First Folio, and in performance probably at least two years longer than that, by the Middletonian adaptation. Unlike my imagined art conservationists with their high-tech equipment, Jowett and Taylor have no means to discern the traces of adaptation except close examination of the clues provided by the only surviving textual witness, the Folio edition of 1623. Alerted to the possibility that something might be amiss with this particular textual production by a well-known crux – the Duke's 'place and greatness' speech in the first scene of Act 4 has long been considered inadequate to cover the offstage dialogue between Mariana and Isabella – they begin to examine more fully the whole sequence of events leading up to this six-line soliloquy. This makes them notice that there are other respects in which this scene seems unusual, even suspicious. For example, the song the Boy sings to Mariana turns up in a longer version in Fletcher's *Rollo, Duke of Normandy*, where it seems well-suited to the dramatic context rather than awkwardly coming out of nowhere at the beginning of a new act; Mariana, a character previously mentioned but not staged, is not named until well after Isabella's entrance later in the scene, and she introduces a plot contradiction in her first speech by suggesting that this Friar (a disguise the Duke has recently assumed) has 'often' been a comfort to her; and the writing of her first exchange with the Duke – about twenty-five lines – is both flat and uncharacteristic of Shakespeare in terms of metre, rhyme, and vocabulary.[25] As they explain elsewhere in this study, interpolations by another professional dramatist are betrayed 'not by exercrable [*sic*] badness, but by superfluousness, by bad joins, and by unShakespearian dramatic technique'.[26]

Analysis of those places in which the Folio text of *Measure for Measure* seems inconsistent with itself and speculation about how this sequence of action might look if one imagined it without act breaks and with the opening twenty-five lines of the fourth act removed reveal a quite different narrative shape: 'a single scene of over 600 lines' that allows the action to run 'without interruption from the Duke's great speech of admonition to Claudio ("Be absolute for death") until his exit with Mariana and Isabella, at the end of what the Folio calls Act 4, Scene 1'.[27] Once one sees what Jowett and Taylor describe as 'the satisfying wholeness of this sweep of action', the solution to the crux that initiated the textual investigation becomes likewise apparent. The adapter, probably preparing the work for a Blackfriars revival and so needing to accommodate an act break, created a strong opening to what is now the fourth act by patching in a song and a bit of new dialogue before returning to the entrapment plot in which Mariana is about to be entangled. What became the end of Act 3 was likewise rounded out with the relocation of the long rhyming soliloquy that begins 'He who the sword of Heaven will bear' from its place covering Mariana's and Isabella's offstage dialogue. Their unheard conversation was then covered with the shorter soliloquy ('Oh place and greatness') that the 'sword of Heaven' speech took the place of. This is an elegant piece of reconstruction that provides a clear motive – the need to introduce act breaks for a Blackfriars revival – along with simplicity of execution on the part of the adapter, since undoing the work of adaptation 'depends on only two emendations: the omission of TLN 1769–96 (4.1.1–25) as an interpolation, and the transposition of the Duke's two soliloquies (a consequence of that interpolation)'.[28]

Having found what they believe is a process of adaptation lying behind one textual crux, Jowett and Taylor are disposed to wonder if the same explanation might likewise account for a workable, but odd, sequence early in the first act when first Mistress Overdone then Lucio have knowledge of Claudio's imprisonment, moments later only to seem ignorant of it. In the Folio text, Overdone enters to tell Lucio and his two friends the news, the gallants exit, then Pompey enters to tell Overdone – to her evident surprise – that Claudio has been arrested for 'groping for trouts in a peculiar river'. The gentlemen then re-enter later in the same scene, where they learn – this time from Claudio himself, and again seemingly to their collective surprise – that he has fallen foul of the newly enforced promiscuity laws. This irregularity along with a verbal texture that in key respects is arguably unShakespearean encourage Jowett and Taylor to interpret the opening seventy-nine lines of Act 1.2 as another interpolation introduced at the same time as the renovations that serve to break the action into acts. This long and otherwise gratuitous episode involving Lucio and the two gentlemen 'dishes up an extra helping of bawdy comedy ... [and] expands the part of Lucio, the play's most memorable and important comic creation', factors that might have seemed advantageous to a playwright adapting the work for a revival.[29] Evidence of adaptation in Act 4 thus gives persuasive force to the possibility of similar intervention at the beginning of Act 1.

As Jowett and Taylor acknowledge, this is a classic 'whodunit'. An 'alleged textual crime' has taken place, and the 'clue[s]' that might allow scholars not only to reconstruct what happened but to find a motive and perpetrator depend on close analysis of the 'mutilate[d]' body of the text/ victim.[30] Their transformation of what is textually evident into textual evidence makes for compelling reading, the choice to recount their research as a slowly unfolding web of connections setting up the strong expectation that analysis of these accumulating clues will lead, finally, to a smoking gun. As a result, the revelation that '*Measure for Measure* suffered major theatrical adaptation in 1621 – at least seventeen years after the play was written, and five years after William Shakespeare was buried', seems especially satisfying. It is precisely the sort of answer that knowledge of the conventions of crime or detective genres anticipates.[31]

And yet Jowett's and Taylor's sifting of the Folio text for anomalous or irregular sequences also betrays a sort of persistent anxiety about potential methodological complaints concerning this sort of editorial sleuthing, a desire to rebut sceptics who would challenge such efforts to piece together past events from surviving textual witnesses. The first stage of their argument investigates the type of manuscript from which the Folio text was printed, and concludes that it must have been a copy of a copy – specifically, a transcription by the scribe, Ralph Crane, of a theatrical playbook. Repeatedly Jowett and Taylor insist that this conclusion relies solely on 'mechanical evidence', 'mechanical criteria', and 'objective evidence'.[32] The implication would seem to be that their analysis of printing-house copy is free of interpretation, and based purely on facts. As they explain the logic of the argument that will follow on from this preliminary diagnosis, 'those who disagree with our interpretation of [the play's critical-cum-textual problems] must either offer an alternative interpretation which can be reconciled with the assumption that Crane copied from a prompt-book, or must themselves provide compelling objective evidence that Crane instead used foul papers. Interpretation must accord with the mechanical evidence; it cannot override it.'[33] However, although spelling variations and quantification of instances of profanity might be regarded as mechanical or objective evidence, such enabling conceptual categories as foul papers and promptbooks (or playbooks) cannot. An important consequence of Jowett's and Taylor's analysis of certain Folio characteristics as symptomatic is that it produces (while seeming merely to reveal) as discrete and stable entities the categories of authorial foul papers and (adapted) theatrical playbook. There is the adapted version that survives in the Folio, and then there is *Measure for Measure* 'as Shakespeare must have plotted it', the 'original sequence' that readers 'familiar with the Folio text may have difficulty in imagining'.[34] The argument is thus not founded on purely 'mechanical evidence', but relies on certain preconceptions about the circulation of manuscripts in the professional theatres, and so on the types of document Jowett and Taylor think *can* be recovered because they assume they *must* have once existed. However, the dramatic manuscripts that have survived from the period more often seem to provide hermeneutic puzzles than clear instances of category differences.

William B. Long and Paul Werstine, among others, have challenged what textual scholars and editors can discern about no longer extant manuscripts based on careful diagnosis of the textual symptoms of an extant printed text.[35] Barbara Mowat pushes this argument a step further, arguing that even if those manuscripts survived, we still would not have the textual certainty or singularity posited by New Bibliographic methodologies – Shakespeare's manuscripts, in other words, had they survived, may not have seemed typical of either foul papers or theatrical playbooks, at least as those categories were posited by Greg, and so they would have continued to pose interpretative problems. Citing the example of Katherine Philips, whose writings survive in manuscript, Mowat notes that 'hard choices' are still required of the editor in terms of interpreting which changes to a poem from one manuscript copy to another represent revision as opposed to errors of transmission introduced either by the author or a scribe: 'The facts of publication in manuscript form – i.e., that manuscripts themselves were copied and recopied, that copying inevitably introduces change – means [*sic*] that editors from manuscripts are as hard pressed to publish "authentic" editions of their authors as is any Shakespeare editor.'[36] James Purkis, studying the peculiar instance of the extant manuscript of Thomas Heywood's *The Captives*, draws a similar conclusion. Purkis argues that this manuscript 'span[s] and resist[s] the categories of "foul papers", "fair copies", and playbooks or "promptbooks"', so providing 'an extraordinary insight into the fluid textual condition of the early modern dramatic text': 'Through its deletions, substitutions, supplementations, and interlined corrections, the manuscript raises questions of textual multiplicity not just in terms of a multiplicity of documents, but within the document itself.'[37] The argument for turning away from editorial procedures that depend on categorizing printed texts as either foul papers or fair copy, 'authorial' or 'theatrical', rests on the position that such analysis may prevent us from perceiving the complex ways dramatic manuscripts were produced and circulated in early modern England. If one resists the implicit binary choice offered by Jowett and Taylor (foul papers or promptbook; if not foul papers, then promptbook) to wonder instead how else manuscripts might have evolved, then their reconstruction of an adapted and unadapted *Measure for Measure* remains a feasible, but finally unprovable, explanation of some features of the Folio text that have seemed troubling to some critics.

My purpose in citing this instance of textual scholarship is not to contribute further to the debate about whether a process of adaptation actually took place around 1619, but to highlight how the case for Middleton's historical 'reshaping' of *Measure for Measure* modifies the work in the present day for modern users. Jowett's and Taylor's explanation of these perceived cruces proposes that users have long misrecognized Shakespeare's work, wrongly taking an instance of partial adaptation that survives in the Folio as the thing itself. Whether or not Jowett and Taylor are right, their argument is illustrative of my point that editorial or actorly fidelity to a text – even the very earliest text – is no assurance that the problem of adaptation has thereby been averted. Textual fidelity is an insufficient gauge of the work's stability in part because any text, even the earliest one, functions only provisionally as a genuine instance, and because modern editors, even those preparing facsimiles, can never copy an existing text but must produce new textual instances that are either taken as the work or rejected as adaptation. To put this a different way, Jowett's and Taylor's research has no physical impact on the Folio text of *Measure for Measure*. Rather, it potentially alters the grounds on which modern producers and consumers evaluate that particular instance of production as genuine or adaptive by changing one's ideas and expectations about *the work*. What is therefore instructive about their research, quite apart from the historicist case for adaptation which one may or may not find persuasive, is the way it prises apart work and text, implicitly demonstrating how the former is a pragmatic concept that *comes after*, rather than antedates, production instances. What one thinks of as *Measure for Measure* provides the necessary standard by which actual instances, textual or theatrical, historical or modern, are produced and appraised. But there remains always the potential for a perceived misalignment that can be realized at any time between one's conception of the work and any particular instance of it, so transforming the previously supposed genuine instance into adaptation, and adaptation into the thing itself. Because the work does not exist somewhere (not even in the First Folio), but always 'survives' somewhere else, it remains susceptible, among other things, to the ways scholars conduct and write textual histories. Inevitably, as conceptions of the work continue to alter over time, so will assessments of what will or should count as either an authentic or an adapted textual production, along with the criteria or terms by which it is recognized.

It therefore follows that methodological responses to the identification of error and decisions about emendation are shaped in powerful ways by editorial recourse to what I would describe as pragmatic notions of the work. The editors of the Oxford Shakespeare, for example, decided to relegate a few speeches of Folio *Measure for Measure* to an appendix called 'Additional Passages', in effect disentangling what Jowett and Taylor regard as the original and reshaped versions in order to present the reader (somewhat paradoxically in the context of a complete works of Shakespeare) with a modern textual instance of the adapted work. On similar grounds, Jowett's edition of *Measure for Measure* for the Oxford Middleton *Collected Works* uses variant fonts to trace simultaneously the revised and unrevised versions, and he makes use of the commentary to draw out matters of adaptation. Jowett's choices continually foreground a process of adaptation, not only making it visible to the reader but even insisting on it by means of the semiotics of the page: 'Alongside the typographical variety within the text of the play, the commentary makes the page visually busy. And it makes the adapted sections occupy a disproportionate number of pages … This is, then, a form of specialized and motivated editing, one might even say polemical editing.'[38] The use of such parallel-text techniques in an edition of a work presented as part of the Middleton canon is motivated in the first instance by issues of authorship – the two-text passages account for segments the editor considers to be written by Shakespeare or revised by Middleton.[39] But as Jowett explains, 'the issue is not simply authorial': 'What might it mean to think of an adapted version of the play as belonging to 1621; in what ways might it belong to this cultural environment and speak differently as a result?'[40] In other words, by producing this 'Shakespearean' work in an unfamiliar manner – by including an instance of it in its entirety as part of another author's canon, and disrupting the smooth reading experience with parallel-text display – Jowett makes available to the modern reader issues of historicity that might not otherwise arise.

Editorial procedures based on what one can infer about manuscripts that are no longer extant have been the object of sharp critique by scholars who challenge as self-realizing the positivist modernism of New Bibliographical ideologies and methodologies. And yet by no means has everyone abandoned the principles of copy-text editing, an awareness of the theoretical debates instead often prompting an adapted, or at least more rhetorically cautious, application of those basic principles. Editorial practices in Shakespeare studies have for a while now thus been at something of a watershed moment – perhaps not a 'crisis', as McLeod characterized it when 'unediting' was on the upswing, but a potential turning point as scholars explore and seek to articulate alternative strategies of textual production.[41] Perhaps the most sustained attempt in Shakespeare studies to develop a practical and theoretical alternative to Gregian-influenced procedures is offered by the New Folger Shakespeare series, prepared by Mowat and Werstine. I therefore want to consider how the New Folger editors – choosing not to write or otherwise rely on textual histories that seek to recover from early printed texts, manuscript authorities – manage to control the problem of adaptation. The larger question that arises from this discussion is whether it is possible to produce a textual instance of Shakespeare's drama *without* appeals to the work.

Editions in the New Folger series are not 'critical', at least so far as that term in a textual studies context is associated with working hypotheses about lost authorial or theatrical manuscripts and Gregian copy-text procedures. But neither are they examples of 'best text' editing, a school of thought closely associated with Greg's contemporary, R. B. McKerrow, who proposed to reconstruct what the author meant to write through judicious emendation of a single surviving text. As Werstine has explained the problem posed by McKerrow's goal, it leaves editors in the impossible position of 'establishing the text of a metaphysical "work" that transcends its evidently imperfect printed states'. His answer to both critical and best-text methodologies is 'to strive for the humanly possible goal of editing one or more of the early printed texts, without claiming to locate either author or work in relation to these printed versions'.[42] Werstine's reluctance to edit on the basis of what one thinks one can say about the author from early printed texts is not, as he puts it, a 'quirk' that makes him 'chronically pessimistic about finding Shakespeare immediately behind his printed plays'. The nature of his objection is evidentiary rather than dispositional: the 'documentary evidence' provided by extant manuscripts from the period 'proves invalid any inferences about the nature of printer's copy that are based on unresolved textual tangles in printed texts'.[43]

The danger is to suppose that because certain historical accounts on which editors have long relied have been challenged as 'narratives', one is disallowed from making claims about the past because there are no facts of history.[44] The theoretical issue, rather, is two-fold. It is not that one cannot discern *anything* about a past moment of production through textual study, but that all facts, as Hugh Grady and Terence Hawkes explain, 'are capable of genuinely contradictory meanings, none of which has any independent, "given", undeniable, or self-evident status'.[45] By adopting different perspectives on the same material, commentators can arrive at competing interpretations of a past event or sequence of events. This is simply to acknowledge that interpretative meaning rests with the historian, not with the documents she studies. The second issue is perhaps more challenging of textual studies as a form of historical investigation, and it centres on the problem of discerning what constitutes in the first place the historical record one seeks to interpret. Which evidence does one decide to include as potentially meaningful or otherwise revealing of a past moment? Basic decisions about how to constitute a field of study shape fundamentally one's sense of that 'past moment' as a discrete event and thus one's research into it. 'History is perhaps the most thoroughly hermeneutic creation of all culture,' Nancy Partner reflects, 'from the "inside" because historians begin by creating a text, the Past, through the interpretive creation of and with evidence; and from the "outside" because they then proceed to explain it.'[46] Or as William Ingram puts it, 'everything regarded as "evidence" is of course *evident* simply by virtue of its existence, but it is not thereby "evidence". Only when we transform it into a meaningful piece of a past whole – however we may conceive that "whole" – does it become "evidence".'[47] That 'past whole', no less than the narratives one tells of it, is itself a construction that takes form by means of scholars choosing, for instance, to include certain surviving documents, but not others, as evidence of it. To shape one's analyses according to Greg's categories of manuscript (foul papers, fair copy, promptbook) presumes and imposes a certain consistent, and probably oversimplified, conception of the historical landscape – in this case, early modern processes of textual transmission in manuscript and print. Given the particularity of the manuscripts that have actually survived from the period – what seems to unite them as a group is each one's exceptional character – the same problem would potentially arise any time one sought to extend to a different textual environment as supposedly 'typical' practice an explanatory framework developed from the individual instance. In such interpretative circumstances, an ongoing metacritical scepticism about accounts of the past, a curiosity about how what is *evident* has been transformed into *evidence* (or else set aside as incidental), signals less a loss of faith in the historical enterprise than a productive engagement with how the discipline might continue to take shape.

The uncertain implications for editorial practice of this debate on historical method mark a major hurdle for modern textual production. Mowat's and Werstine's refusal to make editorial choices on the basis of what one believes can be said about the manuscript(s) that provided copy for an extant printed text is a compelling theoretical starting point for modern textual production. Equally valuably, their ground-breaking work on the New Folger editions has created the opportunity for textual scholars to examine the practical challenges that press into view when one abandons copy-text and best-text strategies. Greg's binary distinction between authorial foul papers and theatrical promptbook was so valuable, and has proven so enduring, in part because hypotheses about the manuscript(s) that lie behind printed texts are hugely enabling in terms of developing a rationale by means of which one can posit and correct error. Using Greg's account in *The Shakespeare First Folio* of the typical symptoms of authorial and theatrical manuscripts as they survive into printed texts, one could diagnose a printed text through analysis of features that Greg identified as significant such as false starts and loose ends, confusions around character names, substitution of an actor's name in place of a character's name, and permissive stage directions.[48] On the basis of this perceived evidence and resulting diagnosis, one could formulate an editorial response, particularly as that would shape the choice of copy-text and strategies of sometimes quite complex emendation. Alternatively, if one refuses to engage in speculation about the manuscript from which a particular printed text derives, one avoids making unfounded evidentiary claims about surviving documents. One can often say *something* about surviving printed texts, but not enough to recover the manuscript document(s) in their particularity, and Werstine's analyses, perhaps most notably, deliberately stop short of attributing the system of changes one can trace between variant texts to a specific agent of production.[49]

However, this caution about the conclusions one chooses to draw from study of textual instances has its own implications for editorial practice, particularly in terms of developing a theory of error. Without a working hypothesis about origins – a foundation on which to explain *how* this text came to look as it does – the basis on which one corrects supposed errors of transmission comes to seem very obviously subjective. Emendation, as noted earlier, is an art not a science, but it is an art that previously has at least seemed grounded in the 'facts' of history: Hero's mother could be removed as a ghost character from *Much Ado about Nothing* since the earliest quarto in which she appears in a massed stage direction was printed from the author's foul papers; 'O, o, o, o, o' could be taken out of an edition of *Hamlet* (or latterly, and according to the same reasoning, left in) since it turns up in the Folio text which is based on the theatrical playbook and so is probably an actor's interpolation; editors could introduce into their editions of *Romeo and Juliet* and *Hamlet* striking Q1 stage directions on the grounds that these early quartos, while otherwise textually unreliable, in some way reflect aspects of early modern performance conventions. Hypotheses about historical origins guide and support the thousands of small and large decisions editors have to make in the course of producing a new text. Without them, when and how one should or might intervene become especially difficult to assess.

Mowat addresses this issue head-on in 'The Problem of Shakespeare's Text(s)'. No longer oriented towards 'the authorial manuscript behind the early printing', the editor is left with two options: either to replicate that printing 'with all its faults' or to prepare 'the editorially, culturally constructed play':[50]

There is little that one can theorize about the editing of Shakespeare's texts once one abandons belief in the controlling power of the manuscript underlying the print. One chooses which early printed text to edit, sticks to that text as closely as is feasible, and adds or substitutes variants or emendations only in specific circumstances, which one then spells out in one's textual introduction. The 'problem' with Shakespeare's texts, in other words, is, for the editor today, no longer so much theoretical as practical, turning on questions of how one chooses.[51]

Mowat provides examples of the common sorts of textual glitches one encounters as an editor and explains how she and Werstine made their choices. Throughout the second quarto of *Hamlet*, the textual version the New Folger editors selected to prepare, the queen is called 'Gertrard'. However, rather than present the reader with a name lacking an existence in this tragedy's cultural afterlife, 'we allow the "Shakespeare" that is culturally constructed to outweigh the Shakespeare that may be reflected in Q2 *Hamlet*, and we name her "Gertrude"'.[52] In *Othello*, a multiple-version play no less textually problematic than *Hamlet*, the metrically short Folio line 'If she be false, heaven mocks itself' is conventionally emended through reference to the 1622 quarto to produce the well-known line 'If she be false, O then heaven mocks itself'. Because the metrically defective line is rhetorically strong, Mowat and Werstine consider the extra foot 'strictly padding' and so choose to leave the Folio reading unemended. However, another short line earlier in the same play – 'That I love the Moor to live with him' – less rhetorically compelling, is filled out through reference to the quarto ('did love') to produce the metrically regular line with which many readers are familiar.[53]

As these examples perhaps suggest, the process of emendation for the New Folger editors is not always in response to perceptions of error or revision: in none of these cases are the editors proposing that an authorial reading has been corrupted through faulty transmission, or that a weak reading was authorially or otherwise revised in a subsequent version. They are not even suggesting that the readings as they appear in Q2 *Hamlet* or F *Othello* are necessarily wrong. These potential emendations are weighed up, and either adopted or rejected, on the basis of whether the received text is considered to offer a preferable reading to the one found in the early printing, the editors then explaining the rationale behind the choices on which they settled. What is striking about this procedure is not that any individual emendation seems right or wrong, but that the method is so obviously subjective, largely dependent on editorial judgement, or taste. One feels cut loose from something that had previously served to anchor the whole decision-making process. This might be a 'freeing' experience, as Mowat has found it,[54] or one might rather feel something of the dismay of the banished Mowbray, with every road open to him except the one that leads home.

The goal of editorial research for the New Folger editors is no longer to seek to recover what they consider editorially fabricated histories of textual origins pre-dating the quartos and 1623 Folio, but to engage with the cultural history that begins with, and has continued to evolve since, the publication of those earliest print witnesses. Both Mowat and Werstine are therefore quite openly hostile to the idea of the 'work', but I nonetheless believe a reconceived version of it underwrites their editorial method.[55] It is implicit, for example, in the argument that '[e]ach of Shakespeare's plays is, by now, a cultural as well as an editorial construct'.[56] As suggested in my opening chapter, 'play' often seems a bit of a fudged term – it is neither text or version, nor quarto, folio, or theatrical enactment. It is all of these, and more. 'Play' unobtrusively does service here not for the work as the author intended it – an ideal text that one can never recover and perhaps never existed except as an editorial objective – but for the work as the editor has formed an opinion about it by means of its production instances. Without recourse to this controlling, pragmatic concept, an editor simply could not make evaluative choices or decisions.

The difference then between New Folger editions and editions broadly inspired by copy-text or best-text rationales in the tradition of the New Bibliography rests in the former's refusal to emplot in a narrative of origins textual details that other editors have construed as evidence. Mowat and Werstine are perhaps particularly alert to Partner's observation that history is 'the most thoroughly hermeneutic creation of all culture', and so especially aware that there is a long tradition of editors creating the past they then proceed to explain. Their response is therefore to make only cautious, and by comparison to other editors restrained, claims about the manuscripts and performances that must have at one time existed. This is not to suggest, however, that Mowat and Werstine themselves write narrative-free history. On the contrary, a particular construction of what I previously described as the 'historical landscape' is implicit in Mowat's and Werstine's decision to base their modern editions on a category of texts that is usually described as 'substantive' – on printed texts that are considered to possess independent authority since they are not apparently straightforward reprints of extant printed texts.

The obvious advantage to choosing one's copy-text from among a group of early printings is that one has a better chance to limit the sorts of changes that are inevitably introduced, either deliberately or accidentally, as the result of successive instances of production. However, I would argue that this procedure also represents a point at which debates about editorial practice in Shakespeare studies have stalled. An underlying belief in the need to found new editions on a work's textual origins – an idea introduced by Malone and transformed by Greg into something approaching an editorial system that has since been both refined and critiqued by textual scholarship – persists as, simply, the proper way to edit. The historicizing impulse is itself no longer historicized but taken for granted as the way to limit innovation or corruption and so to control adaptation. An idea of a textual origin – even for those who question whether a manuscript could ever in practice function as a stable origin, or consider that for practical or theoretical reasons it is irrecoverable[57] – functions pragmatically to define the parameters of the work and so to control the problem of adaptation for purposes of modern textual production. The work is fashioned as existing most authentically in the earliest reliable textual productions one believes can be recovered (whether an extant printed text or combination of texts, or an editorially inferred manuscript), which are then mediated by means of variably interventionist editorial protocols that guide, for example, emendation of error, processes of modernization and standardization, and clarification of staging, procedures that modern readers are implicitly asked to accept as providing potentially improved access to the work. Appeals to history protect editorial instances of a fluid, unfixed work that is perpetually coming into being from coming to seem instances of adaptation, the work's necessary supplement. The modern textual production thus achieves recognition as genuine on the basis of its relation to the work conceived as rooted in (specifically early modern) history.

An editorial practice that would identify the most reliable text by means of chronological priority perhaps needs little explanation or defence in a prevailing historicist climate. However, once one challenges on theoretical and methodological grounds the editorial recovery of manuscript origins to embrace instead the preparation of extant texts as emended through reference to 'the editorially, culturally constructed play', this perhaps previously unquestioned connection between work identity and early modern history becomes potentially a matter for further enquiry. As Mowat's explanation of the decision to emend Gertrard to Gertrude demonstrates, what can be taken as a genuine textual reading is, for the New Folger editors and their readers, at least partly generated through reader *familiarity* with the work in production. The history they 'get right', therefore, is not exclusively located in a past moment seen as defining on the basis of temporal proximity to an author, or agents and circumstances of production contemporary with an author, but is rather conceived as continuing into the present day, with editors giving readers the texts they already recognize as the work. Moreover, if one further avoids the error of collapsing work into (original) text – as already illustrated through Jowett's and Taylor's reclassification of Folio *Measure for Measure* as adaptation, even a text considered for editorial purposes substantive is always measured against one's own actual or pragmatically held beliefs about the work – there seems no necessary reason to prioritize an early chronological moment when preparing a new edition. Historically and culturally speaking, as Grigely has explained, later texts are no less significant than an early quarto or the 1623 Folio and not in any objective sense 'less' the work than any other textual-theatrical instance of production on the work's timeline.

The spectre such a situation raises, of course, is the possibility that cultural familiarity will provide an insufficient control on innovation and corruption, so over time 'reducing' the works to the sort of textual-theatrical productions prepared by the actor-editors of the Reduced Shakespeare Company. In effect, and to return to Goodman's anxieties about the transitivity of identity, this would be the Shakespearean equivalent of transforming Beethoven's *Fifth* into *Three Blind Mice*. What this book has tried to demonstrate, however, is that this condition of uncertainty – what I call the problem of adaptation – is *always* inherent to work production. One never 'gets back' in any historical sense to the work because it is always constructed in a present moment. Extant texts, whether they date to the sixteenth, nineteenth, or twentieth century, like theatrical stagings, are production instances that something else – variously described as the play or the work, or else identified by a title such as *Measure for Measure* – 'survives'. The work is the conceptual construction, pragmatically known and always located somewhere other than at the site of production, that makes it possible to regulate a work's identity and what will count as adaptation. It allows one to assess existing textual instances as more or less genuine, and to generate criteria of error sufficient to justify various forms of editorial emendation; without it, judgement is disabled.

The choice, therefore, to recognize Shakespeare's works in modern editions founded on substantive texts (so excluding some of the early quartos as unreliable, and most publications that post-date the First Folio as derivative or adaptive) is just that – a choice. Distinguishing between substantive and derivative texts is one way a modern readership pragmatically distinguishes between work and adaptation, but, as illustrated by the example of Alexander Pope and other eighteenth-century editors who preferred to base their new editions on recent editions published by their contemporaries, this is more a modern cultural convention than a necessary property of the work in its textual instances, offering a particular construction of authenticity that can itself be contested. That it is not a necessary choice is demonstrated by Jonathan Bate and Sonia Massai, who argue that: 'Once the lopsided, restrictive conception of authorship is overcome, or at least substantially qualified, there remains no reason why editors should defer exclusively to early documents and previous scholarly editions, at the expense of what may then be seen as only superficially "marginal," derivative texts.'[58] Pointing out that the functions of editor and adaptor share key similarities in terms of adjusting a text 'to the different exigencies of the receiving audience', Bate and Massai advocate allowing the work of adaptors (specifically, those close to the age of Shakespeare) to influence editorial decision-making: 'if we attend seriously to the rich tradition of early adaptations, if we treat them as editions and not aberrations, we may still have discoveries to make'.[59]

My claim that editorial theory has stalled around issues of historicity is thus not an argument in favour of editors returning to eighteenth-century ideas of 'improving', or seventeenth-century ideas of 'perfecting', Shakespeare's texts. My purpose, rather, is simply to foreground the point that texts, no less than performances, are not authoritative in and of themselves, but have authority conferred on them through reference to certain culturally accepted criteria that both control work production and serve to distinguish what will count as the 'genuine' and adaptive instance. Many modern editions, as already indicated, are at least implicitly alert to the cultural life of the work as an ongoing historical process editorially shaped for new generations of readers. Whether one considers the local problem of naming characters in *Hamlet* or *1 Henry IV*, or a large-scale decision to present *Measure for Measure* by means of parallel-text display, editors pause over how – and whether – a particular work through textual production might be made, in Jowett's words, to 'speak differently'.[60] Even when, as with the example of Gertrude/Gertrard, the decision is to preserve a traditional and so familiar form, there is an awareness that this is a choice. Continuity in such circumstances, paradoxically, is itself a form of innovation, or, to put this another way, to edit is always, inevitably, to produce something new.

Looking back on past editions it is easy to suppose that progress has been made towards ever more accurate texts and an improved ability to identify fraudulent production. However, the situation is probably rather more circular than linear: modern editions tend better than dated ones to embody expectations of the work. Decisions about spelling offer a ready case in point. Modern spelling editions inevitably sacrifice etymologically significant information and require on the part of editors a certain amount of translation – the grammatical distinction between the singular and plural forms of 'more', for example, has been entirely lost to today's readers and so the familiar modern form is now usually substituted in place of the obsolete 'mo'. This process of updating the language to make it more accessible to readers has been regarded by some commentators as a form of adaptation, a less extreme version of the principles that underpin the 'Shakespeare Made Easy' series, but today anything less than full modernization tends to look old-fashioned.[61] *Either* decision − to modernize or not to modernize − can therefore result in a text that is taken as work adaptation rather than work production. Editors negotiate this situation not by being right (the idea of accuracy in such circumstances is irrelevant), but by either conforming to current production trends or else, as Stanley Wells did with his influential essay 'Old and Modern Spelling', by choosing the right time to make a forceful and persuasive enough intervention in current practices to transform those trends for future users.[62]

As the example of spelling suggests, choices that may once have seemed to provide transparent access to the work in the instance can come to seem problematic as editions age; the other side of this situation is that as the assumptions and expectations of readers continue to evolve, alternative editorial choices not only become feasible but even desirable. T. J. B. Spencer's choice to include in his Penguin edition the clown's quips from the first quarto as part of Hamlet's advice to the players, or Dover Wilson's narrative description of 'the air' in Titania's bower as 'heavy with the scent of blossom', or even Charlton Hinman's bibliographical decision when preparing his facsimile of the First Folio to reproduce corrected pages rather than corrected formes, so creating a version of the Folio that could never have existed in 1623, now seem in their different ways to represent adaptive editorial strategies. Alternatively, to consider the editorial scene in the last quarter of the twentieth century from the perspective of a new century, the Oxford editors' two-text *King Lear* or Michael Warren's *The Complete 'King Lear', 1608–1623* ('*King Lear*' in a box') are currently for many readers unexceptional textual productions of a multiple-version work. As discussed in previous chapters, there is no way to define the essential properties of the work in such a way as to know it objectively in its production instances. Editing, like theatre, is thus a form of modern production that constantly and inevitably flirts with the possibility, and problem, of adaptation.

Since there can be no objectively accurate textual instance, textual studies informs without determining in any necessary way the protocols of editorial production. What is interesting to mark, then, is the way certain textual innovations find an audience at particular moments. This is the respect in which editorial practice has perhaps reached something of an impasse and potential turning point, insofar as ongoing textual innovation seems hedged in on the one side by attempts to represent for modern readers the historicity of the manuscripts that must have once existed (one form of historical truth-claim) and on the other by a methodological insistence that all an editor can reasonably do in light of available evidence is prepare an edition of a substantive text that is alert to the textual guises the work has already assumed (a different kind of historical truth-claim). If the work, however, were conceptually and rhetorically disentangled from ideas of textual origin, the production emphasis might shift from issues surrounding mediations of (a) *past* moment(s) of work production to consideration of the work's *ongoing* development and editors' active contribution to its formation.

This would be to release editorial practice from imperatives to represent in new editions of the works reconstructions of the past. Constructing the work through textual appeals to early modern history is just one possible editorial procedure – even if, at the moment, this procedure 'continues to be accorded all the incontrovertibility of the obvious'.[63] It would be to create ideological space for, and moreover to encourage, forms of culturally engaged editorial practices such as the sorts of feminist intervention posited by Valerie Wayne, for example, when she argues for emending the speech prefixes in Middleton's *A Trick to Catch the Old One* in order to interpolate a name (Jane) for the character known generically as 'Courtesan', or by Barbara Hodgdon when she considers including in her edition of *Taming of the Shrew* a cue for Katherina and Petruchio to exit the final scene separately rather than together.[64] Disentangling text and work also helps to make sense of Ronald Tumelson's provocative argument that, despite evidence amassed by Peter Blayney that seemingly variant readings in some copies of the Folio result from a piece of type deteriorating during the book's printing, Ferdinand will continue to admire his 'wife' *and* praise Prospero as 'wise'.[65] Reflecting on the passage's 'multi-lexicality' both in the critical and editorial traditions and in readings of certain copies of the Folio, Tumelson proposes to 'allow the presence of both readings not only to tempt us from the Eden desired by textual critics but also to haunt our editions and interpretations of the play', a haunting that he shows has long been firmly in place.[66] In terms of the difficult question of print stagings and the integration of performance studies into editorial production, an emphasis on the work as process might embolden editors to introduce production strategies able to stimulate different sorts of readerly engagements with a wide variety of theatrical grammars.[67] In short, to resist the dominant inclination to regard past histories as foundational to editorial labour would be to insist on the realization that textual, no less than theatrical, efforts to recover 'what happened' can only be pursued alongside efforts to shape 'what *is* happening' in terms of work recognition and the ever-shifting boundaries that separate work from adaptation.

Notes

Introduction: the problem of adaptation

1 'A prince among Hamlets: five of *Hamlet*'s admirers select the greatest Danes they have seen', *Times Supplement (The Knowledge)*, 18 February 2006.
2 David Nathan, *Jewish Chronicle*, 16 May 1997, quoted in *Theatre Record*, 7–20 May 1997.
3 Nicholas de Jongh, *Evening Standard*, 9 May 1997, quoted in *Theatre Record*, 7–20 May 1997; Charles Spencer, 'In short, it's Hamlet Lite', *Daily Telegraph*, 12 May 1997.
4 Alex Jennings quoted in Robert Hanks, 'Fellow of infinite jest?', *Independent*, 30 April 1997.
5 This position is discussed at length in Chapter 1.
6 See also Cary Mazer's discussion of the dynamic interplay between the creativities of author and theatre practitioners in 'Not Not Shakespeare: Directorial Adaptation, Authorship, and Ownership'. Mazer unpacks the peculiar issues of ownership and copyright law raised by Joe Calarco's *Shakespeare's R&J*, a legally recognized original work by Calarco that only includes dialogue written by Shakespeare (*Shakespeare Bulletin* 23 (2005): 23–42).
7 Ruby Cohn, *Modern Shakespeare Offshoots* (Princeton, NJ: Princeton University Press, 1976), pp. 3–4.
8 Linda Hutcheon, *A Theory of Adaptation* (London: Routledge, 2006), p. 8.
9 Hutcheon, *A Theory of Adaptation*, p. 9. See also Gérard Genette, *Palimpsests: Literature in the Second Degree* [1982], trans. Channa Newman and Claude Doubinsky (Lincoln, NA: University of Nebraska Press, 1997).
10 Julie Sanders, *Adaptation and Appropriation* (London: Routledge, 2006), p. 62.
11 Sarah Cardwell, *Adaptation Revisited: Television and the Classic Novel* (Manchester: Manchester University Press, 2002), p. 67.
12 *Adaptations of Shakespeare: A Critical Anthology of Plays from the Seventeenth Century to the Present*, ed. Daniel Fischlin and Mark Fortier (London: Routledge, 2000), p. 3.
13 *Adaptations of Shakespeare*, ed. Fischlin and Fortier, p. 17.
14 Cardwell, *Adaptation Revisited*, p. 18.
15 *Adaptations of Shakespeare*, ed. Fischlin and Fortier, p. 7.
16 Hutcheon, *A Theory of Adaptation*, p. 39.
17 The continued currency of such debates is suggested by a recent exchange between R. A. Foakes and W. B. Worthen concerning the supposed meanings of Shakespeare's texts, theatrical production, and the interpretative strategies

of performance theory. See R. A. Foakes, 'Performance Theory and Textual Theory: A Retort Courteous', *Shakespeare* 2:1 (2006): 47–58, and W. B. Worthen, 'Texts, Tools, and Technologies of Performance: A Quip Modest, in Response to R. A. Foakes', *Shakespeare* 2:2 (2006): 208–19.

1 Surviving performance: Shakespeare's contested works

1 James McLaverty, 'The Mode of Existence of Literary Works of Art: The Case of the *Dunciad* Variorum', *Studies in Bibliography* 37 (1984): 82–105, p. 82.

2 Bateson's specific target was Fredson Bowers and his optimistic claim to have proven 'on physical evidence not subject to opinion' that Shakespeare wrote 'sallied', rather than 'sullied' or 'solid', flesh. See F. W. Bateson, 'Modern Bibliography and the Literary Artifact', *English Studies Today*, 2nd ser., ed. G. A. Bonnard (Bern: Francke Verlag, 1961), pp. 67–77.

3 Bateson, 'Modern Bibliography', p. 74.

4 Bateson, 'Modern Bibliography', p. 72.

5 Bateson, 'Modern Bibliography', p. 74. Richard Wollheim characterizes the Idealist theory at the heart of Bateson's approach in three propositions: 'First, that the work of art consists in an inner state or condition of the artist, called an intuition or an expression: secondly, that this state is not immediate or given, but is the product of a process, which is peculiar to the artist, and which involves articulation, organization, and unification: thirdly, that the intuition so developed may be externalized in a public form, in which case we have the artifact which is often but wrongly taken to be the work of art' (*Art and Its Objects* (Harmondsworth: Penguin, 1968), pp. 52–3).

6 Jerome J. McGann, *The Textual Condition* (Princeton, NJ: Princeton University Press, 1991), p. 81.

7 McLaverty, 'The Mode of Existence', p. 105.

8 McLaverty, 'The Mode of Existence', p. 82.

9 McLaverty, however, to a much greater extent than either McGann or D. F. McKenzie, remains invested in the importance of authorial intentions, arguing that presentational features such as typeface and layout are important not because one wishes to include in modern editions non-authorial material, but because authors deliberately use such features of the book to generate particular effects ('The Concept of Authorial Intention in Textual Criticism', *The Library*, 6th ser., 6 (1984): 121–38, p. 131).

10 For a critique of the ideological and interpretatively limiting implications of editorial practice, see Alan C. Dessen, *Recovering Shakespeare's Theatrical Vocabulary* (Cambridge: Cambridge University Press, 1995); Margaret Jane Kidnie, 'Text, Performance, and the Editors: Staging Shakespeare's Drama', *Shakespeare Quarterly* 51 (2000): 456–73; Leah S. Marcus, *Unediting the Renaissance: Shakespeare, Marlowe, Milton* (London: Routledge, 1996); Randall McLeod [Random Clod], 'Information upon Information', *Text* 5 (1991): 241–81; Stephen Orgel, *The Authentic Shakespeare and Other Problems of the Early Modern Stage* (London: Routledge, 2002), esp. pp. 1–5 and 15–20.

11 Orgel, *The Authentic Shakespeare*, p. 16. See also David Scott Kastan, *Shakespeare and the Book* (Cambridge: Cambridge University Press, 2001); McLeod, 'Information upon Information'; Marcus, *Unediting the Renaissance*; Margreta de Grazia and Peter Stallybrass, 'The Materiality of the Shakespearean Text', *Shakespeare Quarterly* 44 (1993): 255–83.

12 See, for example, Edward Pechter's reservations about claims that 'materiality' will revolutionize literary studies in 'Making Love to Our Employment; Or, the Immateriality of Arguments about the Materiality of the Shakespearean Text', *Textual Practice* 11 (1997): 51–67. Pechter's article led to a flurry of rejoinders, including Margreta de Grazia and Peter Stallybrass, 'Love among the Ruins: Response to Pechter', *Textual Practice* 11 (1997): 69–79; Graham Holderness, Bryan Loughrey, and Andrew Murphy, 'Busy Doing Nothing: A Response to Edward Pechter', *Textual Practice* 11 (1997): 81–87; Pechter, 'All You Need Is Love (Dah Dahdah Dahdah): A Response to Margreta de Grazia, Peter Stallybrass, Graham Holderness, Bryan Loughrey and Andrew Murphy', *Textual Practice* 11 (1997): 331–4.

13 D. C. Greetham highlights the practical problems presented by a sociology of text in *Theories of the Text* (Oxford: Oxford University Press, 1999), pp. 45–7; Paul Eggert, in 'Document and Text: The "Life" of the Literary Work and the Capacities of Editing', more emphatically suggests that McGann has a theory of textual production but not an editorial rationale, arguing that a sociology of text logically disables any form of editorial practice (*Text* 7 (1994): 1–24, p. 16). In 'The Editorial Problem of Final Authorial Intention', G. Thomas Tanselle distinguishes between the types of editorial methodology suitable for 'historical document[s]' and 'a work of literary art': whereas 'an exact transcript' is often desirable for the former, in the latter case only a clear reading text 'can represent (or attempt to represent) the author's intention' (*Selected Studies in Bibliography* (Charlottesville, VA: University Press of Virginia, 1979), pp. 309–53, pp. 347–8). Henry Woudhuysen offers an excellent discussion of some of these competing editorial priorities with particular reference to facsimile reproductions in '"Work of Permanent Utility": Editors and Texts, Authorities and Originals', in *Textual Performances: The Modern Reproduction of Shakespeare's Drama*, ed. Lukas Erne and Margaret Jane Kidnie (Cambridge: Cambridge University Press, 2004), pp. 37–48. On facsimile reproduction as a form of editorial mediation of the artifact, and its problems, see Eggert, 'Document and Text', pp. 19–20; G. Thomas Tanselle, *A Rationale of Textual Criticism* (Philadelphia, PA: University of Pennsylvania Press, 1989), p. 54; Woudhuysen, '"Work of Permanent Utility"', pp. 37–8, 45–7.

14 Nelson Goodman, *Languages of Art: An Approach to a Theory of Symbols*, 2nd edn (Indianapolis and Cambridge: Hackett Publishing Company, 1976), p. 113.

15 Goodman, *Languages of Art*, p. 116.

16 Goodman, *Languages of Art*, pp. 115–16.

17 John Carey, *What Good Are the Arts?* (London: Faber and Faber, 2005), p. 245.

18 Goodman, *Languages of Art*, p. 122.

19 This extends Goodman's discussion of musical composition (pp. 113–14) to drama.

20 Goodman, *Languages of Art*, p. 178.

21 Goodman, *Languages of Art*, p. 186.

22 Jenefer Robinson, 'Languages of Art at the Turn of the Century', *The Journal of Aesthetics and Art Criticism* 58 (2000): 213–18, p. 217.

23 Goodman, *Languages of Art*, pp. 186–7.

24 W. W. Greg, 'The Rationale of Copy-Text', *Studies in Bibliography* 3 (1950): 19–36. See also Tanselle, 'Editorial Problem', for a summary of how intentionality bears on eclectic editing (pp. 309–10).

25 The textual dilemmas presented here have been summarized from instances cited by Tanselle in 'Editorial Problem'. These sorts of questions characterize

debates at the heart of textual scholarship and are the subject of an extensive literature. Some of the more influential statements include Greetham, *Theories*; Jerome J. McGann, *A Critique of Modern Textual Criticism* (Charlottesville, VA: University Press of Virginia, 1992); McLaverty, 'Concept'; Peter L. Shillingsburg, 'Text as Matter, Concept, and Action', *Studies in Bibliography* 44 (1991): 31–82; Hans Zeller, 'A New Approach to the Critical Constitution of Literary Texts', *Studies in Bibliography* 28 (1975): 231–64. John Bryant presents an abstract model of the work as an 'ontology of process' that tracks the dynamic relations among textual versions and adaptations in *The Fluid Text: A Theory of Revision and Editing for Book and Screen* (Ann Arbor, MI: University of Michigan Press, 2002, p. 61). However, for Bryant and as distinct from my argument for the work as process, 'the original text' as defined by authorial intentions remains firmly distinguished from subsequent 'cultural revision or adaptation' (p. 110), his model thus returning to a conception of authority already familiar from the essays, for instance, of Tanselle.

26 Michael D. Friedman, 'In Defense of Authenticity', *Studies in Philology* 99 (2002): 33–56, p. 39.
27 Wollheim, *Art and Its Objects*, p. 91.
28 Wollheim, *Art and Its Objects*, p. 21.
29 Wollheim, *Art and Its Objects*, p. 94.
30 As Wollheim is careful to insist, 'there is nothing that can be predicated of a performance of a piece of music [i.e., the token] that could not also be predicated of that piece of music itself [i.e., the type]. This point is vital' (97–8).
31 Wollheim, *Art and Its Objects*, p. 98.
32 Wollheim, *Art and Its Objects*, p. 98.
33 Wollheim controversially extends this discussion to criticism: what performance interpretation brings to drama, critical interpretation brings to art as various as drama, novels and paintings (*Art and Its Objects*, pp. 100–7). In all of these cases, interpretation has the potential to transform one's perception of the work of art. A later generation's changed estimation of the brushwork of Titian and Velázquez, for example, brings 'hitherto extraneous' details of the work within an understanding of its aesthetics; likewise, a perception of Iago's 'homosexuality', 'not open to earlier generations', suddenly comes to play a role in the structure of *Othello* (pp. 104–5). The position that criticism shapes meaning and that every age will reinvent Shakespeare's plays in its own likeness is familiar (see especially Gary Taylor, *Reinventing Shakespeare: A Cultural History from the Restoration to the Present* (London: Vintage, 1991), and Terence Hawkes, *Meaning by Shakespeare* (London: Routledge, 1992)). However, to draw a formal equation between theatrical performance and critical analysis seems problematic. Critics since Wollheim have sometimes drawn on the position in an effort to free theatre from an injunction to reproduce faithfully the supposed 'truth' of the text, arguing that the meaning of the text in performance is as varied as its meaning in essays and books (see Barbara Hodgdon, 'Parallel Practices, or the *Un*-Necessary Difference', *The Kenyon Review* 7:3 (1985): 57–65, and David McCandless, *Gender and Performance in Shakespeare's Problem Comedies* (Bloomington and Indianapolis, IN: Indiana University Press, 1997)). While I have sympathy with the desire to release performance from narrow text-based definitions of 'authentic' representation, this construction of the work seems self-defeating, since it establishes an implicit hierarchy in which the work-as-text is prioritized as origin over its derivative (critical/theatrical)

expressions. This undercuts, as does Wollheim, precisely what makes the dramatic work different from the work of literature – its peculiar ability to exist simultaneously in the distinct media of text and performance.

34 Wollheim, *Art and Its Objects*, p. 97.

35 Wollheim, *Art and Its Objects*, p. 95.

36 Michael Bristol and Kathleen McLuskie, with Christopher Holmes, eds, *Shakespeare and Modern Theatre: The Performance of Modernity* (London: Routledge, 2001), p. 1.

37 Thomas Clayton, 'Theatrical Shakespearegresses at the Guthrie and Elsewhere: Notes on "Legitimate Production"', *New Literary History* 17 (1986): 511–38, p. 519; John Russell Brown, 'Free Shakespeare', *Shakespeare Survey* 24 (1971): 127–35, p. 133.

38 Greetham, *Theories*, p. 35.

39 Clayton, 'Theatrical Shakespearegresses', pp. 529, 536. The next quotation is from Thomas Clayton, '"Balancing at Work": (R)evoking the Script in Performance and Criticism', in *Shakespeare and the Sense of Performance: Essays in the Tradition of Performance Criticism in Honor of Bernard Beckerman*, ed. Marvin and Ruth Thompson (Newark, DE: University of Delaware Press, 1989), pp. 228–49, pp. 235–6.

40 Jay L. Halio, *Understanding Shakespeare's Plays in Performance* (Manchester: Manchester University Press, 1988), pp. 29–30.

41 Friedman, 'In Defense of Authenticity', p. 38, and Richard Hornby, *Script into Performance: A Structuralist View of Play Production* (Austin and London: University of Texas Press, 1977), p. 107, emphasis in originals.

42 Goodman, *Languages of Art*, pp. 186–7.

43 See, for example, Goodman, *Languages of Art*, pp. 177–221; Joseph Margolis, *Art and Philosophy* (Brighton: Harvester Press, 1980), pp. 118–19; Wollheim, *Art and Its Objects*, pp. 97–103.

44 McCandless, *Gender and Performance*, p. 8.

45 Clayton, 'Theatrical Shakespearegresses', p. 517.

46 Friedman, 'In Defense of Authenticity', p. 53.

47 Anthony Grafton, *Forgers and Critics: Creativity and Duplicity in Western Scholarship* (Princeton, NJ: Princeton University Press, 1990), p. 126.

48 Grafton, *Forgers and Critics*, p. 127.

49 See for instance, Russ McDonald's implicit critique of students' use of such series as comparable to eating the menu and not the food in a great restaurant in 'Planned Obsolescence or Working at the Words', in *Teaching Shakespeare: Passing It On*, edited G. B. Shand (Chichester: Wiley-Blackwell, 2009), pp. 25–42, p. 41. *1 Henry IV*, ed. Alan Durband, Shakespeare Made Easy (New York: Baron's Educational Series, 1985).

50 *The Taming of the Shrew*, ed. G. R. Hibbard (London: Penguin, 1968); *The Taming of the Shrew*, ed. Ann Thompson (Cambridge: Cambridge University Press, 1984); *The Taming of the Shrew*, ed. H. J. Oliver (Oxford: Oxford University Press, 1982); *The Taming of the Shrew*, ed. Brian Morris (London: Methuen, 1981).

51 *The First Quarto of Othello*, ed. Scott McMillan, New Cambridge Shakespeare – The Early Quartos (Cambridge: Cambridge University Press, 2001).

52 Greetham, *Theories*, p. 35.

53 Joseph Grigely, *Textualterity: Art, Theory, and Textual Criticism* (Ann Arbor: University of Michigan Press, 1995), p. 110.

54 Jorge Luis Borges, 'Pierre Menard, Author of the *Quixote*', *Labyrinths: Selected Stories and Other Writings*, ed. Donald A. Yates and James E. Irby, Preface by André Maurois (London: Penguin, 1970), pp. 62–71. Grigely's discussion is indebted to Arthur C. Danto's now classic aesthetic analysis of this story, especially to his insight that 'works are in part constituted by their location in the history of literature as well as by their relationships to their authors, and these are often dismissed by critics who urge us to pay attention to the work itself'. See Arthur C. Danto, *The Transfiguration of the Commonplace: A Philosophy of Art* (Cambridge, MA: Harvard University Press, 1981), esp. pp. 35–6.

55 Grigely, *Textualterity*, p. 99.

56 Grigely, *Textualterity*, pp. 94–5.

57 Grigely, *Textualterity*, p. 100.

58 'What is important about such formulas is that they remind us we do not normally conceive a book in terms of itself as a work, but in terms of its texts, or in any case the specific texts with which we have had encounters … If then we consider a work as a nontangible idea represented by a sequential series of texts – whether these texts are inscribed or performed, whether they are authorized or not – then we might be able to make more out of Goodman's original question [about forgery]' (*Textualterity*, pp. 100–1).

59 Grigely, *Textualterity*, p. 99.

60 Grigely, *Textualterity*, p. 119.

61 Grigely, *Textualterity*, p. 110, his emphasis.

62 Wollheim, *Art and Its Objects*, p. 25.

63 Grigely, *Textualterity*, p. 119.

64 Susan Wilsmore, 'The Literary Work Is Not Its Text', *Philosophy and Literature* 11 (1987), p. 309.

65 See Roland Barthes, 'The Death of the Author', trans. Geoff Bennington, in *Modern Criticism and Theory: A Reader*, ed. David Lodge (Harlow: Longman, 1988, repr. 1996), pp. 167–72, and 'From Work to Text', trans. S. Heath, in *Modern Literary Theory: A Reader*, ed. Philip Rice and Patricia Waugh, 3rd edn (London: Arnold, 1996), pp. 191–7.

66 Stanley Wells and Gary Taylor with John Jowett and William Montgomery, eds, *William Shakespeare: The Complete Works* (Oxford: Clarendon Press, 1986), p. xxxvii.

67 Kastan, *Shakespeare and the Book*, p. 3, and Chapter 1.

68 Grigely, *Textualterity*, p. 89.

69 Wilsmore, 'The Literary Work Is Not Its Text', p. 307.

2 Defining the work through production, or what adaptation is not

1 When exactly a literary or dramatic work should be considered finished is a question closely tied to the theoretical problems associated with versions, and is the subject of an extensive body of literature. See, for example, Hershel Parker, 'The Text Itself – Whatever That Is', *Text* 3 (1987): 47–54; James Thorpe, *Principles of Textual Criticism* (San Marino: Huntington Library, 1972); Jerome J. McGann, *A Critique of Modern Textual Criticism* (Charlottesville and London: University Press of Virginia, 1992); G. Thomas Tanselle, 'The Editorial Problem of Final Authorial Intention', *Selected Studies in Bibliography* (Charlottesville: University Press of Virginia, 1979), pp. 309–53.

2 Examples of the latter practice, where workshopped or devised theatre led to texts that could serve as the basis for subsequent performance, include plays

'by' Caryl Churchill, Complicite Theatre, and Robert Lepage, whose *Elsinore* was published in *Canadian Theatre Review*. The fluidity between text and performance becomes more visible with the advent of new technologies; Andy Lavender, for example, notes that when Lepage's one-man show *Needles and Opium* was remounted by an Italian company, Lepage relied on video recordings as 'the final authority for restaging' (*Hamlet in Pieces: Shakespeare Reworked by Peter Brook, Robert Lepage, Robert Wilson* (London: Nick Hern Books, 2001), p. 135).

3 Brian Vickers, for example, invokes as a criticism of the second edition of the Oxford *Complete Works* a 'growing consensus' that 'the variations between the two texts [of *King Lear*] are not so great as to constitute two separate plays; that the alterations are theatrical, not authorial; and that the play loses more than it gains' ('By other hands', *Times Literary Supplement*, 11 August 2006, pp. 10–12, p. 12).

4 Vickers is thus engaged with the Oxford editors in a debate about the boundaries of the work that cannot be finally won or lost. The perceived shape of the work – whether, for instance, one sees in the texts of *King Lear* a single unity or multiple versions – rests not on facts and evidence, but on critical judgement as informed by ideological and aesthetic considerations of interpretation. Indeed it is the need to persuade, as opposed to an ability finally to prove, that perhaps accounts for the polemical tone in which competing arguments about versions are frequently conducted – falling foul of the faults of character he holds up for reproof, Vickers, for example, vilifies Gary Taylor for being sarcastic, proud, and employing a style of argumentation that marks a return to the 'adversarial rhetoric' and 'vicious *ad hominem* attacks' of eighteenth-century scholarship.

5 Ralph Berry, *On Directing Shakespeare: Interviews with Contemporary Directors* (London: Croom Helm, 1977), p. 71. Quoted in Halio, *Understanding Shakespeare's Plays*, p. 12.

6 Peter Hall, *Peter Hall's Diaries*, ed. John Goodwin (London: Hamish Hamilton, 1983), pp. 177, 254, and Stanley Wells, *Royal Shakespeare* (Manchester: Manchester University Press, 1977), p. 9; both are quoted in Eric Rasmussen, 'The Revision of Scripts', in *A New History of Early English Drama*, ed. John D. Cox and David Scott Kastan (New York: Columbia University Press, 1997), pp. 441–60, p. 445.

7 Warchus in interview with Rupert Christiansen ('Art for theatre's sake', *Daily Telegraph*, 11 October 1996).

8 Doran cut the short scene in which the Duke of Florence justifies to the Dumaine brothers his cause for war (3.1).

9 Robert Smallwood, 'Shakespeare Performances in England, 1997', *Shakespeare Survey* 51 (1998): 219–55, p. 242.

10 Georgina Brown, 'Shakespeare in the cold light of day', *Mail on Sunday Review*, 1 June 1997; Robert Gore-Langton, *Express*, 15 May 1997, quoted in *Theatre Record*, 7–20 May 1997; Michael Billington, 'Get shorter', *Guardian*, 10 May 1997.

11 'Bravado' is the term used by Andrew Billen, 'So Hamlet drops the bullets from the gun. Then he gets the giggles', *Observer Review*, 11 May 1997; the other quotations are from John Peter, *Sunday Times*, 18 May 1997, quoted in *Theatre Record*, 7–20 May 1997.

12 Gore-Langton, *Express*.

13 Ann O'Bryan, *Hamlet, A CurtainUp Review*, 2 January 1998, and Lyn Gardner, 'Ban the bard', *Guardian*, 8 May 1997, allude to what they expect will be the outrage of 'purists'.

14 This soliloquy is not printed in the Folio; some modern editions based on the Folio include it as an appendix (see, especially, *William Shakespeare: The Complete Works*, ed. Stanley Wells and Gary Taylor with John Jowett and William Montgomery (Oxford: Oxford University Press, 1986), and *Hamlet*, ed. G. R. Hibbard (Oxford: Oxford University Press, 1987)).

15 Alex Jennings interviewed by John Morrish, 'To be the Prince at last', *Sunday Telegraph*, 27 April 1997. On the production's naturalism, see Kate Bassett, 'From Elsinore to a Spanish court', *Daily Telegraph*, 10 December 1997; Alastair Macaulay, *Financial Times*, 14 May 1997, quoted in *Theatre Record*, 7–20 May 1997; Benedict Nightingale, 'Cuts that forget the play's the thing', *Times*, 6 December 1997; James Treadwell, *Spectator*, 17 May 1997, quoted in *Theatre Record*, 7–20 May 1997.

16 'Hamlet as domestic drama', *Daily Mail*, 6 December 1997.

17 *Hamlet*, dir. Matthew Warchus, 1997, Promptbook, Royal Shakespeare Company archives, Shakespeare Centre Library, Stratford-upon-Avon, England, first performance 8 May 1997.

18 *Hamlet*, dir. Warchus, Promptbook.

19 *Henry V*, dir. Kenneth Branagh (1989); *Hamlet*, dir. Kenneth Branagh (1996).

20 Quoted in Christiansen, 'Art for theatre's sake'.

21 Jennings interviewed by Morrish, 'To be the Prince at last': 'The rehearsals have reached an interesting stage. "We are giving up fighting for lines that have been cut," [Jennings] says, laughing. And cut they certainly have been. "Oh yes, heftily. It's short and modern ... and hopefully sweet. And very intelligently done, I think. But I would quite like to say, 'O, that this too too solid flesh would melt ... '"' (ellipses in original). Jennings also mentions the omission of the opening of this soliloquy in his interview with Robert Hanks ('Fellow of infinite jest?', *Independent*, 30 April 1997).

22 John Gross, *Sunday Telegraph*, 11 May 1997, quoted in *Theatre Record*, 7–20 May 1997.

23 Matthew Warchus interviewed by Gardner, 'Ban the Bard'.

24 Robert Butler, for example, notes: 'You can tell something is up from the entries in the programme ... Hang on, you think: what children, what party, what film sequence? They were never in my edition' ('Warchus puts his Art into his Hamlet', *Independent on Sunday*, 11 May 1997).

25 Alan Dessen instead interprets this credit as evidence of adaptation, and offers a short summary of how Warchus conflated, departed from, and supplemented the early texts (*Rescripting Shakespeare: The Text, the Director, and Modern Productions* (Cambridge: Cambridge University Press, 2002), pp. 16–17).

26 Programme, *Hamlet*, dir. Matthew Warchus, Royal Shakespeare Company, first performance 8 May 1997.

27 Programme, *Hamlet*, dir. Warchus.

28 Gross, *Sunday Telegraph*.

29 For discussion of the play's stage traditions, including choices made by Forbes-Robertson, see *Hamlet*, ed. Robert Hapgood, Shakespeare in Production (Cambridge: Cambridge University Press, 1999), pp. 7, 44.

30 Hapgood, pp. 74–5; Michael Billington, *Guardian*, 21 November 1989, cited in Hapgood, p. 75.

31 Lloyd Rose, '"Hamlet," Cut to the Quick', *Washington Post*, 12 June 1998; Benedict Nightingale, *Times*, 10 May 1997, quoted in *Theatre Record*, 7–20 May 1997.

32 For discussion of Eyre's production as 'bristl[ing] with intelligence and good ideas', 'tremendous', 'thoroughly sensible and thoroughly alive', see Michael Billington, 'Human Prince', *Guardian*, 5 April 1980; James Fenton, 'A tremendous "Hamlet"', *Sunday Times*, 6 April 1980; Robert Cushman, 'On the razor's edge', *Observer*, 6 April 1980. Benedict Nightingale, naming his top ten actors in the role in 2008, ranks Jonathan Pryce's performance in third spot ('Some day my Prince will come', *Times*, 18 February 2008).

33 J. C. Trewin, *Five and Eighty Hamlets* (London: Century Hutchinson, 1987), p. 168.

34 Programme notes, *Hamlet*, dir. Adrian Noble, Royal Shakespeare Company, first performance 12 December 1992.

35 Anthony B. Dawson, *Hamlet*, Shakespeare in Performance (Manchester: Manchester University Press, 1995), p. 12. Dawson provides an illuminating discussion of the Noble/Branagh production, especially in terms of the cultural status it assumed in Britain. The production was based on the edition prepared by Philip Edwards (Cambridge: Cambridge University Press, 1985); ironically, Edwards' introductory material was cited to support textual indeterminacy in the programme for the Warchus production.

36 *Hamlet*, dir. Noble, Programme, 1992.

37 'Wot – No More Shakespeare?', published Roundtable Discussion with Michael Billington, Matthew Warchus, Cicely Berry, Stephen Poliakoff, Simon Reade, and members of the audience, *RSC Magazine* (Summer 1998): 8–9, p. 8. Warchus was clarifying in a roundtable discussion hosted by the RSC what he said to reporters prior to the show's opening (see Gardner, 'Ban the bard').

38 Nightingale, for instance, warns readers not to expect to hear '"oh that this too too solid flesh would melt" or "bid the soldiers shoot" or many a famous and important line in between. Warchus injects a spurious episode in which Derbhle Crotty's Ophelia sends Hamlet back his letters and, shirt open, he bangs despairingly at her door, and another in which Diana Quick's Gertrude, having been read Hamlet's account of his adventures at sea, tells Horatio to "commend a mother's care to him". Yet poor Jennings does not even get the chance to deliver the great soliloquy that begins "how all occasions do inform against me"' ('Cuts that forget the play's the thing'). Gross, commenting on the opening moments, argues that this is an interpretation 'we could none the less live with if it were *just* a cut, or if we felt that the director, Matthew Warchus, was putting something commensurate in its place. What we actually get is Claudius booming out his opening speech from somewhere in the wings, while a home movie of Hamlet's happy childhood is projected on to a screen at the back of the stage. It isn't an obvious improvement on the original' (*Sunday Telegraph*, 11 May 1997).

39 As Noël Carroll explains the relation in an analysis of mass media explicitly indebted to Wollheim's type–token thesis, making theatre is like following a 'recipe' – another commonplace metaphor figures the work as a 'blueprint' for production. See Noël Carroll, *A Philosophy of Mass Art* (Oxford: Clarendon, 1998), pp. 211–12 and footnotes 47–8.

40 Rose, '"Hamlet"'.

41 Michael Coveney, 'The RSC is suffering', *New Statesman*, vol. 127, 10 April 1998; Nightingale, *Times*, 10 May 1997.

42 See, for example, Howard Feinstein, 'Wherefore art thou Leonardo?', *Guardian*, 6 December 1996, and 'Life's a beach, and then you die', *Evening Standard*, 27 March 1997; Geoff Brown, 'Cooler Shakespeare', *Times*, 27 March 1997; Derek Malcolm, 'Romeo and Juliet: Bard's in the 'hood', *Guardian*, 28 March 1997.

43 *Hamlet* is described in the same interview as 'paying homage' to Luhrmann's achievement (see Jasper Rees, 'A cut above the rest', *Independent on Sunday*, 27 April 1997). Luhrmann's *Romeo + Juliet* was released in the United States on 5 November 1996, about seven weeks before Branagh's film *Hamlet*, and in Britain on 28 March 1997.

44 Billington, 'Get shorter'; Brown, 'Shakespeare in the cold light of day'.

45 Alan Riding, 'The Royal Shakespeare: renewing itself under fire', *New York Times*, 17 May 1998.

46 Macaulay, *Financial Times*; LG, 'Hamlet, RSC, Main Theatre, Stratford', *Stratford-upon-Avon Journal*, 22 May 1997. The phrase 'Shakespeare Lite' in the next sentence is adapted from Charles Spencer's description of the Warchus production as 'Hamlet Lite' ('In short, it's Hamlet Lite', *Daily Telegraph*, 12 May 1997).

47 'Wot – No More Shakespeare?', p. 8.

48 Gardner, 'Ban the bard'. Warchus shot to fame with acclaimed RSC productions of *Henry V* and Jonson's *Devil Is an Ass* in 1995–6, and he was returning to the company from London's West End, where he had just directed Tom Courteney and Albert Finney in Yasmina Reza's *Art*, a play that won the Olivier Award for Best Comedy in 1996 before transferring to Broadway.

49 'Shakespeare fatigue' is Riding's term, and he describes it as a 'trendy topic for debate' ('The Royal Shakespeare').

50 John Gross, 'New-minted Moor', *Sunday Telegraph*, 22 February 2004.

51 Charles Spencer, 'Dench delivers a perfect farewell', *Daily Telegraph*, 21 February 2004.

52 Dench had acted more recently with the RSC in London-based productions such as Bertolt Brecht's *Mother Courage* (1984) and Peter Shaffer's *The Gift of the Gorgon* (1993), but her prior appearance onstage in Stratford-upon-Avon dates to her performance of Lady Macbeth opposite Ian McKellan in 1977.

53 Michael Billington, 'All's Well That Ends Well', *Guardian*, 21 February 2004.

54 The quotation is from Spencer, 'Dench delivers'. Those who emphasized the ambiguity of the closing moments included Ian Johns, 'Of trysts and mellow fruitfulness', *Times*, 21 February 2004, and Paul Taylor, 'There is nothing like a dame', *Independent Review*, 15 December 2003.

55 William P. Halstead documents changes made to the text of *All's Well* in twenty-seven copies dating from Bell's acting edition of 1773 to Jon Jory's Oregon Shakespeare Festival promptbook of 1975. See William Halstead, *Shakespeare as Spoken: A Collation of 5000 Acting Editions and Promptbooks of Shakespeare*, 14 vols (Ann Arbor, MI: Published for American Theatre Association by University Microfilms International, 1977–83), Vol. 4: *The Taming of the Shrew, All's Well That Ends Well, Twelfth Night* (1979).

56 *All's Well that Ends Well*, dir. Greg Doran, Promptbook, Royal Shakespeare Company archive, Shakespeare Centre, Stratford-upon-Avon, first performance 11 December 2003.

57 Colin Chambers, *Inside the Royal Shakespeare Company* (London: Routledge, 2004), p. 91.

58 The adjective 'humane' was applied to the production by Gross, 'New-minted Moor'; Johns, 'Of trysts and mellow fruitfulness'; Kate Bassett, 'Beauties and beasts – and a morris dance', *Independent on Sunday*, 14 December 2003.

59 Shakespeare, *All's Well That Ends Well*, in *The Complete Works*, ed. Wells *et al.*, 3.2.28.

60 The speech comes at 1.3.124–32. Doran discusses it in terms of the play's potential biographical links to Shakespeare's life in an article published in the *Guardian* that eventually appeared in slightly revised form in the production's programme.

61 John Peter, 'That's moor like it', *Sunday Times*, 29 February 2004.

62 Rhoda Koenig, 'All's Well That Ends Well', *Independent Review*, 24 February 2004; Spencer, 'Dench delivers'; Billington, 'All's Well'; Benedict Nightingale, 'Dame, set and match to Judi Dench', *Times*, 13 December 2003.

63 Spencer, 'Dench delivers'; Billington, 'All's Well'.

64 Duncan Smith, 'Dame back at RSC after 25 years away', *Stratford-upon-Avon Herald*, 11 December 2003, p. 7.

65 Only one review of *All's Well*, Gross's 'New-minted Moor', was accompanied by a photograph that was not of Judi Dench; published at the time of the London transfer, it featured instead a production photograph of Antony Sher as Iago from the other revival under discussion.

66 Nightingale, 'Dame, set and match'.

67 Matt Wolf, 'A widow of opportunity', *Sunday Telegraph*, 30 November 2003; Dench's ranking in the poll is reported in the same article.

68 Preston Witts, '"Cold feet" before the warmest of welcomes', *Stratford-upon-Avon Herald*, 5 February 2004; Smith, 'Dame back'.

69 'All's well as Dame Judi opens library', *Stratford-upon-Avon Journal*, 8 January 2004.

70 Wolf, 'A widow of opportunity'.

71 The announcement is reported in Fiachra Gibbons, 'RSC abandons its roots to lure stars', *Guardian*, 25 May 2001, and analysis of its implications began immediately. See Michael Billington, 'In a world of dazzle, beware a lost identity', *Guardian*, 25 May 2001, and Benedict Nightingale, 'All the world's a new stage', *Times*, 30 May 2001.

72 For a fuller account of the RSC season and how it was adapted during Noble's tenure as artistic director, see Chambers, *Inside the Royal Shakespeare Company*, pp. 96ff., and Steven Adler, *Rough Magic: Making Theatre at the Royal Shakespeare Company*, with a Foreword by Chris Parry (Carbondale and Edwardsville: Southern Illinois University Press, 2001), pp. 80–106.

73 That figure is cited in Jack Malvern, 'RSC plays to bypass London for first time', *Times*, 8 October 2003, and Fiachra Gibbons, 'Homeless RSC faces winter of discontent', *Guardian*, 8 October 2003. The transfer of the Jacobethan season was apparently only made possible through a 'last-minute plea' by Doran to Holt, who reportedly told him, 'I'm going to do it darling, because it's impossible' (James Christopher, '"The RSC made a mistake"', *Evening Standard*, 12 December 2002).

74 Malvern, 'RSC plays'; Gibbons reports complaints on Whatsonstage.com from cast members who perceive that their season was simply written off by senior management ('Homeless RSC').

75 Alison Roberts, 'Now we're much more nimble. We're fitter', *Evening Standard*, 27 February 2001.

76 Gibbons, 'RSC abandons its roots'.

77 Billington, 'In a world of dazzle'; Nightingale, 'All the world's a new stage'.

78 Roy Hattersley describes how 'loose talk from the RSC' about building a theatre village led to fears of the transformation of Stratford into a theme park: 'The critics' imaginary fears were confirmed when Kris Kliszewicz, a local businessman, announced that he intended to create "Tudor Stratford". Kliszewicz's only connection with the RSC is one meeting with the company, arranged (perhaps foolishly) "out of courtesy" [in January 2002]. But allegations of his involvement persist, prejudicing attempts to demonstrate the practical need for change' ('A sea of woes', *Guardian*, 7 October 2002).

79 See James Morrison, 'Once more unto the Barbican for RSC', *Independent on Sunday*, 13 January 2002, and Louise Jury, 'Financial drama at RSC eased as debts are reduced by half', *Independent*, 13 December 2003.

80 Lyn Gardner, 'Now buy the T-shirt … ', *Guardian*, 27 February 2001.

81 In separate articles published in *Shakespeare Quarterly*, Miriam Gilbert and Stanley Wells weigh up the reasons for, and implications of, Noble's model of change, arriving at quite different conclusions. See Miriam Gilbert, 'The Leasing-out of the RSC', *Shakespeare Quarterly* 53 (2002): 512–24, and Stanley Wells, 'Awaking Your Faith', *Shakespeare Quarterly* 53 (2002): 525–35.

82 Dalya Alberge, 'Cusack attacks "exclusivity" of British theatre', *Times*, 9 January 2002; see also 'MPs baulk at bill for RSC "village"', *Independent on Sunday*, 10 March 2002.

83 The allocation of Lottery money for the Stratford theatre redevelopment project was given initial conditional approval in mid-March 2002 (David Benedict, 'Is the RSC safe in his hands?', *Observer Review*, 31 March 2002).

84 See, for instance, the objections voiced by Peter Holland and Russell Jackson in Alexa Baracaia, 'RSC governor backs strike action', *Stage*, 6 September 2001, and Michael Dobson's description of the company as 'a subsidized conventional impresario' in 'Shakespeare Performances in England, 2001', *Shakespeare Survey* 55 (2002), 285–321, p. 285.

85 John Peter, 'Bloodbath at the RSC', *Sunday Times (Culture)*, 18 November 2001.

86 Michael Billington, 'Something rotten in Stratford', *Guardian*, 6 March 2002.

87 Sheridan Morley, 'Stratford's chaotic shambles', *Spectator*, 16 March 2002.

88 Quoted from the RSC mission statement that appeared at the front of the 2000 programmes.

89 James Morrison, 'RSC chief is wrong, say theatre knights', *Independent on Sunday*, 24 March 2002.

90 Billington, 'Something rotten'.

91 Kate Bassett, 'You guys moaned, but my changes are sound', *Independent on Sunday*, 18 February 2001.

92 Adrian Noble, 'We must reinvent theatre for a generation raised on television', *Independent*, 26 March 2002.

93 The *Henry VI* plays opened in Stratford after seventeen, rather than the usual twenty-one, weeks for rehearsal (Daniel Rosenthal, 'The power behind the throne', *Independent*, 13 December 2000), and the tetralogy closed in London on 26 May 2001.

94 Rhoda Koenig praises the 'clarity and intelligence' with which all the actors speak the verse ('A truly terrific history', *Independent*, 15 December 2000), while Charles Spencer says: 'The cast, often doubling their roles, achieve a superb sense of ensemble … It's a magnificent, ambitious event that … displays the

RSC at the very top of its game' ('Gripped by a 12-hour bloodfest', *Daily Telegraph*, 15 December 2000). Benedict Nightingale, arguing that this tetralogy defines 'This England' as 'one of the RSC's major landmarks', praises how Boyd has 'transformed his cast into a splendidly versatile ensemble' ('Power and the gory', *Times*, 27 April 2001).

95 Stanley Wells argues that even if The Other Place had been sold out during the highly acclaimed new work season of 2001 (box office receipts in fact averaged just over sixty per cent), 'every seat sold and paid for would have been subsidized to the tune of something like £50' ('Awaking Your Faith', p. 529).

96 See Adrian Noble, 'All's Well', *Guardian*, 3 October 2001; Gardner, 'Now buy the T-shirt …'; Bassett, 'You guys moaned'.

97 Dobson, 'Shakespeare Performances in England, 2001', p. 286; 'Brave new world', *Economist*, 1 December 2001; Billington, 'In a world of dazzle'.

98 Michael Billington, 'Not a crisis, but the curtain rising on a promising era', *Guardian*, 29 July 2003.

99 Peter, 'Bloodbath at the RSC'.

100 Dobson, 'Shakespeare Performances in England, 2001', p. 286; Michael Boyd, interviewed by Rupert Christiansen, 'Noble ambitions?', *Daily Telegraph*, 30 April 2002.

101 Noble, 'All's Well'.

102 Charles Spencer, 'The RSC's brave new world', *Daily Telegraph*, 22 September 2001.

103 Wells, 'Awaking Your Faith', p. 526.

104 Cordula Kempe noticed that Noble, in contrast to the previous year, did not mention it in his annual programme greeting ('The Royal Shakespeare Company and Its Future: A Submission' (October 2001), p. 6 (Shakespeare Institute Library, p/box 203)). The word's omission from the page explaining the company's history, goals, and future made headline news in 2002, when it was mentioned by Sam West while collecting an Olivier Award for *Hamlet* (Alexa Baracaia, 'West affirms RSC criticism', *Stage*, 14 February 2002); see also Dobson, 'Shakespeare Performances in England, 2001', p. 286. However, a review of programmes from 1985 shows that the term 'ensemble' was introduced as a feature of the story of the company as late as 2000. Although the following year the word disappears from the body of the article, the subheadline announces: 'The Royal Shakespeare Company is one of the world's best-known theatre ensembles'.

105 Peter Hall interviewed by Patrick Miles, 'Chekhov, Shakespeare, the Ensemble and the Company', *New Theatre Quarterly* 11 (1995): 203–10, p. 208.

106 Miles, 'Chekhov, Shakespeare, the Ensemble and the Company', pp. 205, 207.

107 Benedict Nightingale, 'Reduced Shakespeare Co', *Times*, 22 March 2002; Billington, 'Something rotten in Stratford'.

108 Jeremy Austin, 'Dench joins critics of RSC reform', *Stage*, 18 April 2002. Dench's letter is reproduced in full in Kempe, 'The Royal Shakespeare Company and Its Future'.

109 The RSC was given a rise of 5.5 per cent compared to hikes of 16.5 per cent and 34 per cent for the National and Donmar respectively. See Dalya Alberge, 'Paltry grant adds to RSC woes', *Times*, 26 March 2003, and David Lister, 'Another tragedy at the Royal Shakespeare Company', *Independent*, 29 March 2003.

110 David Smith, 'RSC battles to keep £13m grant as its crown slips', *Observer*, 16 November 2003. Smith prefaces the Hillier quotation with the comment: 'Some observers have already begun to "think the unthinkable". Last week, the London Assembly's culture, sport and tourism committee raised the once unimaginable question of what failings would cause the Arts Council to axe its £13.3 million grant to the RSC. Until recently £1.8m of that was conditional on a London presence. The council made clear it still expected the RSC to perform in London.' Kate Kellaway argues that the implication of comments on the RSC deficit by Nicola Thorold of the Arts Council 'is understood by all: the RSC's annual grant from the Arts Council of £13m must, this year, extend to include the capital ... If the RSC were to fail to find a London base by October 2004, the [London Assembly Culture Committee] would urge the Arts Council to review its funding arrangements' ('Where to be or not to be?', *Observer Review*, 11 January 2004).

111 Smith, 'RSC battles'.

112 Riding, 'The Royal Shakespeare'.

113 Simon Callow, 'Thrift, Horatio, thrift! And stuff the quality', *Independent (Weekend Review)*, 14 November 1998.

114 Coveney, 'The RSC is suffering'.

115 George Bernard Shaw, reviewing a production of *All's Well That Ends Well* by the Irving Dramatic Club, London, 2 February 1895. See *Shaw on Shakespeare: An Anthology of Bernard Shaw's Writings on the Plays and Production of Shakespeare*, ed. and with an introduction by Edwin Wilson (London: Cassell, 1962), p. 10.

116 David Maddox, 'Insiders head list for top RSC job', *Stratford-upon-Avon Herald*, 11 July 2002.

117 Peter, 'That's moor like it'. Two days later, looking forward to the summer programme, Jim Burke described the RSC as 'getting back to basics with a mouth-watering season of Shakespeare's grandest tragedies' ('Blockbusting Bard to triumph again', *Metro*, 2 March 2004). Before the show opened, Michael Billington characterized Boyd's leadership as a return 'to 1960s basics' ('Bold plans signal new era for Stratford', *Guardian*, 30 September 2003).

118 J. L. Styan, *All's Well That Ends Well*, Shakespeare in Performance (Manchester: Manchester University Press, 1984), p. 24. The pervasiveness of this advertisement is suggested by reviewers at the time of the London transfer who insist this is a strong company performance, not a star turn. Rhoda Koenig's description of Dench's face 'glower[ing], *alone*, from the posters' (my emphasis) makes it clear that she has the advertising publicity in mind, as the production poster portrayed the Countess framed by the faces of the other lead actors. See Koenig, 'All's Well', and Ian Johns, 'Of trysts and mellow fruitfulness'.

119 Peter, 'That's moor like it'; Gross, 'New-minted Moor'.

120 Charles Spencer, 'All rise for Dame Judi', *Daily Telegraph*, 13 December 2003.

121 Gross, 'New-minted Moor'.

3 Entangled in the present: Shakespeare and the politics of production

1 Charles Marowitz, *The Marowitz Shakespeare: Adaptations and Collages of* Hamlet, Macbeth, The Taming of the Shrew, Measure for Measure, *and* The Merchant of Venice (New York and London: Marion Boyars, 1978), p. 13.

2 Marowitz, *The Marowitz Shakespeare*, p. 13.

3 Marowitz, *The Marowitz Shakespeare*, p. 12.

4 Marowitz, *The Marowitz Shakespeare*, p. 12.

5 Peter Erickson, *Rewriting Shakespeare, Rewriting Ourselves* (Berkeley: University of California Press, 1991).

6 Helen Gilbert and Joanne Tompkins, *Post-Colonial Drama: Theory, Practice, Politics* (London: Routledge, 1996), p. 16.

7 Gilbert and Tompkins, *Post-Colonial Drama*, p. 18.

8 Peter Widdowson, '"Writing back": Contemporary Re-visionary Fiction', *Textual Practice* 20 (2006): 491–507, pp. 505–6.

9 Martin Orkin, 'Possessing the Book and Peopling the Text', in *Post-colonial Shakespeares*, ed. Ania Loomba and Martin Orkin (London: Routledge, 1998), pp. 186–204, p. 187.

10 Orkin, 'Possessing the Book', p. 187.

11 Widdowson, '"Writing back"', p. 501.

12 John Thieme, 'A Different "Othello Music": Djanet Sears's *Harlem Duet*', in *Performing National Identities: International Perspectives on Contemporary Canadian Theatre*, ed. Sherrill Grace and Albert-Reiner Glaap (Vancouver: Talonbooks, 2003), 81–91, p. 81.

13 Gilbert and Tompkins, *Post-Colonial Drama*, p. 51.

14 The visual layout of the programme to *Elsinore* implies that 'Variations on Shakespeare's *Hamlet*' might be read as a subtitle. In his 'Director's Note', Lepage likens *Elsinore* to a preliminary 'sketch' (*Elsinore*, dir. Robert Lepage, Programme, Royal National Theatre, first performance 4 January 1997).

15 Joyce Green MacDonald, 'Finding *Othello*'s African Roots through Djanet Sears's *Harlem Duet*', in *Approaches to Teaching Shakespeare's* Othello, ed. Peter Erickson and Maurice Hunt (New York: Modern Language Association of America, 2005), pp. 202–8, p. 208.

16 Michel de Certeau, *The Possession at Loudun*, trans. Michael B. Smith, with a Foreword by Stephen Greenblatt (Chicago: University of Chicago Press, 2000), p. 227.

17 Djanet Sears, *Harlem Duet* (Toronto: Scirocco Drama, 1997), pp. 12, 14.

18 Sears, *Harlem Duet*, pp. 14–15.

19 See especially Ric Knowles, 'Shakespeare, 1993, and the Discourses of the Stratford Festival, Ontario', *Shakespeare Quarterly* 45 (1994): 211–25, and Margaret Jane Kidnie, '"What world is this?": *Pericles* at the Stratford Festival of Canada, 2003', *Shakespeare Quarterly* 55 (2004): 307–19. For an insightful discussion of the spatial and cultural dynamics of the Stratford main stage, see Denis Salter, 'Acting Shakespeare in Postcolonial Space', in *Shakespeare, Theory, and Performance*, ed. James C. Bulman (London: Routledge, 1996), pp. 113–32, pp. 118–23.

20 Evelyn Myrie relates, for example, that, despite 'numerous unkept promises to [her]self' to get to Stratford, it was *Harlem Duet* that finally compelled her and some friends to go. Once at Stratford, they were welcomed by 'three local young black women': 'They sensed that we were from out of town and rushed up to greet us. "Hello, Hello," they said. "It's good to see you all … we don't see many of us around here."' We chuckled as we walked along to be a part of Stratford history' ('Stratford play breaks new multicultural ground', *Hamilton Spectator*, 17 July 2006). Gary Smith likewise comments: 'There is little doubt the play is attracting black people to Stratford. The day I saw it the theatre was almost full and there were far more people of colour than us pale-faced

whites' ('Stratford's *Harlem Duet* deserves to be seen', *Hamilton Spectator*, 26 August 2006).

21 Martin Morrow, 'Of Cast Iron and Steam', *Canadian Review of Books* 36:1 (January–February 2007): 38, and Smith, 'Stratford's *Harlem Duet* deserves to be seen'.

22 Djanet Sears in interview with Clifton Joseph, '*Harlem Duet*: the Stratford Festival opens its first all-black production', *The National*, Canadian Broadcasting Corporation, air date 30 June 2006. I am grateful to Bonnie Brown, the programme's producer, for sharing with me a transcript of this interview.

23 Sears, *Harlem Duet*, pp. 22–3.

24 Sears, *Harlem Duet*, p. 17.

25 Sears, *Harlem Duet*, p. 14.

26 Sears, *Harlem Duet*, pp. 73–4.

27 Paul Gilroy, *Against Race: Imagining Political Culture beyond the Color Line* (Cambridge, MA: Harvard University Press, 2000), p. 23.

28 Gilroy, *Against Race*, p. 40.

29 Sears, *Harlem Duet*, p. 73. Gilroy talks about a 'common humanity' in *Against Race*, p. 15.

30 Sears, *Harlem Duet*, p. 70.

31 Sears, *Harlem Duet*, p. 44.

32 Peter Dickinson, 'Duets, Duologues, and Black Diasporic Theatre: Djanet Sears, William Shakespeare, and Others', *Modern Drama* 45 (2002): 188–208, p. 200.

33 Homi Bhabha, 'Of Mimicry and Man: The Ambivalence of Colonial Discourse', *October* 28 (1984): 125–33, p. 130, emphasis in original.

34 Jyotsna Singh, 'Othello's Identity, Postcolonial Theory, and Contemporary African Rewritings of *Othello*', in *Women, 'Race', and Writing in the Early Modern Period*, ed. Margo Hendricks and Patricia Parker (London: Routledge, 1994), pp. 287–99, p. 292.

35 Frantz Fanon, *Black Skin, White Masks*, trans. Charles Lam Markmann (New York: Grove Press, 1967), p. 69.

36 Sears, *Harlem Duet*, p. 66. See Fanon, *Black Skin, White Masks*, p. 111.

37 Sears, *Harlem Duet*, p. 103.

38 Jean-François Lyotard, *The Differend: Phrases in Dispute* [1983], trans. Georges Van Den Abbeele, Theory and History of Literature 46 (Minneapolis: University of Minnesota Press, 1988), p. xi.

39 Djanet Sears and Alison Sealy-Smith in interview with Ric Knowles, 'The Nike Method', *Canadian Theatre Review* 97 (1998): 24–30, p. 25. The Nightwood Production ran from 20 April to 18 May 1997.

40 Sears, *Harlem Duet*, p. 35.

41 Sears, *Harlem Duet*, p. 21.

42 Sears, *Harlem Duet*, p. 58.

43 Sears, *Harlem Duet*, p. 73.

44 Sears, *Harlem Duet*, p. 107.

45 Sears, *Harlem Duet*, p. 75, emphasis in original.

46 Sears, *Harlem Duet*, p. 75. See *Harlem Duet*, dir. Djanet Sears, Promptbook, Nightwood Theatre archives, Archival and Special Collections, McLaughlin Library, University of Guelph, first performance 20 April 1997.

47 Sears, *Harlem Duet*, p. 35.

48 James Williams, *Lyotard and the Political* (London: Routledge, 2000), p. 4.

49 Djanet Sears, *Afrika Solo* (Toronto: Sister Vision, 1990), p. 40.

50 Lyotard, *The Differend*, p. 13.

51 Sears, *Harlem Duet*, p. 72.

52 Dickinson and Thieme independently analyse the significance of this audio patterning, Dickinson interpreting it as typical of the call and response patterning typical of the play's 'duets' ('Duets, Duologues, and Black Diasporic Theatre', pp. 191–2), Thieme reading it as 'the tip of an iceberg' that is the 'Othello music' Sears makes integral to her play's dialogue ('A Different "Othello Music"', p. 87).

53 Sears, *Harlem Duet*, p. 101.

54 Sears, *Harlem Duet*, p. 60.

55 Michel de Certeau, *The Writing of History*, trans. Tom Conley (New York: Columbia University Press, 1988), p. 5.

56 Sears, *Harlem Duet*, pp. 75–6.

57 Sears, *Harlem Duet*, p. 112.

58 Kamal Al-Solaylee, 'Stratford finally changes its tune', *Globe Review*, 16 June 2006, p. R21.

59 Sears, 'nOTES oF a cOLOURED gIRL', p. 14. In 'The Two Texts of *Othello* and Early Modern Constructions of Race', Leah Marcus analyses how 'constructions of race' are 'markedly different' in the quarto (1622) and Folio (1623) texts of *Othello*, particularly as they relate to 'other elements of the play, especially female purity', noting that these differences are smoothed over in modern editorial traditions of conflation (*Textual Performances: The Modern Reproduction of Shakespeare's Drama*, ed. Lukas Erne and Margaret Jane Kidnie (Cambridge: Cambridge University Press, 2004), pp. 21–36, p. 22).

60 Margo Hendricks, 'Civility, Barbarism, and Aphra Behn's *The Widow Ranter*', in *Women, 'Race', and Writing in the Early Modern Period*, ed. Margo Hendricks and Patricia Parker (London: Routledge, 1994), pp. 225–39, p. 229.

61 Emily C. Bartels, '*Othello* and Africa: Postcolonialism Reconsidered', *William and Mary Quarterly*, 3rd ser., 54 (1997): 45–64, p. 61–2.

62 Michael Neill, '"Mulattos," "Blacks," and "Indian Moors": *Othello* and Early Modern Constructions of Human Difference', *Shakespeare Quarterly* 49 (1998): 361–74, pp. 361–2.

63 Michael Neill, 'Unproper Beds: Race, Adultery, and the Hideous in *Othello*', *Shakespeare Quarterly* 40 (1989): 383–412, p. 412.

64 Shakespeare, *Othello*, in *William Shakespeare: The Complete Works*, ed. Stanley Wells and Gary Taylor with John Jowett and William Montgomery (Oxford: Clarendon Press, 1986), 1.1.88–9, 1.3.288–90.

65 See, for example, Linda Charnes, 'Shakespeare, and Belief, in the Future', in *Presentist Shakespeares*, ed. Hugh Grady and Terence Hawkes (London: Routledge, 2007), pp. 64–78, pp. 75–6; Karen Newman, *Fashioning Femininity and English Renaissance Drama* (Chicago: University of Chicago Press, 1991), p. 74; Singh, 'Othello's Identity', pp. 288, 290; Neill, 'Unproper Beds', pp. 406, 410; Michael Neill, '*Othello* and Race', in *Approaches to Teaching Shakespeare's* Othello, ed. Peter Erickson and Maurice Hunt (New York: Modern Language Association of America, 2005), pp. 37–52, pp. 37–8; Joyce Green MacDonald, 'Black Ram, White Ewe: Shakespeare, Race, and Women', in *A Feminist Companion to Shakespeare*, ed. Dympna Callaghan (Oxford: Blackwell, 2000), pp. 188–207, p. 203.

66 Shakespeare, *Othello*, 3.3.232–8.

67 Sears, *Harlem Duet*, p. 113.

68 Sears, *Harlem Duet*, pp. 99, 71.

69 Singh, 'Othello's Identity', p. 299.

70 Hugh Quarshie, *Second Thoughts about* Othello, as quoted in Neill, '*Othello* and Race', pp. 42–3. On the politics of casting and theatrical performance, see also Dympna Callaghan, '"Othello was a white man": Properties of Race on Shakespeare's Stage', in *Alternative Shakespeares*, vol. 2, ed. Terence Hawkes (London: Routledge, 1996), pp. 192–215, and Denise Albanese's discussion of how a 'photonegative' production of *Othello* in Washington in 1997 'makes clear the potentially unintended resonances provided by bodies interacting, put on view, and pressured by the history surrounding the moment of viewing' ('Black and White, and Dread All Over: The Shakespeare Theater's "Photonegative" *Othello* and the Body of Desdemona', in *A Feminist Companion to Shakespeare*, ed. Dympna Callaghan, pp. 226–47, p. 233).

71 Sears, *Harlem Duet*, p. 21.

72 Sears, *Harlem Duet*, p. 100.

73 Sears, *Harlem Duet*, p. 35. Nova Scotia is home to the first free Black community in Canada, a legacy that dates back to the late eighteenth century when slaves who defected to the British to fight against the Americans during the War for Independence were relocated along with other Loyalists to the Maritime provinces. On the deprivation and racial injustice suffered by the Black Loyalists, and the founding of Africville on the northern periphery of Halifax, see Donald H. Clairmont and Dennis William Magill, *Africville: The Life and Death of a Canadian Black Community* [1974], 3rd edn (Toronto: Canadian Scholars' Press, 1999), and James W. St. G. Walker, 'Allegories and Orientations in African-Canadian Historiography: The Spirit of Africville', *Dalhousie Review* 77:2 (1997): 155–77.

74 Sears, *Harlem Duet*, pp. 35, 17.

75 Sears and Smith with Knowles, 'The Nike Method', p. 26.

76 Sears, *Harlem Duet*, p. 117.

77 Sears, *Harlem Duet*, p. 15.

78 Joanne Tompkins, 'Infinitely Rehearsing Performance and Identity: *Africa* [sic] *Solo* and *The Book of Jessica*', *Canadian Theatre Review* 74 (1993): 35–9, p. 36.

79 Tompkins, 'Infinitely Rehearsing', p. 38.

80 Richard Paul Knowles, 'From Dream to Machine: Peter Brook, Robert Lepage, and the Contemporary Shakespearean Director as (Post)Modernist', *Theatre Journal* 50 (1998): 189–206, p. 205.

81 Jennifer Harvie and Erin Hurley, 'States of Play: Locating Québec in the Performances of Robert Lepage, Ex Machina, and the Cirque du Soleil', *Theatre Journal* 51:3 (1999): 299–315, pp. 307–8.

82 Lepage explains an idea of theatre as process in conversation with Alison McAlpine (*In Contact with the Gods? Directors Talk Theatre*, ed. Maria M. Delgado and Paul Heritage (Manchester: Manchester University Press, 1996), pp. 129–57, p. 135).

83 Lyn Gardner, 'Mission impossible', *Guardian*, 19 February 2007.

84 Robert Lepage, *Da Vinci*, Working Script, English adaptation by Linda Gaboriau (May 1987).

85 Janice Kennedy cites this initial running time for *Elseneur* in 'Hamlet: the Canadian sequel', *Ottawa Citizen*, 8 September 1997.

86 Paul Taylor, *Independent*, 26 November 1993.

87 Charles Spencer, *Weekend Telegraph*, 27 November 1993.

88 Robert Lepage, *Elseneur – Elsinore*, Touring Script (1996), Ex Machina archives, La Caserne Dalhousie, Québec City.

89 Lepage productions previously staged at the National were *Tectonic Plates* (1990), *Needles and Opium* (1992), *A Midsummer Night's Dream* (1992–3), and *The Seven Streams of the River Ota* (1996). *Coriolan* played at the Nottingham Playhouse in 1993, but did not transfer to London.

90 This is the figure cited by Martin Hannon and Robert McNeil ('Festival gloom as theatre showpiece cancelled', *Scotsman*, 14 August 1996); Dan Glaister ('Fated, not fêted', *Guardian*, 15 August 1996); Charles Spencer ('To be or not to be at Edinburgh Festival depends on a broken rivet', *Daily Telegraph*, 15 August 1996). Brian McMaster, Chief Executive of the Edinburgh International Festival, refused to speculate on cancellation costs (*Daily Express*, 'A riveting end to the Festival's showpiece', 15 August 1996).

91 The quotations are from Charles Spencer, 'When the machinery stops the show', *Daily Telegraph*, 15 August 1996.

92 Michael Billington, 'Visual feast goes emotionally cold', *Guardian*, n.d.

93 Alastair Macaulay, 'All cut up over Hamlet', *Financial Times*, 7 January 1997.

94 Robert Lepage, as quoted in Andy Lavender, *Hamlet in Pieces: Shakespeare Reworked by Peter Brook, Robert Lepage, Robert Wilson* (London: Nick Hern Books, 2001), p. 108.

95 Nick Curtis, 'Not boldness but sheer arrogance', *Evening Standard*, 6 January 1997.

96 *Elsinore*, based on *Hamlet* by William Shakespeare, adapted by Robert Lepage, produced by Ex Machina (*Canadian Theatre Review* 111 (2002): 89–99).

97 Christopher Innes, 'Beyond Categories (Redefining "mainstream")', in *Beyond the Mainstream*, ed. Peter Paul Schnierer, Contemporary Drama in English, vol. 4, 1996 (Trier: WVT Wissenschaftlicher Verlag Trier, 1997), pp. 55–67, p. 67.

98 Hamlet's first encounter with Rosencrantz and Guildenstern (2.2.243–378), for example, happened before Polonius showed his love letter to the King and Queen (2.2.86–159), rather than after his 'mad' scene with Polonius (2.2.171–211); Ophelia's narrative of Hamlet's visit to her closet was set in counterpoint to Hamlet's 'nunnery' speeches (2.1, 3.1); Gertrude's monologue describing the death of Ophelia (4.7.166–83) was interspersed with snatches of the maid's songs (4.5); and Hamlet's accounts of the pirate attack and his recomposition of the commission to England were conflated (4.6, 5.2). All line numbers are keyed to *Hamlet*, ed. T. J. B. Spencer, The New Penguin Shakespeare (London: Penguin Books, 1980).

99 Richard Paul Knowles, '"The Real of It Would Be Awful": Representing the Real Ophelia in Canada', *Theatre Survey* 39:1 (1998): 21–40.

100 Lepage, as quoted in Lavender, *Hamlet in Pieces*, p. 133.

101 See *A New Variorum Edition of Shakespeare: Hamlet*, ed. H. H. Furness, vol. 1 (Philadelphia: J. B. Lippincott Company, 1877). The emendation can be found, for example, in *Hamlet, Prince of Denmark*, ed. K. Deighton (London: Macmillan, 1891, reprinted 1931), and survives in slightly modified form in the annotation on 'Location' provided by *The Riverside Shakespeare*: 'Elsinore. A guard-platform of the castle' (ed. G. Blakemore Evans with J. J. Tobin, 2nd edn (Boston: Houghton Mifflin Company, 1997)).

102 Ian Shuttleworth, 'Playing games with Hamlet', *Financial Times*, 21 November 1996; Tom McSorley, '*Elsinore*, by Robert Lepage', broadcast on 'All in a Day', CBC Radio 1, 10 September 1997.

103 Lavender, *Hamlet in Pieces*, p. 129.

104 Ric Knowles, 'Reading *Elsinore*: The Ghost and the Machine', *Canadian Theatre Review* 111 (2002): 87–8, p. 87.
105 Glaister, 'Fated, not fêted'.
106 Curtis, 'Not boldness'.
107 Jane Edwardes, 'Elsinore', *TimeOut*, 1 January 1997.
108 Billington, 'Visual feast'.
109 Michael Coveney, 'First person singular', *Observer*, 12 May 1996.
110 Benedict Nightingale, 'Missing the point', *Times*, 6 January 1997.
111 'What draws me to Hamlet is his inability to forge a link between the acts he must undertake and his own thoughts ... [I]sn't it the absence of blind passion that prevents him doing what he has to do? Some might say that this isn't the most important paradox of Hamlet's nature; but for me it is the only one, because it's the one I share' (Lepage, dir., *Elsinore*, Programme, Royal National Theatre, first performance 4 January 1997).
112 Robert Butler, *Independent on Sunday*, 24 November 1996.

4 Adapting media: *ShakespeaRe-Told* by the BBC

1 These quotations are taken from Charles Spencer's review of Robert Lepage's non-performance of *Elsinore* at the Edinburgh Festival ('When the machinery stops the show', *Daily Telegraph*, 15 August 1996), discussed in chapter 3.
2 Complicite and the English Shakespeare Company, like Lepage, have long integrated multi-media components into live performance. Michael Billington comments on intersections between film and theatre throughout the twentieth century, predicting that although '[p]urists may ... argue nostalgically for the integrity of form', the two media will continue to merge ('Star of stage and screen', *Guardian*, 19 November 2003).
3 Some of the more widely influential electronic projects include Early English Books Online, the Internet Shakespeare Editions (http://ise.uvic.ca), Hamlet on the Ramparts (http://shea.mit.edu/ramparts), and archive projects in English literature such as the Dante Gabriel Rossetti Archive (www.rossettiarchive.org) and the William Blake Archive (www.blakearchive.org). An electronic New Variorum Shakespeare is currently in development through the Modern Language Association of America.
4 See, for instance, Jerome J. McGann's influential 'Rationale of Hypertext', first published online in 1995 and reproduced in *Radiant Textuality: Literature after the World Wide Web* (Basingstoke: Palgrave, 2001), pp. 53–74. John Lavagnino counters what he sees as the excesses of 'casual futurological wisdom' of some scholarship on new technology from the 1990s in 'Two Varieties of Digital Commentary', in *Textual Performances: The Modern Reproduction of Shakespeare's Drama*, ed. Lukas Erne and Margaret Jane Kidnie (Cambridge: Cambridge University Press, 2004), pp. 194–209, esp. p. 194.
5 Influential criticism in this field, however, includes *Shakespeare on Television: An Anthology of Essays and Reviews*, ed. J. C. Bulman and H. R. Coursen (Hanover: University Press of New England, 1988); H. R. Coursen, *Watching Shakespeare on Television* (Rutherford, NJ: Fairleigh Dickinson University Press, 1993) and *Shakespeare Translated: Derivatives on Film and TV* (New York: Peter Lang, 2005); Susan Willis, *The BBC Shakespeare Plays: Making the Televised Canon* (Chapel Hill and London: University of North Carolina Press, 1991). See also Michèle Willems, 'Verbal-Visual, Verbal-Pictorial or Textual-Televisual? Reflections

on the BBC Shakespeare Series', in *Shakespeare and the Moving Image*, ed. Anthony Davies and Stanley Wells (Cambridge: Cambridge University Press, 1994), pp. 69–85; Barbara Hodgdon, 'Katherina Bound, or Play(K)ating the Strictures of Everyday Life', in *The Shakespeare Trade: Performances and Appropriations* (Philadelphia: University of Pennsylvania Press, 1998), pp. 1–38; *Shakespeare Survey* 61 (2008), an issue devoted to 'Shakespeare, Sound and Screen'.

6 In addition to the BBC1 productions, BBC4 broadcast as part of the New Shakespeare Season a film based on William Boyd's fictionalized treatment of the sonnets called *A Waste of Shame* (22 November) and *Shakespeare's Happy Endings* (28 November), a mock documentary written and performed by Patrick Barlow on the history of adaptation of Shakespeare's plays. The season was rounded out with Radio 3 productions of *Much Ado About Nothing* (13 November), *Macbeth* (20 November), and *Pericles* (27 November).

7 The dramas were televised on 7, 14, 21, and 28 November, respectively. Six of Chaucer's tales – *The Wife of Bath*, *The Miller's Tale*, *The Knight's Tale*, *The Sea Captain's* [*Shipman's*] *Tale*, *The Pardoner's Tale*, and *The Man of Law's Tale* – were broadcast after the 9 p.m. watershed between 11 September and 16 October 2003. At the British Academy Television Awards (BAFTAs) in 2004, Julie Walters won Best Actress as the Wife of Bath, and *The Canterbury Tales: The Wife of Bath's Tale*, written by Sally Wainwright, was nominated in the category of Best Single Drama.

8 A few individuals worked on multiple productions. *Taming* and *Much Ado*, for example, produced by Diederick Santer, shared personnel responsible for Publicity (Tara Houghton), Artists' Contracts (Thalia Reynolds), Post Production Supervision (Caroline McManus and Alice Greenland), and Sound Recording (Bruce Wills), while Michelle Osborn handled Publicity for *Macbeth* and *Dream*, the two shows produced by Pier Wilkie. The Production Executive for all four dramas was Gordon Ronald.

9 See Charles Marowitz, 'Introduction', *The Marowitz Shakespeare* [1978] (New York: Marion Boyars, 1990), pp. 7–27, pp. 18–19; Michael Billington, *Guardian*, 5 May 1978; Shirley Nelson Garner, '*The Taming of the Shrew*: Inside or Outside of the Joke?', in *'Bad' Shakespeare: Revaluations of the Shakespeare Canon*, ed. Maurice Charney (Rutherford, NJ: Fairleigh Dickinson University Press, 1988), pp. 105–19, esp. p. 106. Ann Thompson describes it as a modern 'problem play' in the introduction to her New Cambridge edition of *Taming of the Shrew* (Cambridge: Cambridge University Press, 1984), p. 21.

10 *Shaw on Shakespeare: An Anthology of Bernard Shaw's Writings on the Plays and Production of Shakespeare*, ed. and with an introduction by Edwin Wilson (London: Cassell, 1962), p. 180.

11 A fictional pedigree is invented for this character on the *ShakespeaRe-Told* website that confirms that the forenames of 'Crick, EARL of CHARLBURY' are 'currently subject to rule by the Family Records Court' (www.bbc.co.uk/drama/shakespeare/tamingoftheshrew/society.shtml, accessed 4 July 2006).

12 A sentimental interpretation of Petruchio was suggested, for example, at the Royal Shakespeare Company in 2003 (dir. Greg Doran), where Petruchio (Jasper Britton) wore a black armband in mourning for the recent death of his father, and delivered his taming soliloquy while seeming to embrace a portrait of his father; Colm Feore at the Stratford Festival of Canada in 1988 (dir. Richard Monette) physically flinched at Katherine's anger and pain, seeming to suffer with his wife through the process of taming.

13 The scriptwriter of *Much Ado*, David Nicholls, was at this time perhaps best known for his work on the award-winning British television series *Cold Feet*, and viewers' expectations of this scene may have been further influenced by memories of the hospital scene in the much-hyped penultimate episode of the final series (9 March 2003). This broadcast attracted huge viewing figures as a result of the producers releasing in advance the information that one of the show's central characters would be killed off.

14 E. Jane Dickson, 'William's Women', BBC *Radio Times*, 5–11 November 2005, pp. 13–15, p. 14. The quotation from Keeley Hawes that follows is from the same source.

15 The tag line is quoted from the front cover of the DVD case (Acorn Video, 2006).

16 Sir Trevor Nunn, quoted in Chris Hastings, 'Nunn lays into BBC for Shakespeare-lite', *Sunday Telegraph*, 9 October 2005.

17 'Wot – No More Shakespeare?', published Roundtable Discussion with Michael Billington, Matthew Warchus, Cicely Berry, Stephen Poliakoff, Simon Reade, and members of the audience, *RSC Magazine* (Summer 1998): 8–9, p. 9. All quotations cited in this paragraph are taken from the same page.

18 Dickson, 'William's Women', p. 14.

19 *Macbeth*, *ShakespeaRe-Told*, broadcast BBC1, 14 November 2005. Transcribed from DVD (Acorn Video, 2006).

20 There are points of contact between this argument about the BBC's scripting of Shakespeare's works for a twenty-first century television audience and Leah S. Marcus' argument about the additions to *Doctor Faustus* changing Marlowe's words in order to preserve a peculiar author-effect that she maintains would seem to later audiences 'more' Marlowe than Marlowe. See *Unediting the Renaissance: Shakespeare, Marlowe, Milton* (London: Routledge, 1996), pp. 38–67.

21 See, for instance, Willems, 'Verbal-Visual, Verbal-Pictorial or Textual-Televisual?'; Stanley Wells, 'Television Shakespeare', *Shakespeare Quarterly* 33 (1982): 261–77, reprinted in *Shakespeare on Television*, ed. Bulman and Coursen, pp. 41–9; Sheldon P. Zitner, 'Wooden O's in Plastic Boxes: Shakespeare and Television', *University of Toronto Quarterly* 51 (1981): 1–12, reprinted in *Shakespeare on Television*, ed. Bulman and Coursen, pp. 31–41.

22 Willems, 'Verbal-Visual, Verbal-Pictorial or Textual-Televisual?', p. 83. See also Stanley Wells' call in 'Television Shakespeare' for full rescripting on the grounds that he would prefer good television to faithful Shakespeare; my argument in this chapter is that it is difficult to keep such oppositions distinct since playing the works in a new medium will bring into question what one can subsequently recognize as 'faithful' Shakespeare.

23 Tony Wilson, *Watching Television: Hermeneutics, Reception and Popular Culture* (Cambridge: Polity Press, 1993), pp. 115–16.

24 John Thornton Caldwell, *Televisuality: Style, Crisis, and Authority in American Television* (New Brunswick, NJ: Rutgers University Press, 1995), esp. pp. 73–102. For the comparison of television to radio, see H. R. Coursen, 'The Bard and the Tube', in *Shakespeare on Television*, ed. Bulman and Coursen, pp. 3–10, p. 6. On some of the problems with reading television as film, see Jason Mittell, 'A Cultural Approach to Television Genre Theory', in *The Television Studies Reader*, ed. Robert C. Allen and Annette Hill (London: Routledge, 2004), pp. 171–81, p. 177.

25 The quotation is from Caldwell, *Televisuality*, p. 92. On television conventions and their continuities, see John Ellis, 'Defining the Medium', in *Tele-Visions: An Introduction to Studying Television*, ed. Glen Creeber (London: British Film Institute Publishing, 2006), pp. 12–19, and Wilson, *Watching Television*, pp. 104–25. In the years since Caldwell first published on 'televisuality', his argument has moved into the popular press, commentators increasingly talking about the shifting balance between film and television. John Patterson and Gareth McLean in 'Move over Hollywood', for example, observe that with series like *The Sopranos*, *24*, and *The West Wing*, television 'has slowly seized the creative initiative from the movies' with 'superbly kinetic and inventive film-making, shot on film, often in wide-screen formats and on location, using big budgets (Lost's opener, for example, cost a record-breaking $10m), special effects and hit-parade soundtracks' (*Guardian*, 20 May 2006).

26 On the centrality of liveness to the aesthetics of television, 'not in the sense that the programmes are literally live, but in the deeper sense that the activity of television broadcasting itself proceeds in the present moment and addresses the present moment', see Ellis, 'Defining the Medium', p. 19.

27 See Anthony Dawson, 'Much Ado about Signifying', *Studies in English Literature 1500–1900* 22 (1982): 211–21, and Nova Myhill, 'Spectatorship in/of *Much Ado about Nothing*', *Studies in English Literature 1500–1900* 39 (1999): 291–311.

28 Such a reading is suggestive of Jean E. Howard's interpretation of *Much Ado* as a work embodying not only metatheatrical, but in some key respects anti-theatrical, attitudes to performance; the medium of production and social circumstances, of course, are greatly revised. See *The Stage and Social Struggle in Early Modern England* (London: Routledge, 1994), pp. 47–72.

29 The continuity announcements at the end of each programme were not identical. The cryptic phrase 'press red now', which presumes a viewer familiarity with digital technology, was heard at the end of *Dream*, the last programme in the series; the introduction to interactivity after *Much Ado* was fuller: 'There's much more ado for digital viewers. Press the red button on your remote now for interviews with the cast and a truly interactive exploration of the themes and language of Shakespeare's work.'

30 Robert McCrum, 'Shakespeare on the BBC? Great. Oh, hang on a moment', *Observer Review*, 6 November 2005. Jonathan Bate, by way of contrast to McCrum, finds in the shows '[g]reat entertainment and intelligent Shakespearean interpretation', 'sky-high' production values, and 'razor-sharp' performances, and he concludes his review by urging the BBC to 'commission more of these films forthwith' ('Skilful Remixes of A Bard for All Seasons', *Times Higher Education Supplement*, 9 December 2005, p. 13).

31 Thomas Sutcliffe, 'Last night's TV: Bard in the background', *Independent*, 22 November 2005, p. 52.

32 'Producer's Intro', *Canterbury Tales*, www.bbc.co.uk/drama/canterburytales/producers_intro.shtml, site accessed 4 May 2006.

33 Susan Willis reports that Cedric Messina, founder and producer 1978–80, had been wrongly quoted as saying the BBC–Time/Life Complete Works series would offer definitive productions of the canon (*The BBC Shakespeare Plays*, p. 16). James C. Bulman, however, reads as synonymous with 'definitive' Messina's explanation in the preface to the BBC editions of the plays that his aim is 'to make the plays, in permanent form, accessible to audiences throughout the world' (see 'The BBC Shakespeare and "House Style"',

Shakespeare Quarterly 35 (1984): 571–81, reprinted in *Shakespeare on Television*, ed. Bulman and Coursen, p. 50).

34 'A public service for all: the BBC in the digital age', 14 March 2006 (www. bbccharterreview.org.uk, accessed 4 May 2006), p. 11.

35 'A public service for all', pp. 4 and 24.

36 The series was shown in Canada over four weeks from 5 March 2006, occupying the Sunday 9:00 p.m. (Eastern) slot.

37 Explaining that digital television is just another form of computer and predicting that systems of information delivery as seemingly distinct as mobile phones, the internet, and television will merge and so transform, Nicholas Negroponte polemically argued as early as 1995 that the 'key to the future of television is to stop thinking about television as television'. See Nicholas Negroponte, *being digital* (New York: Alfred A. Knopf, 1995), pp. 37–50, esp. p. 48.

38 'A public service for all', p. 15.

39 Transcribed from the *ShakespeaRe-Told* website (site accessed August 2006). The material transmitted by digital broadcast was subsequently made available through broadband streaming via the internet to computers in Britain.

5 Textual origins

1 'J! Archive' (www.j-archive.com), accessed 29 March 2007. Clicking on the clues launches the pre-recorded productions of Shakespeare performed by the Reduced Shakespeare Company that were televised on 26 April 2005.

2 Tom Stoppard, *The Fifteen Minute Hamlet* (New York: Samuel French, 1978); this condensed *Hamlet* was later incorporated into Stoppard's *Dogg's Hamlet* (London: Faber, 1980).

3 Jess Borgeson, Adam Long, and Daniel Singer, The Reduced Shakespeare Company's *The Complete Works of William Shakespeare (abridged)*, ed. Professor J. M. Winfield (New York: Applause Books, 1994); see also the DVD/video recording, starring Adam Long, Daniel Singer, and Jess Winfield, directed by Paul Kafno (Acorn Media, 2001).

4 A one-hour version of the *Complete Works* was first performed at the Edinburgh Festival in 1987, and versions of the production have since toured the United States, Canada, and Britain. The *Complete Works* played at the Lillian Bayliss Theatre (London, England) in December 1991, and for an eleven-month engagement in 1992 at the Arts Theatre, London. The RSC opened the show at the Criterion Theatre, London, on 7 March 1996, where it ran until 3 April 2005.

5 *Complete Works*, p. 2.

6 *Complete Works*, p. 4.

7 *Complete Works*, p. 7.

8 *Complete Works*, p. 5.

9 A. R. Braunmuller traces the adoption by H. H. Furness of the 'classic(al) three-layer page-design – text, collation, two-columned commentary' for single volume editions back to the 'increasingly elaborate editions of Greek and Latin authors' in early modern and Enlightenment Europe ('Shakespeares various', in *In Arden: Editing Shakespeare*, ed. Ann Thompson and Gordon McMullan (London: Thomson, 2003), pp. 3–16, p. 11).

10 *Complete Works*, pp. 13, 38, 24.

11 *Complete Works*, pp. 42, 44.

12 See, for instance, Alan C. Dessen, *Elizabethan Stage Conventions and Modern Interpreters* (Cambridge: Cambridge University Press, 1984), and his 'Shakespeare and the Theatrical Conventions of His Time', in *Cambridge Companion to Shakespeare Studies*, ed. Stanley Wells (Cambridge: Cambridge University Press, 1986), pp. 85–99, *Recovering Shakespeare's Theatrical Vocabulary* (Cambridge: Cambridge University Press, 1995), and *Rescripting Shakespeare: The Text, the Director, and Modern Productions* (Cambridge: Cambridge University Press, 2002).

13 Dessen, *Rescripting Shakespeare*, p. 224.

14 Dessen, *Rescripting Shakespeare*, p. 234.

15 Don Weingust, *Acting from Shakespeare's First Folio: Theory, Text and Performance* (London: Routledge, 2006), p. 7.

16 Weingust, *Acting from Shakespeare's First Folio*, p. 83.

17 Weingust, *Acting from Shakespeare's First Folio*, p. 87.

18 Weingust, *Acting from Shakespeare's First Folio*, p. 115. As Alan Galey comments, Freeman corrects what he interprets as typographical error through reference to the early quartos and second to fourth folios, as though the modern era of editorial mediation began 'sometime between F4 … and Nicholas Rowe's first multivolume edition of 1709' ('The Shakespearean Archive: Information's Cultural Work from Early Modern Print to the Electronic New Variorum Shakespeare', unpublished doctoral dissertation, University of Western Ontario, 2006, p. 127). Sonia Massai identifies patterns of editorial corrections in Shakespeare's quartos and folios predating Rowe's edition of 1709, arguing that these mostly anonymous correctors aimed to 'perfect' the text rather than to 'emend' it, as named editors of Shakespeare would do starting from the beginning of the eighteenth century. See *Shakespeare and the Rise of the Editor* (Cambridge: Cambridge University Press, 2007).

19 See Randall McLeod, 'UnEditing Shak-speare', *Sub-Stance* 33–4 (1982): 26–55; [Random Clod], 'Information upon Information', *Text* 5 (1991): 241–81; [Random Cloud], 'The Marriage of Good and Bad Quartos', *Shakespeare Quarterly* 33 (1982): 421–30.

20 Laurie E. Osborne, *The Trick of Singularity:* Twelfth Night *and the Performance Editions* (Iowa City: University of Iowa Press, 1996), p. 43. See also McLeod, 'Information upon Information'.

21 Osborne, *The Trick of Singularity*, p. 44.

22 In *Textual and Literary Criticism* (Cambridge: Cambridge University Press, 1959), p. 68, Bowers argues: 'When we inquire what agent decides to which range we may assign the individual words of Shakespeare's text, just about the only answer is *critical judgement* or *common sense*. No linguistic or bibliographical argument has any operative validity until the results of its application are accepted by the critical judgement.' Taylor's comparison of emendation to an art follows the comment that editors 'promulgate the notion that editing is no more than a matter of judicious *selection*; they obscure the fact that it also depends upon judicious *invention*' (*William Shakespeare: A Textual Companion*, Stanley Wells and Gary Taylor with John Jowett and William Montgomery (Oxford: Clarendon Press, 1987; reprinted with corrections New York and London: Norton, 1997), p. 59).

23 Bowers, *Textual and Literary Criticism*, p. 68.

24 Gary Taylor and John Lavagnino, gen. eds, *Thomas Middleton: The Collected Works* (Oxford: Oxford University Press, 2007), and Gary Taylor and John Lavagnino, gen. eds, *Thomas Middleton and Early Modern Textual Culture: A Companion to the Collected Works* (Oxford: Oxford University Press, 2007).

25 See Gary Taylor and John Jowett, *Shakespeare Reshaped 1606–1623* (Oxford: Clarendon Press, 1993), pp. 139–40, for a full summary of the evidence for interpolation.

26 Taylor and Jowett, *Shakespeare Reshaped*, p. 160.

27 Taylor and Jowett, *Shakespeare Reshaped*, p. 140.

28 Taylor and Jowett, *Shakespeare Reshaped*, p. 151.

29 Taylor and Jowett, *Shakespeare Reshaped*, p. 156.

30 Taylor and Jowett, *Shakespeare Reshaped*, pp. 186, 120, 122.

31 Taylor and Jowett, *Shakespeare Reshaped*, p. 186. The argument is repeated in more concise detail in John Jowett, *Shakespeare and Text* (Oxford: Oxford University Press, 2007), pp. 43–5.

32 Taylor and Jowett, *Shakespeare Reshaped*, p. 119.

33 Taylor and Jowett, *Shakespeare Reshaped*, p. 119.

34 Taylor and Jowett, *Shakespeare Reshaped*, pp. 141, 148.

35 See, for example, William B. Long, 'Stage-directions: A Misinterpreted Factor in Determining Textual Provenance', *Text* 2 (1985): 121–37, and '"A bed / for woodstock": A Warning for the Unwary', *Medieval and Renaissance Drama in England* 2 (1985): 91–118, and Paul Werstine, 'McKerrow's "Suggestion" and Twentieth-century Shakespeare Textual Criticism', *Renaissance Drama* 19 (1988): 149–73, 'Plays in Manuscript', in *A New History of Early English Drama*, ed. John D. Cox and David Scott Kastan (New York: Columbia University Press, 1997), pp. 483–92, and 'Post-theory Problems in Shakespeare Editing', *Yearbook of English Studies* 29 (1999): 106–11.

36 Barbara Mowat, 'The Problem of Shakespeare's Text(s)', *Shakespeare Jahrbuch* 132 (1996): 26–43, p. 30.

37 James Purkis, 'Recognizing the Author in Early Modern English Literature', unpublished doctoral dissertation, University of Birmingham, 2005, p. 144.

38 John Jowett, 'Addressing Adaptation: *Measure for Measure* and *Sir Thomas More*', in *Textual Performances: The Modern Reproduction of Shakespeare's Drama*, ed. Lukas Erne and Margaret Jane Kidnie (Cambridge: Cambridge University Press, 2004), pp. 63–76, pp. 71–2.

39 Jowett clarifies that the two textual strata of 1603–4 and 1621 are distinguished by date, 'in full recognition that the agents involved may not exclusively be Middleton and Shakespeare, but acceptance too that in practice they appear mostly to be so' ('Addressing Adaptation', p. 69).

40 Jowett, 'Addressing Adaptation', p. 69.

41 See Randall McLeod, ed., *Crisis in Editing* (New York: AMS Press, 1994). Edward Pechter returns to this language of crisis to explore if editing is still undergoing 'a *bona fide* paradigm shift' in 'Crisis in Editing?', *Shakespeare Survey* 59 (Cambridge: Cambridge University Press, 2006), pp. 20–38, p. 38.

42 Paul Werstine, 'Housmania: Episodes in Twentieth-century "Critical" Editing of Shakespeare', in *Textual Performances*, ed. Erne and Kidnie, pp. 49–62, p. 59.

43 Werstine, 'Housmania', p. 58.

44 Concerns about the construction of editorial narratives were forcefully articulated by Werstine in his ground-breaking article 'Narratives about Printed Shakespeare Texts: "Foul Papers" and "Bad" Quartos', *Shakespeare Quarterly* 41 (1990): 65–86.

45 Hugh Grady and Terence Hawkes, 'Introduction: Presenting Presentism', in *Presentist Shakespeares*, ed. Hugh Grady and Terence Hawkes (London: Routledge, 2007), pp. 1–5, p. 3.

46 Nancy Partner, 'Making up Lost Time: Writing on the Writing of History', *Speculum* 61 (1986): 90–117, p. 108.

47 William Ingram, 'Introduction: Early Modern Theatre History: Where We Are Now, How We Got Here, Where We Go Next', in *A Handbook on Early Modern Theatre*, ed. Richard Dutton (Oxford: Oxford University Press: forthcoming).

48 The temptation to read only the one-page concluding summary of the characteristics of foul papers and promptbooks flattens out considerably Greg's own highly qualified discussion of the evidence of playbooks in the previous thirty-five pages. See *The Shakespeare First Folio: Its Bibliographical and Textual History* (Oxford: Clarendon Press, 1955), pp. 105–42, esp. p. 142.

49 It is worth noting in this context that Werstine's contribution to the landmark volume *The Division of the Kingdoms*, 'Folio Editors, Folio Compositors, and the Folio Text of *King Lear*', is the only essay in that collection to avoid arguing that *King Lear* was revised by Shakespeare (see *The Division of the Kingdoms: Shakespeare's Two Versions of* King Lear, ed. Gary Taylor and Michael Warren (Oxford: Clarendon Press, 1983), pp. 247–312). Werstine makes this orientation away from authorial agency explicit in 'The Textual Mystery of *Hamlet*', *Shakespeare Quarterly* 39 (1988): 1–26.

50 Mowat, 'The Problem of Shakespeare's Text(s)', p. 41.

51 Mowat, 'The Problem of Shakespeare's Text(s)', p. 43.

52 Mowat, 'The Problem of Shakespeare's Text(s)', p. 42.

53 Mowat, 'The Problem of Shakespeare's Text(s)', pp. 42–3.

54 Mowat, 'The Problem of Shakespeare's Text(s)', p. 34.

55 See, for example, Werstine, 'Housmania', p. 59, and Mowat, 'The Problem of Shakespeare's Text(s)', pp. 34–6.

56 'The Problem of Shakespeare's Text(s)', p. 41.

57 In addition to the manuscript considerations raised by Mowat and Osborne's enquiries into textual historicity, consider W. W. Greg's conclusion 'that in the case of Shakespeare – and the same applies to the Elizabethan drama generally – we cannot hope to achieve a certainly correct text, not so much on account of the uncertainties of transmission – though they are sometimes serious – as because the author may never have produced a definitive text for us to recover' (*The Editorial Problem in Shakespeare: A Survey of the Foundations of the Text*, 3rd edn (Oxford: Clarendon Press, 1954), p. ix).

58 Jonathan Bate and Sonia Massai, 'Adaptation as Edition', in *The Margins of the Text*, ed. D. C. Greetham (Ann Arbor: University of Michigan Press, 1997), pp. 129–51, p. 130.

59 Bate and Massai, 'Adaptation as Edition', pp. 131, 142.

60 For discussion of the Oxford editors' decision to rename Falstaff in *1 Henry IV* Oldcastle, see David Scott Kastan, *Shakespeare after Theory* (London: Routledge, 1999), pp. 93–106.

61 Explaining how modernization, whether partial or complete, 'distort[s] the text', Bowers warns critics not to 'take [their] chances with modernising editors' (*Textual and Literary Criticism*, p. 131). For studies that revisit the merits and compromises of modernization to very different purpose, see Stanley Wells, *Re-editing Shakespeare for the Modern Reader* (Oxford: Clarendon Press, 1984), and David Bevington, 'Modern Spelling: The Hard Choices', in *Textual Performances*, ed. Erne and Kidnie, pp. 143–57.

62 Wells, *Re-editing Shakespeare for the Modern Reader*, pp. 5–31.

63 Margreta de Grazia, *Shakespeare Verbatim: The Reproduction of Authenticity and the 1790 Apparatus* (Oxford: Clarendon Press, 1991), p. 7. Building on the thrust

of de Grazia's research, Wendy Wall critiques the category of the substantive text as part of the 'genealogical quest activated by new bibliographers', and questions how 'an analysis of the play's earliest forms, freed from the organizational straitjacket of a bibliographic family tree, complicate[s] the stories that literary critics tell?' ('De-generation: Editions, Offspring, and *Romeo and Juliet*', in *From Performance to Print in Shakespeare's England*, ed. Peter Holland and Stephen Orgel (Basingstoke: Palgrave Macmillan, 2006), pp. 152–70, pp. 154–5).

64 Valerie Wayne, 'The Sexual Politics of Textual Transmission', in *Textual Formations and Reformations*, ed. Laurie E. Maguire and Thomas L. Berger (Newark: University of Delaware Press, 1998), pp. 179–210, and Barbara Hodgdon, 'New Collaborations with Old Plays: The (Textual) Politics of Performance Commentary', in *Textual Performances*, ed. Erne and Kidnie, pp. 210–23.

65 Ronald A. Tumelson II, 'Ferdinand's Wife and Prospero's Wise', *Shakespeare Survey* 59 (2006): 79–90. See also Peter W. M. Blayney, 'Introduction to the Second Edition', *The Norton Facsimile: The First Folio of Shakespeare*, prepared by Charlton Hinman, with a new introduction by Peter W. M. Blayney, 2nd edn (New York: Norton, 1996), pp. xxvii–xxxiv, p. xxxi.

66 Tumelson II, 'Ferdinand's Wife and Prospero's Wise', p. 89.

67 See, for instance, Hodgdon, 'New Collaborations', and Margaret Jane Kidnie, 'The Staging of Shakespeare's Drama in Print Editions', in *Textual Performances*, ed. Erne and Kidnie, pp. 158–77. A new editorial series of Shakespeare's works, designed to meet the specific readerly needs of theatre practitioners, is forthcoming with Palgrave Macmillan.

Bibliography

Adler, Steven, *Rough Magic: Making Theatre at the Royal Shakespeare Company*, with a Foreword by Chris Parry, Carbondale and Edwardsville: Southern Illinois University Press, 2001.

Albanese, Denise, 'Black and White, and Dread All Over: The Shakespeare Theater's "Photonegative" *Othello* and the Body of Desdemona', in *A Feminist Companion to Shakespeare*, ed. Dympna Callaghan, Oxford: Blackwell, 2000, pp. 226–47.

Alberge, Dalya, 'Cusack attacks "exclusivity" of British theatre', *Times*, 9 January 2002.

—— 'Paltry grant adds to RSC woes', *Times*, 26 March 2003.

Allen, Robert C. and Annette Hill, eds, *The Television Studies Reader*, London: Routledge, 2004.

'All's well as Dame Judi opens library', *Stratford-upon-Avon Journal*, 8 January 2004.

Al-Solaylee, Kamal, 'Stratford finally changes its tune', *The Globe Review*, 16 June 2006, p. R21.

'A prince among Hamlets: five of *Hamlet*'s admirers select the greatest Danes they have seen', *Times Supplement (The Knowledge)*, 18 February 2006.

'A public service for all: the BBC in the digital age', 14 March 2006 (www.bbccharterreview.org.uk, accessed 4 May 2006).

'A riveting end to the Festival's showpiece', *Daily Express*, 15 August 1996.

Austin, Jeremy, 'Dench joins critics of RSC reform', *Stage*, 18 April 2002.

Baracaia, Alexa, 'RSC governor backs strike action', *Stage*, 6 September 2001.

—— 'West affirms RSC criticism', *Stage*, 14 February 2002.

Bartels, Emily C., '*Othello* and Africa: Postcolonialism Reconsidered', *William and Mary Quarterly*, 3rd ser., 54 (1997): 45–64.

Barthes, Roland, 'The Death of the Author', trans. Geoff Bennington, in *Modern Criticism and Theory: A Reader*, ed. David Lodge, Harlow: Longman, 1988, repr. 1996, pp. 167–72.

—— 'From Work to Text', trans. S. Heath, in *Modern Literary Theory: A Reader*, ed. Philip Rice and Patricia Waugh, 3rd edn, London: Arnold, 1996, pp. 191–7.

Bassett, Kate, 'Beauties and beasts – and a morris dance', *Independent on Sunday*, 14 December 2003.

—— 'From Elsinore to a Spanish court', *Daily Telegraph*, 10 December 1997.

—— 'You guys moaned, but my changes are sound', *Independent on Sunday*, 18 February 2001.

Bate, Jonathan, 'Skilful Remixes of A Bard for All Seasons', *Times Higher Education Supplement*, 9 December 2005.

Bate, Jonathan and Sonia Massai, 'Adaptation as Edition', in *The Margins of the Text*, ed. D. C. Greetham, Ann Arbor: University of Michigan Press, 1997, pp. 129–51.

Bateson, F. W., 'Modern Bibliography and the Literary Artifact', *English Studies Today*, 2nd ser., ed. G. A. Bonnard, Bern: Francke Verlag, 1961, pp. 67–77.

Benedict, David, 'Is the RSC safe in his hands?', *Observer Review*, 31 March 2002.

Bennett, Susan, *Performing Nostalgia: Shifting Shakespeare and the Contemporary Past*, London: Routledge, 1996.

Berry, Ralph, *On Directing Shakespeare: Interviews with Contemporary Directors*, London: Croom Helm, 1977.

Bevington, David, 'Modern Spelling: The Hard Choices', in *Textual Performances: The Modern Reproduction of Shakespeare's Drama*, ed. Lukas Erne and Margaret Jane Kidnie, Cambridge: Cambridge University Press, 2004, pp. 143–57.

Bhabha, Homi, 'Of Mimicry and Man: The Ambivalence of Colonial Discourse', *October* 28 (1984): 125–33.

Billen, Andrew, 'So Hamlet drops the bullets from the gun. Then he gets the giggles', *Observer Review*, 11 May 1997.

Billington, Michael, 'All's Well That Ends Well', *Guardian*, 21 February 2004.

—— 'Bold plans signal new era for Stratford', *Guardian*, 30 September 2003.

—— 'Get shorter', *Guardian*, 10 May 1997.

—— *Guardian*, 5 May 1978.

—— *Guardian*, 21 November 1989.

—— 'Human Prince', *Guardian*, 5 April 1980.

—— 'In a world of dazzle, beware a lost identity', *Guardian*, 25 May 2001.

—— 'Not a crisis, but the curtain rising on a promising era', *Guardian*, 29 July 2003.

—— 'Something rotten in Stratford', *Guardian*, 6 March 2002.

—— 'Star of stage and screen', *Guardian*, 19 November 2003.

—— 'Visual feast goes emotionally cold', *Guardian*, n.d.

Blayney, Peter W. M., 'Introduction to the Second Edition', in *The Norton Facsimile: The First Folio of Shakespeare*, prepared by Charlton Hinman, with a new introduction by Peter W. M. Blayney, 2nd edn, New York: Norton, 1996, pp. xxvii–xxxiv.

Borges, Jorge Luis, 'Pierre Menard, Author of the Quixote', in *Labyrinths: Selected Stories and Other Writings*, ed. Donald A. Yates and James E. Irby, Preface by André Maurois, London: Penguin, 1970, pp. 62–71.

Borgeson, Jess, Adam Long, and Daniel Singer, The Reduced Shakespeare Company's *The Complete Works of William Shakespeare (abridged)*, ed. Professor J. M. Winfield, New York: Applause Books, 1994.

Bowers, Fredson, *On Editing Shakespeare and the Elizabethan Dramatists*, n.p.: University of Pennsylvania Library, 1955.

—— *Textual and Literary Criticism*, Cambridge: Cambridge University Press, 1959.

Braunmuller, A. R., 'Shakespeares various', in *In Arden: Editing Shakespeare*, ed. Ann Thompson and Gordon McMullan, London: Thomson, 2003, pp. 3–16.

'Brave new world', *Economist*, 1 December 2001.

Brenton, Howard, *Measure for Measure*, in *Three Plays*, Sheffield: Sheffield Academic Press Ltd, 1989, pp. 89–164.

Bristol, Michael and Kathleen McLuskie, with Christopher Holmes, eds, *Shakespeare and Modern Theatre: The Performance of Modernity*, London: Routledge, 2001.

Brown, Geoff, 'Cooler Shakespeare', *The Times*, 27 March 1997.

Brown, Georgina, 'Shakespeare in the cold light of day', *Mail on Sunday Review*, 1 June 1997.

Brown, John Russell, 'Free Shakespeare', *Shakespeare Survey* 24 (1971): 127–35.

Bryant, John, *The Fluid Text: A Theory of Revision and Editing for Book and Screen*, Ann Arbor: University of Michigan Press, 2002.

Bulman, James C., 'The BBC Shakespeare and "House Style"', *Shakespeare Quarterly* 35 (1984): 571–81. Reprinted in *Shakespeare on Television: An Anthology of Essays and Reviews*, ed. J. C. Bulman and H. R. Coursen, Hanover: University Press of New England, 1988, pp. 50–60.

Bulman, James C. and H. R. Coursen, eds, *Shakespeare on Television: An Anthology of Essays and Reviews*, Hanover: University Press of New England, 1988.

Bunzli, James, 'The Geography of Creation: Décalage as Impulse, Process, and Outcome in the Theatre of Robert Lepage', *The Drama Review* (1999): 79–103.

Burke, Jim, 'Blockbusting Bard to triumph again', *Metro*, 2 March 2004.

Burnett, Linda, '"Redescribing a World": Towards a Theory of Shakespearean Adaptation in Canada', *Canadian Theatre Review* 111 (2002): 5–9.

Butler, Robert, *Independent on Sunday*, 24 November 1996.

—— 'Warchus puts his Art into his Hamlet', *Independent on Sunday*, 11 May 1997.

Caldwell, John Thornton, *Televisuality: Style, Crisis, and Authority in American Television*, New Brunswick, NJ: Rutgers University Press, 1995.

Callaghan, Dympna, '"Othello was a white man": Properties of Race on Shakespeare's Stage', in *Alternative Shakespeares*, vol. 2, ed. Terence Hawkes, London: Routledge, 1996, pp. 192–215.

Callow, Simon, 'Thrift, Horatio, thrift! And stuff the quality', *Independent (Weekend Review)*, 14 November 1998.

Cardwell, Sarah, *Adaptation Revisited: Television and the Classic Novel*, Manchester: Manchester University Press, 2002.

Carey, John, *What Good Are the Arts?* London: Faber and Faber, 2005.

Carroll, Noël, *A Philosophy of Mass Art*, Oxford: Clarendon, 1998.

Cartelli, Thomas, *Repositioning Shakespeare: National Formations, Postcolonial Appropriations*, London: Routledge, 1999.

Chambers, Colin, *Inside the Royal Shakespeare Company*, London: Routledge, 2004.

Chambers, E. K., 'The Disintegration of Shakespeare', London: Published for the British Academy by Oxford University Press, [1924].

Charnes, Linda, 'Shakespeare, and belief, in the future', *Presentist Shakespeares*, ed. Hugh Grady and Terence Hawkes, London: Routledge, 2007, pp. 64–78.

Christiansen, Rupert, 'Art for theatre's sake', *Daily Telegraph*, 11 October 1996.

——— 'Noble ambitions?', *Daily Telegraph*, 30 April 2002.

Christopher, James, '"The RSC made a mistake"', *Evening Standard*, 12 December 2002.

Clairmont, Donald H. and Dennis William Magill, *Africville: The Life and Death of a Canadian Black Community*, [1974], 3rd edn, Toronto: Canadian Scholars' Press, 1999.

Clayton, Thomas, '"Balancing at Work": (R)evoking the Script in Performance and Criticism', in *Shakespeare and the Sense of Performance: Essays in the Tradition of Performance Criticism in Honor of Bernard Beckerman*, ed. Marvin and Ruth Thompson, Newark: University of Delaware Press, 1989, pp. 228–49.

——— 'Theatrical Shakespearegresses at the Guthrie and Elsewhere: Notes on "Legitimate Production"', *New Literary History* 17 (1986): 511–38.

Cohn, Ruby, *Modern Shakespeare Offshoots*, Princeton, NJ: Princeton University Press, 1976.

——— *Retreats from Realism in Recent English Drama*, Cambridge: Cambridge University Press, 1991.

Coursen, H. R., 'The Bard and the Tube', in *Shakespeare on Television: An Anthology of Essays and Reviews*, ed. J. C. Bulman and H. R. Coursen, Hanover: University Press of New England, 1988, pp. 3–10.

——— *Shakespeare Translated: Derivatives on Film and TV*, New York: Peter Lang, 2005.

——— *Watching Shakespeare on Television*, Rutherford, NJ: Fairleigh Dickinson University Press, 1993.

Coveney, Michael, 'First person singular', *Observer*, 12 May 1996.

——— 'The RSC is suffering', *New Statesman*, vol. 127, 10 April 1998.

Curtis, Nick, 'Not boldness but sheer arrogance', *Evening Standard*, 6 January 1997.

Cushman, Robert, 'On the razor's edge', *Observer*, 6 April 1980.

Danto, Arthur C., *The Transfiguration of the Commonplace: A Philosophy of Art*, Cambridge, MA: Harvard University Press, 1981.

Dawson, Anthony B., *Hamlet*, Shakespeare in Performance, Manchester: Manchester University Press, 1995.

——— 'Much Ado about Signifying', *Studies in English Literature 1500–1900* 22 (1982): 211–21.

de Certeau, Michel, *The Possession at Loudun*, trans. Michael B. Smith, with a Foreword by Stephen Greenblatt, Chicago: University of Chicago Press, 2000.

——— *The Writing of History*, trans. Tom Conley, New York: Columbia University Press, 1988.

de Grazia, Margreta, *Shakespeare Verbatim: The Reproduction of Authenticity and the 1790 Apparatus*, Oxford: Clarendon Press, 1991.

de Grazia, Margreta and Peter Stallybrass, 'Love among the Ruins: Response to Pechter', *Textual Practice* 11 (1997): 69–79.

——— 'The Materiality of the Shakespearean Text', *Shakespeare Quarterly* 44 (1993): 255–83.

Deighton, K., ed., *Hamlet, Prince of Denmark*, London: Macmillan, 1891, reprinted 1931.

de Jongh, Nicholas, *Evening Standard*, 9 May 1997, quoted in *Theatre Record*, 7–20 May 1997.

Delgado, Maria M. and Paul Heritage, eds, *In Contact with the Gods? Directors Talk Theatre*, Manchester: Manchester University Press, 1996, pp. 129–57.

Desmet, Christy and Robert Sawyer, *Shakespeare and Appropriation*, London: Routledge, 1999.

Dessen, Alan C., *Elizabethan Stage Conventions and Modern Interpreters*, Cambridge: Cambridge University Press, 1984.

—— *Recovering Shakespeare's Theatrical Vocabulary*, Cambridge: Cambridge University Press, 1995.

—— *Rescripting Shakespeare: The Text, the Director, and Modern Productions*, Cambridge: Cambridge University Press, 2002.

—— 'Shakespeare and the Theatrical Conventions of His Time', in *Cambridge Companion to Shakespeare Studies*, ed. Stanley Wells, Cambridge: Cambridge University Press, 1986, pp. 85–99.

Dickinson, Peter, 'Duets, Duologues, and Black Diasporic Theatre: Djanet Sears, William Shakespeare, and Others', *Modern Drama* 45 (2002): 188–208.

Dickson, E. Jane, 'William's Women', BBC *Radio Times*, 5–11 November 2005, pp. 13–15.

Dobson, Michael, *The Making of the National Poet: Shakespeare, Adaptation, and Authorship, 1660–1769*, Oxford: Clarendon Press, 1992.

—— 'Shakespeare Performances in England, 2001', *Shakespeare Survey* 55 (2002): 285–321.

Donnelly, Pat, 'It's all Lepage – from Hamlet to gravedigger', *Toronto Star*, 11 November 1995.

Doran, Gregory, dir., *All's Well that Ends Well*, Promptbook, Royal Shakespeare Company archive, Shakespeare Centre Library, Stratford-upon-Avon, England, first performance 11 December 2003.

Durband, Alan, ed., *1 Henry IV*, Shakespeare Made Easy, New York: Baron's Educational Series, 1985.

Edwardes, Jane, 'Elsinore', *TimeOut*, 1 January 1997.

Edwards, Philip, ed., *Hamlet*, Cambridge: Cambridge University Press, 1985.

Eggert, Paul, 'Document and Text: The "Life" of the Literary Work and the Capacities of Editing', *Text* 7 (1993): 1–24.

Ellis, John, 'Defining the Medium', in *Tele-Visions: An Introduction to Studying Television*, ed. Glen Creeber, London: British Film Institute Publishing, 2006, pp. 12–19.

Erickson, Peter, *Rewriting Shakespeare, Rewriting Ourselves*, Berkeley: University of California Press, 1991.

Erne, Lukas, *Shakespeare as Literary Dramatist*, Cambridge: Cambridge University Press, 2003.

Erne, Lukas and Margaret Jane Kidnie, eds, *Textual Performances: The Modern Reproduction of Shakespeare's Drama*, Cambridge: Cambridge University Press, 2004.

Escolme, Bridget, *Talking to the Audience: Shakespeare, Performance, Self*, London: Routledge, 2005.

Evans, G. Blakemore with J. J. M. Tobin, eds, *The Riverside Shakespeare* 2nd edn, Boston: Houghton Mifflin Company, 1997.

Fanon, Frantz, *Black Skin, White Masks*, trans. Charles Lam Markmann, New York: Grove Press, 1967.

Feinstein, Howard, 'Wherefore art thou Leonardo?', *Guardian*, 6 December 1996.

Fenton, James, 'A tremendous "Hamlet"', *Sunday Times*, 6 April 1980.

Fischlin, Daniel, 'Nation and/as Adaptation: Shakespeare, Canada, and Authenticity', in *Shakespeare in Canada: 'A World Elsewhere'?*, ed. Diana Brydon and Irena R. Makaryk, Toronto: University of Toronto Press, 2002, pp. 313–38.

Fischlin, Daniel and Mark Fortier, eds, *Adaptations of Shakespeare: A Critical Anthology of Plays from the Seventeenth Century to the Present*, London: Routledge, 2000.

Fiske, John, *Television Culture*, London: Methuen, 1987.

Fiske, John and John Hartley, *Reading Television*, with a new Foreword by John Hartley, London and New York: Routledge, 2003.

Foakes, R. A., 'Performance Theory and Textual Theory: A Retort Courteous', *Shakespeare* 2:1 (2006): 47–58.

Fortier, Mark, 'Undead and Unsafe: Adapting Shakespeare (in Canada)', in *Shakespeare in Canada: 'a world elsewhere'?*, ed. Diana Brydon and Irena R. Makaryk, Toronto: University of Toronto Press, 2002, pp. 339–52.

Freeman, Neil, ed., *The Taming of the Shrew*, New York: Applause Books, 1998.

Friedman, Michael D., 'In Defense of Authenticity', *Studies in Philology* 99 (2002): 33–56.

Furness, H. H., ed., *A New Variorum Edition of Shakespeare: Hamlet*, vol. 1, Philadelphia, PA: J. B. Lippincott Company, 1877.

LG, 'Hamlet, RSC, Main Theatre, Stratford', *Stratford-upon-Avon Journal*, 22 May 1997.

Galey, Alan, 'The Shakespearean Archive: Information's Cultural Work from Early Modern Print to the Electronic New Variorum Shakespeare', unpublished doctoral dissertation, University of Western Ontario, 2006.

Gardner, Lyn, 'Ban the bard', *Guardian*, 8 May 1997.

—— 'Mission impossible', *Guardian*, 19 February 2007.

—— 'Now buy the T-shirt … ', *Guardian*, 27 February 2001.

Garner, Shirley Nelson, '*The Taming of the Shrew*: Inside or Outside of the Joke?', in *'Bad' Shakespeare: Revaluations of the Shakespeare Canon*, ed. Maurice Charney, Rutherford, NJ: Fairleigh Dickinson University Press, 1988, pp. 105–19.

Gaskell, Philip, *From Writer to Reader: Studies in Editorial Method*, Oxford: Clarendon Press, 1978.

Genette, Gérard, *Palimpsests: Literature in the Second Degree*, [1982], trans. Channa Newman and Claude Doubinsky, Lincoln: University of Nebraska Press, 1997.

Gibbons, Fiachra, 'Homeless RSC faces winter of discontent', *Guardian*, 8 October 2003.

—— 'RSC abandons its roots to lure stars', *Guardian*, 25 May 2001.

Gibson, K. Jane, 'Seeing Double: The Map-making Process of Robert Lepage', *Canadian Theatre Review* 97 (1998): 18–23.

Gilbert, Helen and Joanne Tompkins, *Post-Colonial Drama: Theory, Practice, Politics*, London: Routledge, 1996.

Gilbert, Miriam, 'The Leasing-out of the RSC', *Shakespeare Quarterly* 53 (2002): 512–24.

Gilroy, Paul, *Against Race: Imagining Political Culture beyond the Color Line*, Cambridge, MA: Harvard University Press, 2000.

Glaister, Dan, 'Fated, not fêted', *Guardian*, 15 August 1996.

Glavin, John, 'Bulgakov's Lizard and the Problem of the Playwright's Authority', *Text* 4 (1988): 385–405.

Goldberg, Jonathan, 'Textual Properties', *Shakespeare Quarterly* 37 (1986): 213–17.

Goodman, Nelson, *Languages of Art: An Approach to a Theory of Symbols*, 2nd edn, Indianapolis and Cambridge: Hackett Publishing Company, 1976.

Gore-Langton, Robert, *Express*, 15 May 1997, quoted in *Theatre Record*, 7–20 May 1997.

Grady, Hugh, and Terence Hawkes, 'Introduction: Presenting Presentism', in *Presentist Shakespeares*, ed. Hugh Grady and Terence Hawkes, London: Routledge, 2007, pp. 1–5.

Grafton, Anthony, *Forgers and Critics: Creativity and Duplicity in Western Scholarship*, Princeton, NJ: Princeton University Press, 1990.

Grant, Steve, *TimeOut*, 14 May 1997, quoted in *Theatre Record*, 7–20 May 1997.

Greetham, D. C., *Theories of the Text*, Oxford: Oxford University Press, 1999.

Greg, W. W., *The Editorial Problem in Shakespeare: A Survey of the Foundations of the Text*, 3rd edn, Oxford: Clarendon Press, 1954.

—— 'The Rationale of Copy-Text', *Studies in Bibliography* 3 (1950): 19–36.

—— *The Shakespeare First Folio: Its Bibliographical and Textual History*, Oxford: Clarendon Press, 1955.

Grigely, Joseph, *Textualterity: Art, Theory, and Textual Criticism*, Ann Arbor: University of Michigan Press, 1995.

Gross, John, 'New-minted Moor', *Sunday Telegraph*, 22 February 2004.

—— *Sunday Telegraph*, 11 May 1997, quoted in *Theatre Record*, 7–20 May 1997.

Halio, Jay L., *Understanding Shakespeare's Plays in Performance*, Manchester: Manchester University Press, 1988.

Hall, Peter, *Peter Hall's Diaries*, ed. John Goodwin, London: Hamish Hamilton, 1983.

Halstead, William P., *Shakespeare as Spoken: A Collation of 5000 Acting Editions and Promptbooks of Shakespeare*, 14 vols, Ann Arbor, MI: Published for American Theatre Association by University Microfilms International, 1977–83, Vol. 4: *The Taming of the Shrew, All's Well That Ends Well, Twelfth Night* (1979).

'Hamlet as domestic drama', *Daily Mail*, 6 December 1997.

Hanks, Robert, 'Fellow of infinite jest?', *Independent*, 30 April 1997.

Hannon, Martin, and Robert McNeil, 'Festival gloom as theatre showpiece cancelled', *Scotsman*, 14 August 1996.

Hapgood, Robert, ed., *Hamlet*, Shakespeare in Production, Cambridge: Cambridge University Press, 1999.

Hartley, John, *Uses of Television*, London and New York: Routledge, 1999.

Harvie, Jennifer, and Erin Hurley, 'States of Play: Locating Québec in the Performances of Robert Lepage, Ex Machina, and the Cirque du Soleil', *Theatre Journal* 51:3 (1999): 299–315.

Hastings, Chris, 'Nunn lays into BBC for Shakespeare-lite', *Sunday Telegraph*, 9 October 2005.

Hattersley, Roy, 'A sea of woes', *Guardian*, 7 October 2002.

Hawkes, Terence, *Meaning by Shakespeare*, London: Routledge, 1992.

Henderson, Diana E., *Collaborations with the Past: Reshaping Shakespeare across Time and Media*, Ithaca, NY: Cornell University Press, 2006.

Hendricks, Margo, 'Civility, Barbarism, and Aphra Behn's *The Widow Ranter*', *Women, 'Race', and Writing in the Early Modern Period*, ed. Margo Hendricks and Patricia Parker, London: Routledge, 1994, pp. 225–39.

Hibbard, G. R., ed., *Hamlet*, Oxford: Oxford University Press, 1987.

—— *The Taming of the Shrew*, London: Penguin, 1968.

Hodgdon, Barbara, 'Looking for Mr. Shakespeare after "The Revolution": Robert Lepage's Intercultural *Dream* Machine', *Shakespeare, Theory, and Performance*, ed. James C. Bulman, London: Routledge, 1996, pp. 68–91.

—— 'New Collaborations with Old Plays: The (Textual) Politics of Performance Commentary', in *Textual Performances: The Modern Reproduction of Shakespeare's Drama*, ed. Lukas Erne and Margaret Jane Kidnie, Cambridge: Cambridge University Press, 2004, pp. 210–23.

—— 'Parallel Practices, or the *Un*-Necessary Difference', *Kenyon Review* 7:3 (1985): 57–65.

—— *The Shakespeare Trade: Performances and Appropriations*, Philadelphia: University of Pennsylvania Press, 1998.

Holderness, Graham, *Textual Shakespeare: Writing and the Word*, Hatfield: University of Hertfordshire Press, 2003.

Holderness, Graham, Bryan Loughrey, and Andrew Murphy, 'Busy Doing Nothing: A Response to Edward Pechter', *Textual Practice* 11 (1997): 81–7.

Holland, Peter, *English Shakespeares: Shakespeare on the English Stage in the 1990s*, Cambridge: Cambridge University Press, 1997.

—— ed., *From Script to Stage in Early Modern England*, Basingstoke: Palgrave Macmillan, 2004.

—— ed., *Shakespeare, Memory and Performance*, Cambridge: Cambridge University Press, 2006.

Hornby, Richard, *Script into Performance: A Structuralist View of Play Production*, Austin and London: University of Texas Press, 1977.

Howard, Jean E., *The Stage and Social Struggle in Early Modern England*, London: Routledge, 1994.

Hunt, Nigel, 'The Global Voyage of Robert Lepage', *The Drama Review* 33 (1989): 104–18.

Hutcheon, Linda, *A Theory of Adaptation*, London: Routledge, 2006.

Ingram, William, 'Introduction: Early Modern Theatre History: Where We Are Now, How We Got Here, Where We Go Next', in *A Handbook on Early Modern Theatre*, ed. Richard Dutton, Oxford: Oxford University Press, forthcoming.

Innes, Christopher, 'Beyond Categories (Redefining "mainstream")', in *Beyond the Mainstream*, ed. Peter Paul Schnierer, Contemporary Drama in English, vol. 4, 1996, Trier: WVT Wissenschaftlicher Verlag Trier, 1997, pp. 55–67.

Johns, Ian, 'Of trysts and mellow fruitfulness', *Times*, 21 February 2004.

Joseph, Clifton, in interview with Djanet Sears, '*Harlem Duet*: The Stratford Festival opens its first all-black production', *The National*, Canadian Broadcasting Corporation, air date 30 June 2006.

Jowett, John, 'Addressing Adaptation: *Measure for Measure* and *Sir Thomas More*', in *Textual Performances: The Modern Reproduction of Shakespeare's Drama*, ed. Lukas Erne and Margaret Jane Kidnie, Cambridge: Cambridge University Press, 2004, pp. 63–76.

—— 'Editing Shakespeare's Plays in the Twentieth Century', *Shakespeare Survey* 59 (2006): 1–19.

—— *Shakespeare and Text*, Oxford: Oxford University Press, 2007.

Jury, Louise, 'Financial drama at RSC eased as debts are reduced by half', *Independent*, 13 December 2003.

Kastan, David Scott, *Shakespeare after Theory*, London: Routledge, 1999.

—— *Shakespeare and the Book*, Cambridge: Cambridge University Press, 2001.

Kellaway, Kate, 'Where to be or not to be?', *Observer Review*, 11 January 2004.

Kempe, Cordula, 'The Royal Shakespeare Company and Its Future: A Submission', October 2001, Shakespeare Institute Library, p/box 203.

Kennedy, Dennis, ed., *Foreign Shakespeare: Contemporary Performance*, Cambridge: Cambridge University Press, 1993.

Kennedy, Janice, 'Hamlet: The Canadian Sequel', *Ottawa Citizen*, 8 September 1997.

Kidnie, Margaret Jane, 'The Staging of Shakespeare's Drama in Print Editions', in *Textual Performances: The Modern Reproduction of Shakespeare's Drama*, ed. Lukas Erne and Margaret Jane Kidnie, Cambridge: Cambridge University Press, 2004, pp. 158–77.

—— 'Text, Performance, and the Editors: Staging Shakespeare's Drama', *Shakespeare Quarterly* 51 (2000): 456–73.

—— '"What world is this?": *Pericles* at the Stratford Festival of Canada, 2003', *Shakespeare Quarterly* 55 (2004): 307–19.

Knowles, Richard Paul [Ric], 'From Dream to Machine: Peter Brook, Robert Lepage, and the Contemporary Shakespearean Director as (Post)Modernist', *Theatre Journal* 50 (1998): 189–206.

—— 'Reading *Elsinore*: The Ghost and the Machine', *Canadian Theatre Review* 111 (2002): 87–8.

—— '"The Real of It Would Be Awful": Representing the Real Ophelia in Canada', *Theatre Survey* 39:1 (1998): 21–40.

—— 'Shakespeare, 1993, and the Discourses of the Stratford Festival, Ontario', *Shakespeare Quarterly* 45 (1994): 211–25.

Koenig, Rhoda, 'All's Well That Ends Well', *Independent Review*, 24 February 2004.

—— 'A truly terrific history', *Independent*, 15 December 2000.

Lavagnino, John, 'Two Varieties of Digital Commentary', in *Textual Performances: The Modern Reproduction of Shakespeare's Drama*, ed. Lukas Erne and Margaret Jane Kidnie, Cambridge: Cambridge University Press, 2004, pp. 194–209.

Lavender, Andy, *Hamlet in Pieces: Shakespeare Reworked by Peter Brook, Robert Lepage, Robert Wilson*, London: Nick Hern Books, 2001.

Lawson, Mark, 'Changing the Bard', *Guardian (Culture)*, 2 November 2005.

Lepage, Robert, dir., *Da Vinci*, Working Script (May 1987), English adaptation by Linda Gaboriau.

—— *Elseneur – Elsinore*, Touring Script (1996), Ex Machina archives, La Caserne Dalhousie, Québec City.

—— '*Elsinore*, based on *Hamlet* by William Shakespeare, adapted by Robert Lepage, produced by Ex Machina', *Canadian Theatre Review* 111 (2002): 89–99.

—— *Elsinore*, Programme, Royal National Theatre, first performance 4 January 1997.

Levin, Richard, 'Performance-Critics *vs* Close Readers in the Study of English Renaissance Drama', *Modern Language Review* 81 (1986): 545–59.

'Life's a beach, and then you die', *Evening Standard*, 27 March 1997.

Lister, David, 'Another tragedy at the Royal Shakespeare Company', *Independent*, 29 March 2003.

Loewenstein, Joseph, 'The Script in the Marketplace', *Representations* 12 (1985): 101–14; reprinted in *Representing the English Renaissance*, ed. Stephen Greenblatt, Berkeley: University of California Press, 1988, pp. 265–78.

Long, William B., '"A bed / for woodstock": A Warning for the Unwary', *Medieval and Renaissance Drama in England* 2 (1985): 91–118.

—— 'Stage-Directions: A Misinterpreted Factor in Determining Textual Provenance', *Text* 2 (1985): 121–37.

Lyotard, Jean-François, *The Differend: Phrases in Dispute*, [1983], trans. Georges Van Den Abbeele, Theory and History of Literature 46, Minneapolis: University of Minnesota Press, 1988.

Macaulay, Alastair, 'All cut up over Hamlet', *Financial Times*, 7 January 1997.

—— *Financial Times*, 14 May 1997, quoted in *Theatre Record*, 7–20 May 1997.

McCandless, David, *Gender and Performance in Shakespeare's Problem Comedies*, Bloomington and Indianapolis: Indiana University Press, 1997.

McCrum, Robert, 'Shakespeare on the BBC? Great. Oh, hang on a moment', *Observer Review*, 6 November 2005.

MacDonald, Joyce Green, 'Black Ram, White Ewe: Shakespeare, Race, and Women', in *A Feminist Companion to Shakespeare*, ed. Dympna Callaghan, Oxford: Blackwell, 2000, pp. 188–207.

—— 'Finding *Othello*'s African Roots through Djanet Sears's *Harlem Duet*', in *Approaches to Teaching Shakespeare's* Othello, ed. Peter Erickson and Maurice Hunt, New York: Modern Language Association of America, 2005, pp. 202–8.

McDonald, Russ, 'Planned Obsolescence or Working at the Words', in *Teaching Shakespeare: Passing It On*, ed. G. B. Shand, Chichester: Wiley-Blackwell, 2009, pp. 25–42.

McGann, Jerome J., *A Critique of Modern Textual Criticism*, Charlottesville: University Press of Virginia, 1992.

—— *Radiant Textuality: Literature after the World Wide Web*, Basingstoke: Palgrave, 2001.

—— *The Textual Condition*, Princeton, NJ: Princeton University Press, 1991.

McLaverty, James, 'The Concept of Authorial Intention in Textual Criticism', *The Library*, 6th ser., 6 (1984): 121–38.

—— 'The Mode of Existence of Literary Works of Art: The Case of the *Dunciad* Variorum', *Studies in Bibliography* 37 (1984): 82–105.

McLeod, Randall, ed., *Crisis in Editing*, New York: AMS Press, 1994.

—— [Random Clod], 'Information upon Information', *Text* 5 (1991): 241–81.

—— [Random Cloud], 'The Marriage of Good and Bad Quartos', *Shakespeare Quarterly* 33 (1982): 421–30.

—— 'UnEditing Shak-speare', *Sub-Stance* 33–4 (1982): 26–55.

McMillan, Scott, ed., *The First Quarto of Othello*, New Cambridge Shakespeare – The Early Quartos, Cambridge: Cambridge University Press, 2001.

McSorley, Tom, '*Elsinore*, by Robert Lepage', broadcast on 'All in a Day', CBC Radio 1, 10 September 1997.

Maddox, David, 'Insiders head list for top RSC job', *Stratford-upon-Avon Herald*, 11 July 2002.

Malcolm, Derek, 'Romeo and Juliet: Bard's in the 'hood', *Guardian*, 28 March 1997.

Malvern, Jack, 'RSC plays to bypass London for first time', *Times*, 8 October 2003.

Marcus, Leah S., 'The Two Texts of *Othello* and Early Modern Constructions of Race', in *Textual Performances: The Modern Reproduction of Shakespeare's Drama*, ed. Lukas Erne and Margaret Jane Kidnie, Cambridge: Cambridge University Press, 2004, pp. 21–36.

—— *Unediting the Renaissance: Shakespeare, Marlowe, Milton*, London: Routledge, 1996.

Margolis, Joseph, *Art and Philosophy*, Brighton: Harvester Press, 1980.

Marowitz, Charles, *The Marowitz Shakespeare: Adaptations and Collages of* Hamlet, Macbeth, The Taming of the Shrew, Measure for Measure, *and* The Merchant of Venice, New York and London: Marion Boyars, 1978.

Marshall, Cynthia, 'Sight and Sound: Two Models of Shakespearean Subjectivity on the British Stage', *Shakespeare Quarterly* 51 (2000): 353–61.

Massai, Sonia, *Shakespeare and the Rise of the Editor*, Cambridge: Cambridge University Press, 2007.

—— ed., *World-wide Shakespeares: Local Appropriations in Film and Performance*, London: Routledge, 2005.

Mazer, Cary, 'Not Not Shakespeare: Directorial Adaptation, Authorship, and Ownership', *Shakespeare Bulletin* 23 (2005): 23–42.

Miles, Patrick, 'Chekhov, Shakespeare, the Ensemble and the Company', *New Theatre Quarterly* 11 (1995): 203–10.

Mittell, Jason, 'A Cultural Approach to Television Genre Theory', *The Television Studies Reader*, ed. Robert C. Allen and Annette Hill, London: Routledge, 2004, pp. 171–81.

Morley, Sheridan, 'Stratford's chaotic shambles', *Spectator*, 16 March 2002.

Morris, Brian, ed., *The Taming of the Shrew*, London: Methuen, 1981.

Morrish, John, 'To be the Prince at last', *Sunday Telegraph*, 27 April 1997.

Morrison, James, 'Once more unto the Barbican for RSC', *Independent on Sunday*, 13 January 2002.

—— 'RSC chief is wrong, say theatre knights', *Independent on Sunday*, 24 March 2002.

Morrow, Martin, 'Of Cast Iron and Steam', *Canadian Review of Books* 36:1 (January–February 2007), p. 38.

Mowat, Barbara, 'The Problem of Shakespeare's Text(s)', *Shakespeare Jahrbuch* 132 (1996): 26–43, reprinted in *Textual Formations and Reformations*, ed. Laurie E. Maguire and Thomas L. Berger, Newark: University of Delaware Press, 1998, pp. 131–48.

'MPs baulk at bill for RSC "village"', *Independent on Sunday*, 10 March 2002.

Myhill, Nova, 'Spectatorship in/of *Much Ado about Nothing*', *Studies in English Literature 1500–1900* 39 (1999): 291–311.

Myrie, Evelyn, 'Stratford play breaks new multicultural ground', *Hamilton Spectator*, 17 July 2006.

Nathan, David, *Jewish Chronicle*, 16 May 1997, quoted in *Theatre Record*, 7–20 May 1997.

Negroponte, Nicholas, *Being Digital*, New York: Alfred A. Knopf, 1995.

Neill, Michael, '"Mulattos," "Blacks," and "Indian Moors": *Othello* and Early Modern Constructions of Human Difference', *Shakespeare Quarterly* 49 (1998): 361–74.

—— '*Othello* and Race', in *Approaches to Teaching Shakespeare's* Othello, ed. Peter Erickson and Maurice Hunt, New York: Modern Language Association of America, 2005, pp. 37–52.

—— 'Unproper Beds: Race, Adultery, and the Hideous in *Othello*', *Shakespeare Quarterly* 40 (1989): 383–412.

Newman, Karen, *Fashioning Femininity and English Renaissance Drama*, Chicago: University of Chicago Press, 1991.

Nightingale, Benedict, 'All the world's a new stage', *Times*, 30 May 2001.

—— 'Cuts that forget the play's the thing', *Times*, 6 December 1997.

—— 'Dame, set and match to Judi Dench', *Times*, 13 December 2003.

—— 'Missing the point', *Times*, 6 January 1997.

—— 'Power and the gory', *Times*, 27 April 2001.

—— 'Reduced Shakespeare Co', *Times*, 22 March 2002.

—— 'Some day my Prince will come', *Times*, 18 February 2008.

—— *Times*, 10 May 1997, quoted in *Theatre Record*, 7–20 May 1997.

Noble, Adrian, 'All's Well', *Guardian*, 3 October 2001.

—— dir., *Hamlet*, Programme notes, Royal Shakespeare Company, first performance 12 December 1992.

—— 'We must reinvent theatre for a generation raised on television', *Independent*, 26 March 2002.

O'Bryan, Ann, *Hamlet, A CurtainUp Review*, 2 January 1998.

Oliver, H. J., ed. *The Taming of the Shrew*, Oxford: Oxford University Press, 1982.

Orgel, Stephen, *The Authentic Shakespeare and Other Problems of the Early Modern Stage*, London: Routledge, 2002.

Orkin, Martin, 'Possessing the book and peopling the text', in *Post-colonial Shakespeares*, ed. Ania Loomba and Martin Orkin, London: Routledge, 1998, pp. 186–204.

Osborne, Laurie E., 'Rethinking the Performance Editions: Theatrical and Textual Productions of Shakespeare', *Shakespeare, Theory, and Performance*, ed. James C. Bulman, London: Routledge, 1996, pp. 168–86.

—— *The Trick of Singularity:* Twelfth Night *and the Performance Editions*, Iowa City: University of Iowa Press, 1996.

Parker, Hershel, 'The Text Itself – Whatever That Is', *Text* 3 (1987): 47–54.

Partner, Nancy, 'Making up Lost Time: Writing on the Writing of History', *Speculum* 61 (1986): 90–117.

Patterson, John, and Gareth McLean, 'Move over Hollywood', *Guardian*, 20 May 2006.

Pechter, Edward, 'All You Need Is Love (Dah Dahdah Dahdah): A Response to Margreta de Grazia, Peter Stallybrass, Graham Holderness, Bryan Loughrey and Andrew Murphy', *Textual Practice* 11 (1997): 331–4.

—— 'Crisis in Editing?', *Shakespeare Survey* 59, Cambridge: Cambridge University Press, 2006, pp. 20–38.

—— 'Making Love to Our Employment; Or, the Immateriality of Arguments about the Materiality of the Shakespearean Text', *Textual Practice* 11 (1997): 51–67.

—— ed., *Textual and Theatrical Shakespeare: Questions of Evidence*, Iowa City: University of Iowa Press, 1996.

Peter, John, 'Bloodbath at the RSC', *Sunday Times (Culture)*, 18 November 2001.

—— *Sunday Times*, 18 May 1997, quoted in *Theatre Record*, 7–20 May 1997.

—— 'That's moor like it', *Sunday Times*, 29 February 2004.

Purkis, James, 'Recognizing the Author in Early Modern English Literature', unpublished doctoral dissertation, University of Birmingham, 2005.

Rabkin, Gerald, 'Is There a Text on This Stage? Theatre, Authorship, Interpretation', in *Re:Direction – A Theoretical and Practical Guide*, ed. Rebecca Schneider and Gabrielle Cody, London: Routledge, 2002, pp. 319–31.

Rasmussen, Eric, 'The Revision of Scripts', *A New History of Early English Drama*, ed. John D. Cox and David Scott Kastan, New York: Columbia University Press, 1997, pp. 441–60.

Reduced Shakespeare Company, *The Complete Works of William Shakespeare (abridged)*, dir. Paul Kafno, Acorn Media, 2001.

Rees, Jasper, 'A cut above the rest', *Independent on Sunday*, 27 April 1997.

Riding, Alan, 'The Royal Shakespeare: Renewing Itself under Fire', *New York Times*, 17 May 1998.

Roberts, Alison, 'Now we're much more nimble. We're fitter', *Evening Standard*, 27 February 2001.

Robinson, Jenefer, 'Languages of Art at the Turn of the Century', *Journal of Aesthetics and Art Criticism* 58 (2000): 213–18.

Rorty, Richard, *Consequences of Pragmatism (Essays: 1972–1980)*, Minneapolis: University of Minnesota Press, 1982.

Rose, Lloyd, '"Hamlet," Cut to the Quick', *Washington Post*, 12 June 1998.

Rosenthal, Daniel, 'The power behind the throne', *Independent*, 13 December 2000.

Salter, Denis, 'Acting Shakespeare in Postcolonial Space', in *Shakespeare, Theory, and Performance*, ed. James C. Bulman, London: Routledge, 1996, pp. 113–32.

Sanders, Julie, *Adaptation and Appropriation*, London: Routledge, 2006.

—— *Novel Shakespeares: Twentieth-century Women Novelists and Appropriation*, Manchester: Manchester University Press, 2001.

Schafer, Elizabeth, 'Performance Editions, Editing and Editors', *Shakespeare Survey* 59 (2006): 198–212.

Schoch, Richard W., *Not Shakespeare: Bardolatry and Burlesque in the Nineteenth Century*, Cambridge: Cambridge University Press, 2002.

Sears, Djanet, *Afrika Solo*, Toronto: Sister Vision, 1990.

—— *Harlem Duet*, Toronto: Scirocco Drama, 1997.

—— *Harlem Duet*, dir. Djanet Sears, Promptbook, Nightwood Theatre archives, Archival and Special Collections, McLaughlin Library, University of Guelph, first performance 20 April 1997.

—— *Harlem Duet*, dir. Djanet Sears, Programme, Stratford Festival of Canada, first performance 20 June 2006.

Sears, Djanet and Alison Sealy-Smith in interview with Ric Knowles, 'The Nike Method', *Canadian Theatre Review* 97 (1998): 24–30.

ShakespeaRe-Told, Broadcast BBC November 2005, Acorn Video, 2006.

Shaw, George Bernard, *Shaw on Shakespeare: An Anthology of Bernard Shaw's Writings on the Plays and Production of Shakespeare*, ed. and with an introduction by Edwin Wilson, London: Cassell, 1962.

Shillingsburg, Peter L., *Scholarly Editing in the Computer Age: Theory and Practice*, 3rd edn, Ann Arbor: University of Michigan Press, 1996.

——'Text as Matter, Concept, and Action', *Studies in Bibliography* 44 (1991): 31–82.

Shuttleworth, Ian, 'Playing games with Hamlet', *Financial Times*, 21 November 1996.

Singh, Jyotsna, 'Othello's Identity, Postcolonial Theory, and Contemporary African Rewritings of *Othello*', in *Women, 'Race', and Writing in the Early Modern Period*, ed. Margo Hendricks and Patricia Parker, London: Routledge, 1994, pp. 287–99.

Smallwood, Robert, 'Shakespeare Performances in England, 1997', *Shakespeare Survey* 51 (1998): 219–55.

Smith, David, 'RSC battles to keep £13m grant as its crown slips', *Observer*, 16 November 2003.

Smith, Duncan, 'Dame back at RSC after 25 years away', *Stratford-upon-Avon Herald*, 11 December 2003.

Smith, Gary, 'Stratford's *Harlem Duet* deserves to be seen', *Hamilton Spectator*, 26 August 2006.

Spencer, Charles, 'All rise for Dame Judi', *Daily Telegraph*, 13 December 2003.

—— 'Dench delivers a perfect farewell', *Daily Telegraph*, 21 February 2004.

—— 'Gripped by a 12-hour bloodfest', *Daily Telegraph*, 15 December 2000.

—— 'In short, it's Hamlet Lite', *Daily Telegraph*, 12 May 1997.

—— 'The RSC's brave new world', *Daily Telegraph*, 22 September 2001.

—— 'To be or not to be at Edinburgh Festival depends on a broken rivet', *Daily Telegraph*, 15 August 1996.

—— *Weekend Telegraph*, 27 November 1993.

—— 'When the machinery stops the show', *Daily Telegraph*, 15 August 1996.

Spencer, T. J. B., ed., *Hamlet*, rev. edn, London: Penguin, 1996.

Steen, Shannon and Margaret Werry, 'Bodies, Technologies, and Subjectivities: The Production of Authority in Robert Lepage's *Elsinore*', *Études Théâtrales / Essays in Theatre* 16 (1998): 139–51.

Stoppard, Tom, *Dogg's Hamlet*, in *The Real Inspector Hound and Other Entertainments*, London: Faber and Faber, 1993.

—— *The Fifteen Minute Hamlet*, New York: Samuel French, 1978.

—— *Jumpers*, New York: Grove Press, 1972.

Styan, J. L., *All's Well That Ends Well*, Shakespeare in Performance, Manchester: Manchester University Press, 1984.

Sutcliffe, Thomas, 'Last Night's TV: Bard in the background', *Independent*, 22 November 2005.

Tanselle, G. Thomas, 'The Editorial Problem of Final Authorial Intention', in *Selected Studies in Bibliography*, Charlottesville: University Press of Virginia, 1979, pp. 309–53.

—— *A Rationale of Textual Criticism*, Philadelphia: University of Pennsylvania Press, 1989.

Taylor, Gary, *Reinventing Shakespeare: A Cultural History from the Restoration to the Present*, London: Vintage, 1991.

—— 'The Renaissance and the End of Editing', in *Palimpsest: Editorial Theory in the Humanities*, ed. George Bornstein and Ralph G. Williams, Ann Arbor: University of Michigan Press, 1993, pp. 121–40.

Taylor, Gary, and John Jowett, *Shakespeare Reshaped 1606–1623*, Oxford: Clarendon Press, 1993.

Taylor, Gary, and John Lavagnino, gen. eds, *Thomas Middleton: The Collected Works*, Oxford: Oxford University Press, 2007.

—— *Thomas Middleton and Early Modern Textual Culture: A Companion to the Collected Works*, Oxford: Oxford University Press, 2007.

Taylor, Paul, *Independent*, 26 November 1993.

—— 'There is nothing like a dame', *Independent Review*, 15 December 2003.

Thieme, John, 'A Different "Othello Music": Djanet Sears's *Harlem Duet*', in *Performing National Identities: International Perspectives on Contemporary Canadian Theatre*, ed. Sherrill Grace and Albert-Reiner Glaap, Vancouver: Talonbooks, 2003, pp. 81–91.

Thompson, Ann, ed., *Taming of the Shrew*, Cambridge: Cambridge University Press, 1984.

Thompson, Ann, and Gordon McMullan, eds, *In Arden: Editing Shakespeare*, London: Thomson Learning, 2003.

Thorpe, James, *Principles of Textual Criticism*, San Marino: Huntington Library, 1972.

Tompkins, Joanne, 'Infinitely Rehearsing Performance and Identity: *Africa* [sic] *Solo* and *The Book of Jessica*', *Canadian Theatre Review* 74 (1993): 35–9.

Treadwell, James, *Spectator*, 17 May 1997, quoted in *Theatre Record*, 7–20 May 1997.

Trewin, J. C., *Five and Eighty Hamlets*, London: Century Hutchinson, 1987.

Trousdale, Marion, 'A Trip through the Divided Kingdoms', *Shakespeare Quarterly* 37 (1986): 218–23.

Tumelson II, Ronald A., 'Ferdinand's Wife and Prospero's Wise', *Shakespeare Survey* 59 (2006): 79–90.

Vickers, Brian, 'By other hands', *Times Literary Supplement*, 11 August 2006, pp. 10–12.

Walker, James W. St. G., 'Allegories and Orientations in African-Canadian Historiography: The Spirit of Africville', *Dalhousie Review* 77:2 (1997): 155–77.

Wall, Wendy, 'De-generation: Editions, Offspring, and *Romeo and Juliet*', in *From Performance to Print in Shakespeare's England*, ed. Peter Holland and Stephen Orgel, Basingstoke: Palgrave Macmillan, 2006, pp. 152–70.

Wallach, Allan, *Hamlet, A CurtainUp Review*, 23 May 1998.

Warchus, Matthew, dir., *Hamlet*, Programme, Royal Shakespeare Company archives, Shakespeare Centre Library, Stratford-upon-Avon, England, first performance 8 May 1997.

—— dir., *Hamlet*, Promptbook, Royal Shakespeare Company archives, Shakespeare Centre Library, Stratford-upon-Avon, England, first performance 8 May 1997.

Warren, Michael, *The Complete 'King Lear', 1608–1623*, Berkeley, Los Angeles and London: University of California Press, 1989.

Wayne, Valerie, 'The Sexual Politics of Textual Transmission', in *Textual Formations and Reformations*, ed. Laurie E. Maguire and Thomas L. Berger, Newark: University of Delaware Press, 1998, pp. 179–210.

Weil, Jr., Herbert S., 'The Options of the Audience: Theory and Practice in Peter Brook's "Measure for Measure"', *Shakespeare Survey* 25 (1972): 27–35.

Weingust, Don, *Acting from Shakespeare's First Folio: Theory, Text and Performance*, London: Routledge, 2006.

Wells, Stanley, 'Awaking Your Faith', *Shakespeare Quarterly* 53 (2002): 525–35.

—— *Re-editing Shakespeare for the Modern Reader*, Oxford: Clarendon Press, 1984.

—— *Royal Shakespeare*, Manchester: Manchester University Press, 1977.

—— 'Television Shakespeare', *Shakespeare Quarterly* 33 (1982): 261–77.

Wells, Stanley and Gary Taylor with John Jowett and William Montgomery, eds, *William Shakespeare: The Complete Works*, Oxford: Clarendon Press, 1986.

—— *William Shakespeare: A Textual Companion*, Stanley Wells and Gary Taylor with John Jowett and William Montgomery, Oxford: Clarendon Press, 1987; reprinted with corrections New York and London: Norton, 1997.

Werstine, Paul, 'Folio Editors, Folio Compositors, and the Folio Text of *King Lear*', in *The Division of the Kingdoms: Shakespeare's Two Versions of* King Lear, ed. Gary Taylor and Michael Warren, Oxford: Clarendon Press, 1983, pp. 247–312.

—— 'Housmania: Episodes in Twentieth-century "Critical" Editing of Shakespeare', in *Textual Performances: The Modern Reproduction of Shakespeare's Drama*, ed. Lukas Erne and Margaret Jane Kidnie, Cambridge: Cambridge University Press, 2004, pp. 49–62.

—— 'McKerrow's "Suggestion" and Twentieth-century Shakespeare Textual Criticism', *Renaissance Drama* 19 (1988): 149–73.

—— 'Narratives about Printed Shakespeare Texts: "Foul Papers" and "Bad" Quartos', *Shakespeare Quarterly* 41 (1990): 65–86.

—— 'Plays in Manuscript', in *A New History of Early English Drama*, ed. John D. Cox and David Scott Kastan, New York: Columbia University Press, 1997, pp. 483–92.

—— 'Post-theory Problems in Shakespeare Editing', *Yearbook of English Studies* 29 (1999): 106–11.

—— 'The Textual Mystery of *Hamlet*', *Shakespeare Quarterly* 39 (1988): 1–26.

Wheale, Nigel, 'Culture Clustering, Gender Crossing: *Hamlet* Meets Globalization in Robert Lepage's *Elsinore*', in *Shakespeare and His Contemporaries in Performance*, ed. Edward J. Esche, Aldershot: Ashgate, 2000, pp. 121–35.

Whelehan, Imelda, 'Adaptations: The Contemporary Dilemmas', in *Adaptations: From Text to Screen, Screen to Text*, ed. Deborah Cartmell and Imelda Whelehan, London: Routledge, 1999, pp. 3–19.

Widdowson, Peter, '"Writing back": Contemporary Re-visionary Fiction', *Textual Practice* 20 (2006): 491–507.

Willems, Michèle, 'Verbal-Visual, Verbal-Pictorial or Textual-Televisual? Reflections on the BBC Shakespeare Series', in *Shakespeare and the Moving Image*, ed. Anthony Davies and Stanley Wells, Cambridge: Cambridge University Press, 1994, pp. 69–85.

Williams, James, *Lyotard and the Political*, London: Routledge, 2000.

Willis, Susan, *The BBC Shakespeare Plays: Making the Televised Canon*, Chapel Hill and London: University of North Carolina Press, 1991.

Wilsmore, Susan, 'The Literary Work Is Not Its Text', *Philosophy and Literature* 11 (1987): 307–16.

Wilson, Edwin, ed., *Shaw on Shakespeare: An Anthology of Bernard Shaw's Writings on the Plays and Production of Shakespeare*, London: Cassell and Co. Ltd, 1962.

Wilson, Tony, *Watching Television: Hermeneutics, Reception and Popular Culture*, Cambridge: Polity Press, 1993.

Witts, Preston, '"Cold feet" before the warmest of welcomes', *Stratford-upon-Avon Herald*, 5 February 2004.

Wolf, Matt, 'A widow of opportunity', *Sunday Telegraph*, 30 November 2003.

Wollheim, Richard, *Art and Its Objects*, Harmondsworth: Penguin, 1968.

Worthen, W. B., *Shakespeare and the Authority of Performance*, Cambridge: Cambridge University Press, 1997.

—— *Shakespeare and the Force of Modern Performance*, Cambridge: Cambridge University Press, 2003.

—— 'Texts, Tools, and Technologies of Performance: A Quip Modest, in Response to R. A. Foakes', *Shakespeare* 2:2 (2006): 208–19.

Worthen, W. B. with Peter Holland, *Theorizing Practice: Redefining Theatre History*, Basingstoke: Palgrave Macmillan, 2003.

'Wot – No More Shakespeare?', published Roundtable Discussion with Michael Billington, Matthew Warchus, Cicely Berry, Stephen Poliakoff, Simon Reade, and members of the audience, *RSC Magazine* (Summer 1998): 8–9.

Woudhuysen, Henry, '"Work of permanent utility": Editors and Texts, Authorities and Originals', in *Textual Performances: The Modern Reproduction of Shakespeare's Drama*, ed. Lukas Erne and Margaret Jane Kidnie, Cambridge: Cambridge University Press, 2004, pp. 37–48.

Zeller, Hans, 'A New Approach to the Critical Constitution of Literary Texts', *Studies in Bibliography* 28 (1975): 231–64.

Zitner, Sheldon P., 'Wooden O's in Plastic Boxes: Shakespeare and Television', *University of Toronto Quarterly* 51 (1981): 1–12.

Index

Related titles from Routledge

A Theory of Adaptation
Linda Hutcheon

Are we living in the age of adaptation? In contemporary cinema, of course, there are enough adaptations – based on everything from comic books to the novels of Jane Austen – to make us wonder if Hollywood has run out of new stories. But if you think adaptation can be understood by using novels and films alone, you're wrong. Today there are also song covers rising up the pop charts, video game versions of fairy tales, and even roller coasters based on successful movie franchises.

Despite their popularity, however, adaptations are usually treated as secondary and derivative. Whether in the form of a Broadway musical or a hit television show, adaptations are almost inevitably regarded as inferior to the "original." But are they?

Here, renowned literary scholar Linda Hutcheon explores the ubiquity of adaptations in all their various media incarnations – and challenges their constant critical denigration. Adaptation, Hutcheon argues, has always been a central mode of the story-telling imagination and deserves to be studied in all its breadth and range as both a process (of creation and reception) and a product unto its own.

Persuasive and illuminating, *A Theory of Adaptation* is a bold rethinking of how adaptation works across all media and genres that may put an end to the age-old question of whether the book was better than the movie, or the opera, or the theme park.

ISBN 13: 978-0-415-96794-5 (hbk)
ISBN 13: 978-0-415-96795-2 (pbk)

Available at all good bookshops
For ordering and further information please visit:
www.routledgeliterature.com

Related titles from Routledge

Adaptation and Appropriation
Julie Sanders

Series: New Critical Idiom

From the apparently simple adaptation of a text into film, theatre or a new literary work, to the more complex appropriation of style or meaning, it is arguable that all texts are somehow connected to a network of existing texts and art forms.

Adaptation and Appropriation explores:

- multiple definitions and practices of adaptation and appropriation

- the cultural and aesthetic politics behind the impulse to adapt

- diverse ways in which contemporary literature and film adapt, revise and reimagine other works of art

- the impact on adaptation and appropriation of theoretical movements, including structuralism, post-structuralism, postcolonialism, post-modernism, feminism and gender studies

- the appropriation across time and across cultures of specific canonical texts, but also of literary archetypes such as myth or fairy tale.

Ranging across genres and harnessing concepts from fields as diverse as musicology and the natural sciences, this volume brings clarity to the complex debates around adaptation and appropriation, offering a much-needed resource for those studying literature, film or culture.

ISBN13: 978-0-415-31171-7 (hbk)
ISBN13: 978-0-415-31172-4 (pbk)

Available at all good bookshops
For ordering and further information please visit:
www.routledge.com

Related titles from Routledge

Alternative Shakespeares 3
Edited by Diana E. Henderson

This volume takes up the challenge embodied in its predecessors, *Alternative Shakespeares* and *Alternative Shakespeares 2*: to identify and explore the new, the changing, the radically 'other' possibilities for Shakespeare Studies at our particular historical moment.

Alternative Shakespeares 3 introduces the strongest and most innovative of the new directions emerging in Shakespearean scholarship – ranging across performance studies, multimedia and textual criticism, concerns of economics, science, religion, and ethics – as well as the 'next step' work in areas such as postcolonial and queer studies that continue to push the boundaries of the field. The contributors approach each topic with clarity and accessibility in mind, enabling student readers to engage with serious 'alternatives' to established ways of interpreting Shakespeare's plays and their role in contemporary culture.

The expertise, commitment and daring of this volume's contributors shine through each essay, maintaining the progressive edge and real-world urgency that are the hallmark of *Alternative Shakespeares*. This volume is essential reading for students and scholars of Shakespeare who seek an understanding of current and future directions in this ever-changing field.

Contributors include: Kate Chedgzoy, Mary Thomas Crane, Lukas Erne, Diana E. Henderson, Rui Carvalho Homem, Julia Reinhard Lupton, Willy Maley, Patricia Parker, Shankar Raman, Katherine Rowe, Robert Shaughnessy and W. B. Worthen.

Diana E. Henderson is Professor of Literature at MIT.

ISBN 13: 978-0-415-42332-8 (hbk)
ISBN 13: 978-0-415-42333-5 (pbk)
ISBN 13: 978-0-203-93409-8 (ebk)

Available at all good bookshops
For ordering and further information please visit:
www.routledgeliterature.com

eBooks – at www.eBookstore.tandf.co.uk

A library at your fingertips!

eBooks are electronic versions of printed books. You can store them on your PC/laptop or browse them online.

They have advantages for anyone needing rapid access to a wide variety of published, copyright information.

eBooks can help your research by enabling you to bookmark chapters, annotate text and use instant searches to find specific words or phrases. Several eBook files would fit on even a small laptop or PDA.

NEW: Save money by eSubscribing: cheap, online access to any eBook for as long as you need it.

Annual subscription packages

We now offer special low-cost bulk subscriptions to packages of eBooks in certain subject areas. These are available to libraries or to individuals.

For more information please contact
webmaster.ebooks@tandf.co.uk

We're continually developing the eBook concept, so keep up to date by visiting the website.

www.eBookstore.tandf.co.uk